Languag

Language demonstrates structure while at the same time showing considerable variation at all levels: languages differ from one another while still being
shaped by the same principles; utterances within a language differ from one
another while still exhibiting the same structural patterns; languages change
over time, but in fairly regular ways. This book focuses on the dynamic processes that create languages and give them their structure and their variance.
Joan Bybee outlines a theory of language that directly addresses the nature of
grammar, taking into account its variance and gradience, and seeks explanation in terms of the recurrent processes that operate in language use. The
evidence is based on the study of large corpora of spoken and written language, and what we know about how languages change, as well as the results
of experiments with language users. The result is an integrated theory of language use and language change which has implications for cognitive processing and language evolution.

JOAN BYBEE is Distinguished Professor Emerita in the Department of
Linguistics at the University of New Mexico. Her previous publications
include *Phonology and Language Use* (Cambridge, 2001) and *Frequency of
Use and the Organization of Language* (2007).

Language, Usage and Cognition

Joan Bybee

University of New Mexico

CAMBRIDGE
UNIVERSITY PRESS

CAMBRIDGE UNIVERSITY PRESS
Cambridge, New York, Melbourne, Madrid, Cape Town, Singapore,
São Paulo, Delhi, Tokyo, Mexico City

Cambridge University Press
The Edinburgh Building, Cambridge CB2 8RU, UK

Published in the United States of America by Cambridge University Press, New York

www.cambridge.org
Information on this title: www.cambridge.org/9780521616836

First published 2010
3rd printing 2011

Printed in the United Kingdom at the University Press, Cambridge

A catalogue record for this publication is available from the British Library

Library of Congress Cataloguing in Publication data
Bybee, Joan L.
  Language, usage, and cognition / Joan Bybee.
    p. cm.
  Includes bibliographical references and index.
  ISBN 978-0-521-85140-4 – ISBN 978-0-521-61683-6 (pbk.)
  1. Language and languages–Usage.   2. Cognitive grammar.
  3. Linguistc change.   I. Title.
  P301.B84 2010
  415–dc22   2010003266

ISBN 978-0-521-85140-4 Hardback
ISBN 978-0-521-61683-6 Paperback

Contents

Figures

Tables

Acknowledgements

A researcher's primary debt is to her teachers, students and colleagues, with whom she has exchanged ideas, critiques and inspiration over the years. In my case, a whole community of linguists exploring functional issues, dia-chronic change, typology and usage effects are cited in the pages of this work for contributing to it through their example and support. This book is based on a forty-year tradition of functional-typological and cognitive linguistics and is dedicated to the men and women who during this period showed the courage to think outside the (black!) box. The book aspires to sum up their work from my own perspective, to apply a consistent set of hypotheses to phonology, mor-phosyntax and semantics, and to formulate specific new hypotheses about how domain-general processes contribute to the structuring of language.

As for contributions of a more personal nature, I am honoured to name two of my closest friends and colleagues, Sandra Thompson and Rena Torres Cacoullos, who lent personal support and provided their scholarly perspective on drafts of various chapters. I also thank Clay Beckner, who worked with me on Chapters 5 and 8, and came up with much of the data and many of the argu-ments cited in Chapter 8 (as we collaborated on a paper on a similar topic). I am also grateful to Ben Sienicki for technical support and to Shelece Easter-day for constructing the index.

Finally, to my family and friends, who support my activities in many ways, and to my husband, Ira Jaffe, I extend heartfelt thanks.

1   A usage-based perspective on language

'The more it changes, the more it stays the same'

1.1   The nature of language

Sand dunes have apparent regularities of shape and structure, yet they also exhibit considerable variation among individual instances, as well as gradience and change over time. If we want to gain understanding of phenomena that are both structured and variable, it is necessary to look beyond the mutable surface forms to the forces that produce the patterns observed. Language is also a phenomenon that exhibits apparent structure and regularity of patterning while at the same time showing considerable variation at all levels: languages differ from one another while still being patently shaped by the same principles; comparable constructions in different languages serve similar functions and are based on similar principles, yet differ from one another in specifiable ways; utterances within a language differ from one another while still exhibiting the same structural patterns; languages change over time, but in fairly regular ways. Thus it follows that a theory of language could reasonably be focused on the dynamic processes that create languages and give them both their structure and their variance.

A focus on the dynamic processes that create language also allows us to move away from an exclusive focus on linguistic structures and formulate a broader goal: to derive linguistic structure from the application of domain-general processes. In this context, domain-general processes would be those that can be shown to operate in areas of human cognition other than language. The goal of this book is to explore the possibility that the structural phenomena we observe in the grammar of natural languages can be derived from domain-general cognitive processes as they operate in multiple instances of language use. The processes to be considered are called into play in every instance of language use; it is the repetitive use of these processes that has an impact on the cognitive representation of language and thus on language as it is manifested overtly. In this book, then, facts about usage, cognitive processing and language change are united to provide an explanation for the observed properties of linguistic structures.

When linguistic structure is viewed as emergent from the repeated application of underlying processes, rather than given a priori or by design, then language can be seen as a complex adaptive system (Hopper 1987, Larsen-Freeman 1997, Ellis and Larsen-Freeman 2006). The primary reason for viewing language as a complex adaptive system, that is, as being more like sand dunes than like a planned structure, such as a building, is that language exhibits a great deal of variation and gradience. Gradience refers to the fact that many categories of language or grammar are difficult to distinguish, usually because change occurs over time in a gradual way, moving an element along a continuum from one category to another. Continua such as that between derivation and inflection, between function words and affixes, between productive and unproductive constructions, illustrate this gradience. Variation refers to the fact that the units and structures of language exhibit variation in synchronic use, usually along the continuous paths of change that create gradience.

1.2   Gradience and variation in linguistic structure

This section presents some examples of the type of gradience and variation that motivate a view of language as a complex adaptive system. These examples are only a few of the many that one could identify as showing gradience and variation among the members of a particular type of linguistic unit – morphemes (section 1.2.1), language-specific categories – English auxiliaries (section 1.2.2), or variation in instantiations of a particular construction – *I don't* + VERB (section 1.2.3).

1.2.1   Units: morphemes

All types of units proposed by linguists show gradience, in the sense that there is a lot of variation within the domain of the unit (different types of words, morphemes, syllables) and difficulty setting the boundaries of the unit. Here I will use morphemes as an example. In their canonical instantiations morphemes involve a constant form associated with a constant meaning. A good example is *happy,* a lexical morpheme. In general, lexical morphemes are less problematic than grammatical morphemes, exhibiting more regularity of form and meaning. However, there are still problematic lexical morphemes which change their meaning and nature depending upon the company they keep. Consider *go,* which often occurs as a simple lexical morpheme, but also occurs in many other constructions, for instance, *go ahead (and), go wrong, go bad, go boom, let's go have lunch,* the famous *be going to* and the quotative *go (and I go 'what do you mean?')* in which its lexical status is quite diminished. We return in Chapter 6 to a discussion of how lexical morphemes become grammatical.

Grammatical morphemes are classically defined as closed class items. Since classes are defined in terms of the properties of constructions, grammatical morphemes are those which are restricted to particular positions in constructions. As a class of unit, grammatical morphemes are highly variable. At the highest level, we find variance across languages in the types of grammatical morphemes that occur. Form and meaning both differ in systematic ways. All languages have function words – non-bound units that express grammatical functions such as tense, aspect, interrogation, negation, and so on. All languages probably also have at least some derivational affixes (Bybee 1985). However, not all languages have inflectional affixes (defined as affixes that belong to obligatory categories). Among those that do have inflection, we traditionally distinguish between agglutinative and fusional languages on the basis of the degree of fusion, allomorphy and irregularity found among the inflectional affixes. Given this range of variation among languages, what similarities do we find among them?

The similarities are apparent in the clines of morphological types, where languages occupy different zones on the cline, ranging from analytic (isolating) to agglutinative to inflectional. The similarities are also apparent in the diachronic processes that create grammatical morphemes, the processes subsumed under the heading 'grammaticalization' (see Chapter 6) by which separate words become affixes and these affixes can become more and more fused with a stem.

Within languages, these same categories can be identified, though rigid distinctions among them are often difficult to make. Gradience is illustrated by the difficulty in determining whether adverbial *–ly* in English is inflectional or derivational (Bybee 1985) or whether the negative particle and its contracted form *–n't* is a clitic or affix (Zwicky and Pullum 1983). Within derivational morphology we find interesting differences not just among affixes, but even considering the same affix in different combinations. The *–ness* suffix in *business* is much less analysable than the same suffix on *happiness*. Hay 2001, 2002 shows that there are even more subtle differences, such as that between the analysability of the suffix in *swiftly* and *softly*.

Grammatical morphemes are bordered by words on the one hand and phonemes on the other. The familiar case of periphrastic expressions using what once were words, such as the perfect *have* + PAST PARTICIPLE, illustrate this gradience, but cases that are not usually cited are cases such as the word *way* in the construction exemplified by *Powell knows how to thread his way between conflicting views.*[1] Since *way* is the only word that can occur in this position in this construction, it qualifies as a grammatical morpheme. However, since it does not fulfil any of the functions traditionally associated with grammatical morphemes, it is more readily recognized as a word. Thus grammatical morphemes that are developing out of words constitute one side of the gradient, and on the other side are grammatical morphemes that are losing their meaningful status and becoming just part of the phonology of the word. Hopper 1994 discusses a number of such cases (see also Greenberg 1978b). One example is the second syllable of English *seldom*, which was previously the dative plural marker attached to the adjective *seld* 'strange, rare' and now is a meaningless part of the word.

The variation and gradience in the category of 'grammatical morpheme' is a direct result of the processes of change that affect morphemes and shape their properties of form and meaning. Lexical morphemes can become grammatical morphemes in the process of grammaticalization (as when the lexical morpheme *go* becomes part of the future construction *be going to*), and in this process gradually become more dependent upon and eventually fused with surrounding material. Derivational morphemes are formed when two words are used together in a compound-like fashion; thus *–ly* came from the noun *líç-* meaning 'body' which produced a compound meaning 'having the body of'. The second part of this compound gradually reduced, spread to more and more nouns and adjectives and generalized its meaning in the process.

Of course, these processes of change are well known and quite taken for granted. What is not so well appreciated, however, is what they tell us about the cognitive processing that is used in language. They tell us something about how language use affects storage in memory and the organization of that storage (Bybee and McClelland 2005, McClelland and Bybee 2007). In the chapters of this book we will be examining the tendencies that are at work when language is being processed. Rather than taking the gradience just illustrated as a descriptive problem, let us consider it the very essence of the phenomenon and think of language as ever being affected by language use and the impact that experience has on the cognitive system.

1.2.2   *Language-specific categories that are heterogeneous and gradient: the English auxiliary*

The English auxiliary sequence is worthy of close scrutiny because it appears to be a very good example of a well-behaved linguistic structure that is involved in certain clear rules. In Chapter 7 I examine the way this structure and the associated rules or constructions (of subject–auxiliary inversion and negation) came into being in the sixteenth century. There we will see that a number of gradual changes, some of them only remotely related at first, led to the formation of the auxiliary and its related constructions. This study brings to light the fact that the element that inverts with the subject and takes negation following it is actually a diverse structural class, including the set of modal auxiliaries (more comments on this set below) which appear with an unmarked main verb form; two constructions that each take a different form of the main verb: the

Progressive (BE + ING) and the Perfect (HAVE + EN); and one element, the copula, which is actually the main verb in the predicates in which it appears. This category also formerly contained (and still does in some dialects) the possessive *have* and indeed many other verbs. Thus the members of the category of auxiliary items in English are quite diverse, being neither structurally nor functionally uniform.

Moreover, the category itself has less than discrete boundaries. The elements mentioned – the modals, the Progressive *be*, the Perfect *have* and the copula – are quite categorically members of this class of items, but the verbs *dare* and *need* sometimes behave as though they were members of the category and sometimes behave as though they were ordinary main verbs. This gradience is not just some passing stage; rather these two verbs have straddled the two categories since the time the category of auxiliary started to differentiate from the category of main verb (some five centuries ago, see Chapter 7).

In addition, the members of the category of modal auxiliary are also diverse and show variation, especially in function. While most express modality, either agent-oriented, ability or root possibility (*can* and *could*), obligation (*must*, *shall* and *should*) or epistemic (*may, might, could*), some also express tense (*will* and *shall* for future) or tense and aspect (*would* for past habitual).

This class of items with very similar structural properties expresses a wide range of different meanings. Such a category is not unusual in the languages of the world. Bybee 1986 surveyed tense, aspect and modality inflections in fifty languages and found that it is actually rather uncommon for position classes to correspond directly to meaning categories. This heterogeneity is not specific to affixes and auxiliaries; prepositions also show many differences in behaviour, with *of*, the most common, often not behaving much like a preposition at all (Sinclair 1991) and complex prepositions (such as *on top of, in spite of*) showing mixed behaviour between containing two prepositions and a noun and functioning as a unit (Chapter 8).

1.2.3 Specific instances of construction vary: *I don't know, I don't inhale*

The types of gradience and variation discussed in the preceding subsections are well-known from the literature (as noted above), but the final type of gradience I want to discuss has only more recently received attention as a phenomenon that a linguistic theory needs to reckon with. In this subsection we focus on the fact that, at times, specific instances of constructions (with particular lexical items included in them) take on behaviour different from the general construction.

Consider the two expressions *I don't know* and *I don't inhale*. They appear to be structurally identical, each one having a first-person-singular pronoun followed by the negated form of the *do* auxiliary and an unmarked main verb. They both exhibit the same phonetic variation in that the initial stop of *don't* can become a flap and the final [t] is usually deleted in both cases. But in addition to this, the first expression *I don't know* also has number of other variant properties that the second expression does not share. Even though *I don't know* can certainly have the meaning that is predictable from the sum of its parts, it is also often used as a discourse marker, mollifying the force of the previous assertions and letting the listener know that the speaker is willing to give up the floor (Scheibman 2000). In this discourse-pragmatic usage, the phrase is also more likely to have further phonetic reduction than in its more semantically transparent usage. The further reduction involves the vowel of *don't* which becomes a schwa. The most extreme reduction which occurs in this phrase is the loss of the initial stop [d]. Neither of these changes occur when the main verb is a less frequent verb such as *inhale* (Bybee and Scheibman 1999). See Chapter 2 for further discussion of reduction and semantic changes in high-frequency expressions.

1.2.4   The role of gradience and variation

To these few examples, one could add many more: the difficulty of defining units such as 'segment', 'syllable' and even 'word', the problem with the notion of 'clause' when clauses take so many shapes, and the fact that grammaticality judgements show gradience and variation across speakers. The existence of gradience and variation does not negate the regular patterning within languages or the patterning across languages. However, it is important not to view the regularities as primary and the gradience and variation as secondary; rather the same factors operate to produce both regular patterns and the deviations. If language were a fixed mental structure, it would perhaps have discrete categories; but since it is a mental structure that is in constant use and filtered through processing activities that change it, there is variation and gradation.

1.3   Domain-general processes

Language is one of the most systematic and complex forms of human behaviour. As such it has given rise to many different theories about what it is used for (thinking vs. communicating), how it has evolved (abruptly or gradually), where its structure comes from (innate structures vs. language use) and what types of processes underlie its structure (those specific to language vs. those applicable in many cognitive domains). Here we consider the last question – are the processes that give us linguistic structure specific to language or are they processes that also apply in other cognitive domains? The best strategy for answering this question is to start first with domain-general processes and see how much of linguistic structure can be explained without postulating processes specific to language. If this quest is even partially successful, we will have narrowed down the possible processes that have to be specific to language. The opposite strategy of assuming processes specific to language will not lead to the discovery of how domain-general processes contribute to linguistic structure.

As mentioned above, a consequence of viewing language as a complex adaptive system and linguistic structure as emergent (Lindblom et al. 1984, Hopper 1987) is that it focuses our attention not so much on linguistic structure itself, as on the processes that create it (Verhagen 2002). By searching for domain-general processes, we not only narrow the search for processes specific to language, but we also situate language within the larger context of human behaviour.

The domain-general cognitive processes studied in this book are categorization, chunking, rich memory storage, analogy and cross-modal association. This list is not meant to exhaust the cognitive processes involved in language, nor to deny that there might be processes specific to language that will be discovered; the list represents the processes that have proven useful in understanding some aspects of language that have particularly interested me.

Categorization is the most pervasive of these processes as it interacts with the others. By categorization I mean the similarity or identity matching that occurs when words and phrases and their component parts are recognized and matched to stored representations. The resulting categories are the foundation of the linguistic system, whether they are sound units, morphemes, words, phrases or constructions (see Chapters 2, 4, 5 and 8). Categorization is domain-general in the sense that perceptual categories of various sorts are created from experience independently of language.

Chunking is the process by which sequences of units that are used together cohere to form more complex units. As a domain-general process chunking helps to explain why people get better at cognitive and neuromotor tasks with practice. In language, chunking is basic to the formation of sequential units expressed as constructions, constituents and formulaic expressions. Repeated sequences of words (or morphemes) are packaged together in cognition so that the sequence can be accessed as a single unit. It is the interaction of chunking with categorization that gives conventional sequences varying degrees of analysability and compositionality (Chapters 3 and 8).

Rich memory refers to the memory storage of the details of experience with language, including phonetic detail for words and phrases, contexts of use, meanings and inferences associated with utterances. Categorization is the process by which these rich memories are mapped onto existing representations (Chapter 2). Memory for linguistic forms is represented in exemplars, which are built up from tokens of language experience that are deemed to be identical. The primary claim of exemplar representation is that each experience with language has an impact on cognitive representations. Non-linguistic memories also have an impact on cognitive representations and on neurological structure (Nader et al. 2000).

Analogy is the process by which novel utterances are created based on previously experienced utterances. Analogy also requires categorization; the parts of previously experienced tokens must be parsed into units that are aligned and categorized before novel utterances can be formed from them. Analogy is domain-general and has been studied in terms of relational structures on visual stimuli, such as scenes, shapes and colours (Gentner 1983, Gentner and Markman 1997).

The list of domain-general processes also includes the ability to make cross-modal associations that provide the link between meaning and form. Ellis (1996) discusses this most basic principle as James' Law of Contiguity (James 1950 [1890]) by which co-occurring experiences tend to be associated in cognition. Ellis goes on to point out that

The implicit, automatic pattern-detection processes that occur within these modalities of representation entail that any such cross-modal association typically occur between the highest chunked levels of activated nodes. Thus to extend Morton's (1967) example, the adult looking at his or her watch when the post falls through the mail slot each morning learns an association that mail time is 8:30 a.m., not one between envelopes and the big hand of the watch. (1996: 110)

Thus meaning is assigned to the largest chunk available – a word, a phrase or a construction. Note that inferences made from the context of particular utterances can also come to be associated with particular sequences, giving rise to changes in meaning (see Chapters 3, 6, 8 and 10).

Chapters 2 through 5 of this book discuss these domain-general processes and the way that their iterative application in language use creates the categories and units of language, sequential structures such as constructions and constituents. It is also shown that variations in analysability and compositionality as well as the productive and creative use of language are derivable from these same processes. Chapters 6 through 8 examine in more detail how these same processes apply in cases of language change, especially in cases of grammaticalization, in the creation of new constructions and in changes in constituent structure. Chapter 10 is devoted to discussing the consequences of these proposals for our understanding of the meaning of grammatical categories. Chapter 11 considers the way similarities among languages arise through application and interaction of domain-general processes during language use in particular cultural contexts.

1.4   Usage-based grammar

In Bybee 2006a I proposed that grammar be thought of as the cognitive organization of one's experience with language. To cast this in terms that linguists are accustomed to dealing with, we need to provide this theory with levels, units and processes that create new utterances. As we will see in the subsequent chapters, the 'construction' as defined in various works by Fillmore and colleagues, Goldberg and Croft (Fillmore et al. 1988, Goldberg 1995, 2006, Croft 2001) provides a very appropriate unit for morphological and syntactic representation. The crucial idea behind the construction is that it is a direct form–meaning pairing that has sequential structure and may include positions that are fixed as well as positions that are open. Thus one can speak of the passive construction, the ditransitive construction or more specific constructions such as those illustrated by these examples:

(1) It *drove* the producer *mad.*
(2) Bantam corkscrewed his *way* through the crowd. (Israel 1996)

These are particular examples of more general constructions; the first is a resultative construction using a particular verb, *drive,* along with a set of adjectives meaning 'crazy' (see Chapters 2 and 5) and the other has a fixed word *way,* along with a verb indicating how a path was created and a locative phrase.

As constructions pair form and meaning, the grammar does not contain modules for syntax as separate from semantics, nor does it provide for derivational histories of surface forms. Even the phonology can be directly represented in the construction in cases of special phonological reduction that occurs in specific constructions (see Chapter 3). The levels of abstraction found in a usage-based grammar are built up through categorization of similar instances of use into more abstract representations (Langacker 1987, 2000).

Since constructions are based firmly on generalizations over actual utterances, their pairing with an exemplar model is rather straightforward, as shown in Chapter 2. Particular instances of constructions impact cognitive representations; thus the token frequency of certain items in constructions (such as the high frequency of *that drives me crazy* in American English), as well as the range of types (what different adjectives can occur in this same construction) determines representation of the construction as well as its productivity. The evidence that specific instances of constructions impact representation includes the fact that these instances can change gradually into new, independent constructions, through repetition (Chapters 2, 6 and 8). In addition, it is shown that the frequency of specific instances of constructions has an impact on the categories formed for the schematic slots in constructions (Chapters 2 and 5).

Because each instance of language use impacts representation, variation and gradience have a direct representation in the language-user's system. In an exemplar model, all variants are represented in memory as exemplar clusters. Such clusters can change gradually, representing the changes that language undergoes as it is used. Thus change is postulated to occur as language is used rather than in the acquisition process (Chapters 6, 7 and 8).

1.5   Sources of evidence

In usage-based theory, where grammar is directly based on linguistic experience, there are no types of data that are excluded from consideration because they are considered to represent performance rather than competence. Evidence from child language, psycholinguistic experiments, speakers' intuitions, distribution in corpora and language change are all considered viable sources of evidence about cognitive representations, provided we understand the different factors operating in each of the settings that give rise to the data.

Given the complex adaptive systems orientation of the research reported here, it should come as no surprise that much of the argumentation is based on examples that demonstrate tendencies in language change. Since language change is as operable and evident in the present as in the past, the data can as well come from modern corpora, corpora with a shallow time depth (e.g. the twentieth century) or from documents that are centuries old. Understanding processes and directions of change provides us with insight into the individual's (synchronic) cognitive system for language. Since I am assuming that even the individual's system is dynamic and changing, changes on both a large and a small scale point to the processing abilities put into play in language use.

Equally important is the role played by language change in explanation. Since all patterns of linguistic structure have an evolutionary history, part of the explanation for why languages have particular structures must involve reference to how these structures arose. One could paraphrase Dobzhansky's (1964: 449) famous statement about biology and evolution by saying 'nothing in linguistics makes any sense except in the light of language change'. One advantage of the complex adaptive systems approach is that the cognitive processes proposed for use in processing language are the same processes that lead to change. Thus explanation on the synchronic and diachronic dimensions is united.

For the present work, the primary sources of data have been corpora of spoken or written language. As the work has evolved over several years, corpora have been used as they became available. For contemporary English, I have used data from *Switchboard* (Godfrey et al. 1992), the *British National Corpus* (Davies 2004), the *Time Magazine* (Davies 2007) corpus and more recently the *Contemporary Corpus of American English* (Davies 2008). I have accessed these corpora both for quantitative data and for individual examples (rather than making up examples). For Spanish the *Corpus Oral de Referencia del Español Contemporáneo* was used as well as a written corpus of fifteen novels assembled by Halvor Clegg at the Humanities Research Center at Brigham Young University. There is no question that access to such large corpora has vastly improved our appreciation of the experience that users have with language.

1.6   Precursors

Like all scholarly work, this book is more a synthesis of previous work than
it is truly original. It is based on a long tradition in American linguistics arising from empirical studies of functional and typological topics. Within two
decades of Chomsky's proposal of the autonomy of syntax (Chomsky 1957,
1965), a strong new tradition of explicitly studying the functions of grammatical constructions had arisen (Givón 1973, Hooper and Thompson 1973, Li
1976). From the very beginning, this work integrated typological and cross-
linguistic considerations, with the goal of understanding language change and
using it as explanation for language-specific synchronic states, as well as the
distribution of language types (Givón 1971, 1979, Li 1975, 1977, Greenberg
et al. 1978). Work in this tradition continues to the present, ever extending its
scope to explain more aspects of grammar through reference to meaning and
discourse function (Hopper and Thompson 1980, 1984, Du Bois 1987, and
other more recent works too numerous to list).

An important development out of this tradition was the surge in studies of
grammaticalization across languages, beginning in the 1970s but really growing in the 1980s (Givón 1979, Lehmann 1982, Heine and Reh 1984, Bybee
1985) and continuing to the present. This work not only identified common
cross-linguistic paths of change for grammaticalizing constructions (Givón
1979, Bybee et al. 1994, Heine et al. 1991, Heine and Kuteva 2002), but it
also identified the dominant mechanisms of change operating as constructions
grammaticalize: bleaching or generalization of meaning (Givón 1973, 1975,
Lord 1976), pragmatic inferencing (Traugott 1989), phonetic reduction (Bybee
2003b), and changes in category and constituent structure (Heine et al. 1991,
Haspelmath 1998). Because these changes take place during language use, and
because many of them depend upon repetition or frequency of use, these studies of grammaticalization processes have led to a re-examination of the nature
of grammar itself. This re-examination reveals that grammar can be affected
by language use, thus giving rise to the idea of a usage-based grammar, which
is the central theme of this book.

In a quite independent development, researchers interested in the form of
synchronic grammar began to examine the idea of treating morphosyntactic
structure in terms of surface-oriented constructions that directly associate form
with meaning (Langacker 1987, Fillmore et al. 1988, Goldberg 1995, Croft
2001). This more surface-oriented approach to grammar provides an appropriate unit of morphosyntax for the description and explanation of the grammaticalization process (Bybee 2003b, Traugott 2003). From the properties of
constructions in language use we can approach the gradient notions of analysability, compositionality, and productivity (Langacker 1987, Clausner and
Croft 1997). As noted above, a usage-based interpretation of constructions as

built up from stored exemplars of language use is the basis of the concept of grammar developed in this book.

For a usage-based theory, quantitative studies become extremely important for the understanding of the breadth of experience with language. The variationist tradition started by Labov (1966, 1972), while aimed at understanding how social factors interact with phonology and grammar, also provides appropriate methodology for the study of grammatical variation and change (see, for instance, Poplack and Tagliamonte 1996, Torres Cacoullos 1999, 2000). More recently, the development of large corpora of contemporary spoken and written discourse as well as historical texts, makes it possible to test hypotheses about the effects of usage on grammar (e.g. Sinclair 1991, Jurafsky 1996, Gregory et al. 1999, Jurafsky et al. 2001). One outcome of corpus linguistics is the renewed interest in formulaic language (Erman and Warren 2000, Wray 2002 and others), which shows how very specific the speaker's knowledge of the language is. The vast knowledge of word combinations and constructions, as well as their specific meanings and sometimes variable phonetic shapes, demonstrates that our linguistic models must contain considerable detail about usage.

Finally, the application of ideas from the theory of complex adaptive systems to language fits well with the Greenbergian tradition of identifying paths of change and the mechanisms behind them (Greenberg 1969, 1978b). The first such explicit proposal appears in Lindblom et al. 1984, with an independent proposal of Hopper 1987 that grammar be viewed as emergent, rather than fixed, discrete and a priori. Further explicit proposals for viewing language as a complex adaptive system appear in Larsen-Freeman 1997 and Ellis and Larsen-Freeman 2006.

1.7   Questions that are asked in this framework

Every theory has a set of assumptions that underlie its research questions and a set of goals that determine what questions are asked. The goals of this book follow the directive of Lindblom et al., who urge us to 'DERIVE LANGUAGE FROM NON-LANGUAGE!' (1984: 187; emphasis in original). We do this by looking behind linguistic structure for the domain-general cognitive processes that give rise to structure. As these processes apply in language use, we are also investigating the ways that experience with language affects its representation; thus we ask: how does frequency of use affect structure? And how does the particular – the actual instances of use – relate to the general – the cognitive representations of language?

The interest in the interaction of use with process allows us also to investigate how constructions arise and change and in effect, formulate and provide some answers to the question of where grammar comes from. At the same time we can also ask more specific questions about words, phrases and constructions concerning their semantic, pragmatic and phonetic form, their analysability, compositionality and productivity. The current book, then, outlines a theory of language that directly addresses the nature of grammar, taking into account its variance and gradience, and seeks explanations in terms of the recurrent processes that operate in language use.

2 Rich memory for language: exemplar representation

2.1 Introduction

Central to the usage-based position is the hypothesis that instances of use impact the cognitive representation of language. Throughout this book arguments for an exemplar representation of language will be given, including the arguments that exemplar representations keep track of usage, allow for the representation of gradience in structures, and allow for gradual change. In demonstrating the properties of exemplar models, the present chapter will emphasize one aspect of exemplar representation – the fact that exemplars are considered to register details about linguistic experience. Exemplar representations are rich memory representations; they contain, at least potentially, all the information a language user can perceive in a linguistic experience. This information consists of phonetic detail, including redundant and variable features, the lexical items and constructions used, the meaning, inferences made from this meaning and from the context, and properties of the social, physical and linguistic context.

We see in this chapter that recent research in phonetic categorization, voice recognition, sociophonetics, lexical diffusion of sound change, grammaticalization, and verbatim recall all point to the retention of considerable linguistic detail in cognitive representations. The interesting questions to be addressed here and in the rest of this book are how the brain deals with this detail, how it handles similarities and differences among tokens of input and registered exemplars and how repetition of tokens affects representations.

2.2 Contrast with the parsimonious storage of generative theory and its structuralist precursors

2.2.1 The structuralist tradition

The position that memory representations for language are rich in detail could not be more different from the structural and generative traditions of the twentieth century. These traditions are firmly committed to the idea that redundancies and variation are extracted from the signal and code and discarded rather than stored in memory. There are several motivations in these frameworks for accepting this position. The patterns that constitute the structure of language can be observed across different lexical items and different contexts; the identification of such patterns by linguists entails abstracting away from specific instances and finding just the right information to characterize the pattern as a rule. It follows, then, that the regularities do not have to be registered with specific lexical items; thus the lexical items contain only the idiosyncratic information.

Despite certain warnings about the need for a more highly specified lexicon (Jackendoff 1975), the basic practice of removing predictable information from storage has continued. Such a practice is not necessarily plausible when one tries to consider what speakers or learners might actually do. Langacker 1987 argues that a necessary prerequisite to forming a generalization is the accumulation in memory of a set of examples upon which to base the generalization. Once the category is formed or the generalization is made, the speaker does not necessarily have to throw away the examples upon which the generalization is based. If linguistic memory is like memory for experience in other domains, it is unlikely that specific instances are completely discarded once a generalization is made (see below).

As stated in the first chapter it is the goal of usage-based theory to seek explanations in terms of domain-general cognitive processes. Thus we should try to establish whether general properties of memory and its organization can be applied to language. In this regard, another argument for abstract, redundancy-free representations was important in the past. Earlier, linguists believed that limitations on memory were such that any redundancies and non-significant detail, as well as particular tokens of language use, would be excluded from permanent memory representations. Indeed, beliefs about memory limitations fuelled the search for ever simpler types of representation. In the discussion following a 1972 presentation, Roman Jakobson commented on the necessity of binary representations for language:

This notion of binarism is essential; without it the structure of language would be lost. When there are two terms in opposition, the two are always present in one's awareness. Just imagine the dozens and dozens of grammatical cases in the languages of the Caucasus. Without these oppositions, the speakers of these languages would be exhausted. (Jakobson 1990: 321)

Jakobson is not giving speakers enough credit. We now know that speakers know tens or even hundreds of thousands of words, and just as many, if not more, prefabricated expressions which these words fit into, expressions such as *bright daylight, pick and choose, interested in, disposed to,* and so on. It is clear that the brain's capacity is impressively large. Two or three dozen case markers (many of which are probably restricted to specific constructions) pose no problem for normal speakers.

2.2.2   *A role for imitation*

In the innatist tradition espoused by Chomsky and colleagues, the role of imitation in language acquisition was argued to be quite minimal and unimportant. Much was made of the fact that children often produce utterances that they could never have heard from an adult. The underlying message in these arguments seems to be that since we are human beings (and therefore quite superior to other animals) and since language is so complex, we simply could not learn it by any means as trivial as imitation; rather, there must be much higher-order types of cognitive activities responsible for language and its complex structure.

The problems with this argument are (i) the assumption that imitation is a low-level activity or ability, and (ii) the assumption that the use of imitation would preclude other cognitive mechanisms. First, if imitation were such a low-level ability, one would expect non-humans to be better at it. Yet the evidence suggests that the ability to imitate among non-humans is quite limited. Apes and monkeys are capable of some imitation, perhaps based on the presence of mirror neurons in their brains, but their imitative capacities seem far below those of humans (Tomasello et al. 1993, Donald 1998, Arbib 2003). While chimps, for instance, have been shown to imitate other chimps and humans, the process is 'long and laborious ... compared to the rapidity with which humans can acquire novel sequences' (Arbib 2003: 193). Arbib distinguishes simple from complex imitations, where the former is limited to short novel sequences of object-oriented actions while the latter, for example, imitating a song or dance, involves parsing, recognizing variations and coordinating the various parts. Complex imitation, then, involves many of the same processes needed to acquire language.

As Donald (1991, 1998) points out, imitation and its higher level counterpart, mimesis, provide the foundation for the homogeneity that is characteristic of human cultures. Bates et al. 1991 emphasize the importance of imitation for human learning in contrast to that of other primates by citing the experiment in which a human infant and a chimpanzee infant were raised in the same human household. They say 'Alas, the experiment was put in jeopardy several times because of its unintended effects on Donald (the human infant-JB): Whereas the chimpanzee made relatively little progress in imitation of Donald, the human child imitated and made productive use of many chimpanzee behaviors!' (Bates et al. 1991: 48).

Of course, imitation can be very important to language without precluding other cognitive processes essential to language. No one would claim that imitation alone is sufficient for transmitting language; in addition, it is necessary to have the generative capacity that allows the imitated sequences to be used productively in new situations. Recognizing a high level of skill at imitating along with the ability to segment, categorize and recombine gives us a better chance at explaining how language works.

2.2.3   Early experimental results

Certain experimental results reinforced the notion of abstract representations. Work on categorical perception in the 1970s emphasized the boundaries between phonetic categories (Liberman et al. 1957, Studdert-Kennedy et al. 1970) showing that subjects could discriminate between stimuli that were acoustically from different phonemes better than stimuli that were within the acoustic range of a single phoneme, even if the former were no farther apart than the latter. This reinforced the notion that the importance of phonemes was discriminating among words: once the discriminating task of the phonetics was accomplished, details of the acoustic form could be discarded.

Subsequent research on different sorts of tasks, however, has shown that subjects are also able to discriminate stimuli within categories and rank them for goodness of fit for the category (Miller 1994). In fact, Miller's work suggests that 'phoneme' may not be the relevant level of categorization, as she has found graded internal structure even in categories that are determined by context, such as the voice onset timing of a syllable-initial [t] in an open vs. closed syllable. In addition, there appear to be multiple acoustic cues that determine category membership and these are in a trading relation – if one is diminished but another augmented the subjects deem the stimuli to be within the category. This sensitivity to phonetic detail suggests categories based on numerous experienced tokens. Evidence to be presented below on adult language change points to a continuing updating of categories based on the phonetic properties of experience with language.

Another experimental finding that reinforced notions about the abstract nature of representation for language came from psycholinguistic experiments on verbatim recall. The results of these experiments in the 1960s and 1970s were widely interpreted as showing that language users do not retain information about the morpho-syntactic form of an utterance they have processed; rather they retain only the meaning or gist of the utterance (Sachs 1967, Bransford and Franks 1971). It was thought that surface syntax is remembered only under certain circumstances: when subjects are warned that there would be a memory test after exposure (Johnson-Laird et al. 1974); when the test immediately follows hearing the sentences (Reyna and Kiernan 1994); when the sentences are highly salient or 'interactive' (Murphy and Shapiro 1994), or when the sentences are isolated and not integrated into a semantically coherent passage (Anderson and Bower 1973, among others).

Gurevich et al. (forthcoming) point out that although these studies were generally interpreted as demonstrating the lack of retention of the verbatim form of experienced tokens, in fact the results actually provide some indication that the surface form of sentences is not necessarily totally lost. In their own experiments, Gurevich et al. had subjects listen to a story and then immediately asked them to indicate 'yes' or 'no' to whether written clauses appearing on the computer screen were exactly the same as clauses they heard in the story. The results were an overall mean of 72 per cent correct, indicating above chance verbatim recall. In a second set of experiments, Gurevich et al. asked subjects to retell the stories they had heard (without being previously warned that this would occur). In their retelling, subjects used from 9 per cent (N = 33) to 22.3 per cent (N = 144) matches to clauses in the original story (depending upon which of several stories they heard), indicating that the verbatim form of heard clauses is indeed not totally lost. Even after a 2-day delay, subjects reproduced verbatim 17 per cent of the clauses heard in the story.

Gurevich et al. were spurred to take up the issue of verbatim memory because of the emerging evidence in linguistics that cognitive representations are sensitive to aspects of experience, such as frequency of use (see Bybee 1985, 2007, among others). A plausible way to represent the impact of tokens of usage on representation is to propose that each token of use strengthens the representation of a particular item, whether it be a word, a string of words, or a construction (Bybee 1985 for morphology). While the effects of frequency are often not noted until some degree of frequency has accumulated, there is no way for frequency to matter unless even the first occurrence of an item is noted in memory. Otherwise, how would frequency accumulate? It cannot be the case that items are not registered until they achieve a certain level of frequency, because we would not know if they had achieved this frequency unless we were 'counting' from the beginning, by registering instances in memory (Bybee 2006a, Gurevich et al. forthcoming). Thus the verbatim form of an experienced token must have some (possibly small) impact on cognitive representation, even if it cannot be recalled accurately afterwards. The fact that any verbatim recall is documented supports this point.

Finally, debates in the categorization literature between the view of categories as characterized by abstractions versus the view of categories as groups of exemplars bears on the same question. Early work in natural categorization identified what have come to be called 'prototype effects'. These effects arise from graded category membership in which some members of categories are considered better or more central members than others. Experiments by Eleanor Rosch (1973, 1975) demonstrated that within a culture, subjects show considerable agreement on which items are considered to be good examples of a category. Prototype effects have been demonstrated to be pervasive in language (Lakoff 1987, Taylor 1995). One interpretation of these effects is that people build up an abstract prototype of a category with which the central member or members share more features than the marginal members do.

It turns out that reference to particular members of categories, or exemplars, can also produce the same effects. Medin and Schaffer 1978 demonstrate this in experiments showing that similarity even to a marginal member facilitates assignment of category membership. Thus if a person is already familiar with an ostrich and has assigned it to the category of 'bird' the assignment of an emu to the same category is facilitated, despite the fact that an emu is as far from the prototype of 'bird' as an ostrich is.

Further evidence for rich memory storage comes from the finding that people are aware that certain features tend to co-occur WITHIN a particular category. For instance, people implicitly know that if a bird sings, it is much more likely to be a small bird than a large bird (Malt and Smith 1984). This detailed, intra-category knowledge is not explainable if people only represent the category using an abstract 'bird' prototype, while discarding knowledge of individual exemplars.

Given these findings about phonetic categories, verbatim recall and categorization as a domain-general process, which indicate that the cognitive representation of language is influenced by specific tokens of language use and the considerable detail contained in these tokens, we proceed now to describe in more detail how the phonology, morphology and syntax of language are treated in an exemplar model, providing at the same time further arguments for exemplar representation.

2.3   Exemplar models in phonology

Exemplar representations have been most fully explored in phonetics and phonology, where models for both perception and production have been proposed. These models assume that every token of experience has some effect on memory storage and organization for linguistic items (Johnson 1997, Pierrehumbert 2001, 2002, Bybee 2001a, 2002b, 2006a). Tokens of linguistic experience are categorized and matched with similar tokens of experience which have previously been stored as exemplars. Thus an exemplar is built up from a set of tokens that are considered by the organism to be the same on some dimension. For instance, each of the phonetic forms of a word that are distinguishable are established in memory as exemplars; new tokens of experience that are the same as some existing exemplars are mapped on to it, strengthening it. Then all the phonetic exemplars of a word are grouped together in an exemplar cluster which is associated with the meanings of the word and the contexts in which it has been used, which themselves form an exemplar cluster (Pierrehumbert 2002, Bybee 2006a). The meanings, inferences and aspects of the context relevant to meaning are also stored with exemplars. Sometimes particular phonetic forms are associated with particular meanings or contexts of use, but more commonly a word is represented as a set of phonetic exemplars with a small range of variation associated directly with a set of meanings.

2.3.1   The Reducing Effect of frequency

A major argument in favour of exemplar models is the fact that words that contain the same phonetic subsequences can have different ranges of variation due to gradual change. A robust finding that has emerged recently in quantitative studies of phonetic reduction is that high-frequency words undergo more change or change at a faster rate than low-frequency words. High-frequency words have a greater proportion of consonant deletion in the case of American t/d-deletion (Gregory et al. 1999, Bybee 2000b) as well as in Spanish intervocalic [ð]-deletion (Bybee 2001a). Unstressed vowels are more reduced in high-frequency words, as shown in Fidelholtz 1975 for English and Van Bergem 1995 for Dutch, and are more likely to delete (Hooper 1976). In addition, there is some evidence for a frequency effect in vowel shifts (Moonwomon 1992, Labov 1994, Hay and Bresnan 2006; see Bybee 2002b for discussion).[1] As Bybee 2000b, 2001a and Pierrehumbert 2001 point out, these facts have a natural place in an exemplar model if we also postulate a bias towards lenition (articulatory reduction) that operates on tokens of use. Words that are used more often are exposed to the bias more often and thus undergo change at a faster rate. The leniting bias is a result of practice: as sequences of units are repeated, the articulatory gestures used tend to reduce and overlap. A number of studies have now shown quantitatively that in cases of variation and ongoing change, high-frequency words with the appropriate phonetic context tend to show more change, both in the proportion of changed variants found in a corpus and in the degree to which the phonetic change has progressed.

Exemplar models provide a natural way to model this frequency effect (an early proposal is found in Moonwomon 1992). If the phonetic change takes place in minute increments each time a word is used and if the effect of usage is cycled back into the stored representation of the word, then words that are used more will accumulate more change than words that are used less. Such a proposal depends upon words having a memory representation that is a phonetic range, that is, a cluster of exemplars (Bybee 2000b, 2001, Pierrehumbert 2001), rather than an abstract phonemic representation. Pierrehumbert 2001 presents a formal exemplar model of lenition that leads to gradual change in exemplar clusters due to a leniting bias affecting words each time they are used.

Each word does not change in totally idiosyncratic ways, but rather follows the general direction of change for the language. For instance, all medial [t] and [d] in American English are subject to flapping before an unstressed vowel. It is not the case that some [t]s and [d]s become fricatives, others glottal stops and so on; rather the phonetic properties of words are associated with one another (Pierrehumbert 2002) leading to both lexically specific variation and patterned variation across lexical items. This patterned variation can be described with exemplars formed from subsequences of words, such as syllables, consonants or

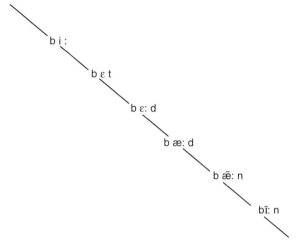

Figure 2.1 Lexical connections for the [b] in *bee, bet, bed, bad, ban, bin*

vowels. Continuing the notation of Bybee 1985, 2001a, we can show relations across words as connecting lines between shared features, as in Figure 2.1.

2.3.2   *Sociophonetic variation*

In recent studies in phonetic variation dubbed 'sociophonetics', researchers argue for exemplars or rich memory for language (Foulkes and Docherty 2006). The same argument applies to subphonemic variation reported in many sociolinguistic studies over the decades in which it is shown that certain phonetic renderings of, for example, American English /r/, or the diphthongs /au/ and /aj/, are associated in certain regions with social class affiliation (Labov 1966, 1972). In order for a certain phonetic form to be associated with males or females, upper or lower socioeconomic class, or geographic regions, these details of pronunciation experienced in oneself and others must be registered in memory and indexed to individuals or classes of individuals. In fact, experimental results suggest that even information about the voice quality of the individual speaker is retained in memory at least for a while (Goldinger 1996).

2.3.3   *Change in adult phonology*

Given exemplar representations and the hypothesis that each token of experience has some impact on memory because it either strengthens an existing exemplar or adds another exemplar to a cluster, it follows that adult pronunciations can undergo change over time. Of course for a child or language learner, each new token of experience can have a much larger impact on representation than it can for an adult, who has already built up a large store of exemplars. Thus changes in adults will be subtle and probably rather slow under most conditions. But change is possible. Sankoff and Blondeau 2007 compared data from the same speakers of Montreal French from 1971 and 1984 with regard to their rate of use of apical [r] (the conservative form) and dorsal or posterior [R], the innovative form. Of the thirty-two individuals studied, ten maintained categorical or near-categorical use of [R] and ten remained categorical or near-categorical in their use of [r]. Another three maintained a fairly constant rate of variation. Of greatest interest are the other nine who all showed significant change over the thirteen years. Seven of these moved from variable to categorical use of [R] and two moved from categorical use of /r/ to 65–66 per cent use of [R].

The data show individual differences, some of which may be due to the particular social situation the person is in and some possibly due to other types of individual differences. The evidence, however, points clearly to the possibility of adult change. Another striking case is reported in Harrington 2006, who studied the recorded Christmas speeches of Queen Elizabeth II over a 50-year period. An examination of the vowels in these recordings shows a change from the earlier Received Pronunciations toward Southern British English, the dialect most popular with younger speakers.

Even among adult speakers, then, the addition of new exemplars to the store of exemplars may have an impact on a speaker's pronunciation, as would be predicted by the rich memory model outlined earlier.

2.4   Morphology

2.4.1   Networks of associations

In an exemplar model, relations can be formed on various levels and along various dimensions. For instance, a word, which consists of a cluster of phonetic exemplars as well as a set of semantic exemplars, can be considered a unit which can then be related to other words in various ways. Words form relations along phonetic dimensions, as in Figure 2.1, as well as along semantic dimensions. In Bybee 1985, 1988a, I argued that morphological relations are emergent from relations formed among words due to their semantic and phonetic similarity. In Figure 2.2 emergent morphological relations are illustrated using the example of some English Past Tense verbs with the /d/ allomorph. The similarity of the final consonant and the similarity of meaning, that is, the fact that all the verbs register past–tense meaning, lead to the identification of the suffix.

In Figure 2.3, the morphological structure of the word *unbelievable* is made apparent by mapping the relations it has with other words with which it shares phonetic and semantic features.

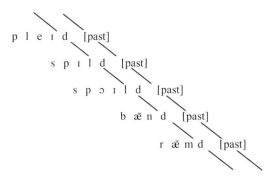

Figure 2.2 Phonological and semantic connections yield Past in *played, spilled, spoiled, banned, rammed*

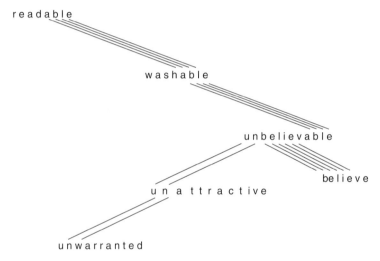

Figure 2.3 The internal structure of *unbelievable* as a derivative of its relations with other words

One advantage of this approach to morphological analysis is that it does not require that a word be exhaustively analysed into morphemes. For instance, the Past Tense form *had* in English may have a connection to the general Past suffix via its final consonant, even though the remaining part of the word, [hæ] is not a morpheme in itself. Similarly, *capable* appears to have the *–able* suffix appropriately signalling an adjective even though *cap-* by itself does not mean anything.

Morphological relations as diagrammed here are gradient in their strength due to differences in both semantic and phonetic similarity. As is well known, words related through derivational morphology may lose some semantic similarity to their bases. The causes of such semantic shifts and changes in degrees of relatedness are discussed in Chapter 3.

As noted above, an exemplar representation is highly redundant; even complex items that can be generated by regular rules may have memory storage. The question posed by this framework is not whether some complex unit is stored in memory or not; the questions to be asked concern the strength of the representation and the strength of its association with other representations, both paradigmatic and syntagmatic, all of which are variable. The property of rich memory representation in this model is extremely important in describing and explaining the way that particular words, sequences of words and constructions accrue particular properties when they are used in context. For instance, at the word level, two words with the same apparent structure, for example verbs sporting a semi-productive prefix such as *re-* or *un-* may have very different degrees of compositionality due to their frequency relations with their base verb and other factors, such as contexts of use. Thus Hay 2001 points out that *refurbish* and *rekindle* have very different relations with *furbish* and *kindle* respectively based on the fact that *refurbish* is much more frequent than *furbish* but *rekindle* is less frequent than *kindle*. Such a difference in the strength of relations among words is handled nicely in an exemplar model with networks of associations, while in structural models this level of detail is completely overlooked.

At a higher level, multi-word sequences such as *dark night* or *pick and choose* have no real idiosyncrasies of meaning and yet are known to be familiar, conventional expressions requiring memory storage. There are also constructions with no real idiosyncrasies of form that nonetheless have accrued pragmatic and semantic properties that must be registered in memory. We turn to these in the discussion below.

2.4.2   The Conserving Effect of token frequency

Exemplar models allow a natural expression of several effects of high token frequency: because exemplars are strengthened as each new token of use is mapped onto them, high-frequency exemplars will be stronger than low-frequency ones, and high-frequency clusters – words, phrases, constructions – will be stronger than lower frequency ones. The effects of this strength (lexical strength [Bybee 1985]) are several: first, stronger exemplars are easier to access, thus accounting for the well-known phenomenon by which high-frequency words are easier to access in lexical decision tasks. Second, high-frequency, morphologically complex words show increased morphological stability.

By morphological stability I refer to two phenomena in linguistic change (both identified by Mańczak 1980 and discussed in Bybee and Brewer 1980 and Bybee 1985). First, frequent forms resist regularizing or other morpho-logical change with the well-known result that irregular inflectional forms tend to be of high frequency. Assuming that regularization occurs when an irregular form is not accessed and instead the regular process is used, it is less likely that high-frequency inflected forms would be subject to regularization. Second, the more frequent of the members of a paradigm tends to serve as the basis of new analogical formations; thus the singular of nouns is the basis for the formation of a new plural (*cow, cows*) rather than the plural serving as the basis for a new singular (*kine* [the old plural of *cow*] does not yield a new singular **ky*). Similarly, the present form serves as the basis for a regularized past and not vice versa. (See Tiersma 1982 and Bybee 1985 for discussions of some add-itional cases that support the frequency argument.)

2.5   Syntax

2.5.1   Word strings

Strings of words can be analysed in a network of relations. While an idiom such as *pull strings* has its own metaphorical meaning, it is nevertheless associated with the words *pull* and *strings* as independent words, as shown in Figure 2.4 (see Nunberg, Sag and Wasow 1994 for arguments to this effect).

As with morphology, the relations diagrammed as connecting lines in these figures can be of varying strengths. Certain factors, which will be dis-cussed in Chapter 3, are influential in the maintenance or loss of these lexical connections.

When two or more words are often used together, they also develop a sequen-tial relation, which we will study as 'chunking' in the next chapter. The strength of the sequential relations is determined by the frequency with which the two words appear together.[2] As we will see, the frequency with which sequences of units are used has an impact on their phonetic, morpho-syntactic and semantic properties.

2.5.2   Constructions

Exemplars and exemplar clusters can be formed at various levels of complex-ity. There are exemplars below the level of the word that correspond to phon-etic sequences that occur within words, such as syllable onsets or rhymes. Constructions also have exemplar representations, but these will be more com-plex, because, depending upon how one defines them, most or all constructions are partially schematic – that is, they have positions that can be filled by a var-iety of words or phrases. In addition, many constructions allow the full range of inflectional possibilities on nouns, adjectives and verbs, so that inflectional

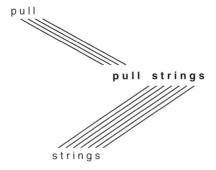

Figure 2.4 An idiom as analysable into component words

positions are schematic, too, with the result that particular exemplars of constructions can differ substantially from one another. However, constructions also usually have some fixed parts which are crucial to the establishment of the exemplar cluster.

Representing grammatical patterns in constructions is particularly appropriate in an exemplar model, since constructions are direct pairings of form with meaning with no intermediate level of representations, such as phrase structure rules would provide. This is appropriate because what language users experience is specific instances or tokens of constructions. They map similar tokens onto one another to establish exemplars and these exemplars group together to form categories that represent both the fixed and schematic slots in constructions. The meaning of a construction is also represented by a set of exemplars which are built up by accessing the meaning of the lexical items used plus the overall meaning in context. As we will see in Chapter 4, constructions are used with novel lexical items and in novel ways through referencing by analogy previously experienced exemplars of the construction.

Consider for example a resultative construction studied by Boas 2003 (cf. a set of 'become' constructions in Spanish as analysed by Bybee and Eddington 2006; see Chapters 4 and 5). This construction uses the verb *drive* with an adjective or prepositional phrase expressing a meaning such as 'drive crazy'. Particular tokens found in the British National Corpus (BNC) include:

(1) It drives me crazy.
(2) they drive you mad
(3) that drives me mad
(4) The death of his wife the following year drove him mad.
(5) A slow-witted girl drove him mad.
(6) It drove the producer mad.
(7) A couple of channels that used to drive her up the wall.
(8) This room drives me up the wall.

The construction consists of a subject position that apparently allows any noun phrase to occur. This is followed by an inflected form of the verb *drive* and a noun phrase that plays the role of experiencer and thus has an animate, usually human, referent. This noun phrase can presumably be of any form, but it is most commonly a pronoun. The adjectives illustrated here are *crazy, mad* and *up the wall;* the others that occur in the BNC are semantically related to these (see Boas 2003).

For illustration, the eight tokens represented above could each be considered exemplars which are grouped together with their identical parts mapped onto one another and their schematic parts forming categories as follows:

(9)

$$
\text{SUBJECT} \quad \text{[DRIVE]} \left\{ \begin{array}{l} \textit{me} \\ \textit{you} \\ \textit{him} \\ \textit{her} \\ \textit{the producer} \end{array} \right\} \left\{ \begin{array}{l} \textit{mad} \\ \textit{crazy} \\ \textit{up the wall} \end{array} \right\}
$$

The category of SUBJECT has not been represented with actual exemplars because it appears to take any NP. Presumably NP is a category that can be developed on the basis of the exemplars that occur in other constructions (Croft 2001). Of course, even here, some realizations of the subject will be more frequent than others. For instance, *that* or *it* might be particularly frequent. [DRIVE] is a notation intended to show that any inflected form of the verb *drive* may appear, in addition to any of the other auxiliary or emerging auxiliary constructions (e.g. *used to, gonna* …). The enlarged font of [DRIVE] represents the strength it acquires by occurring in all instances of the construction. *Mad* and *crazy* are similarly represented enlarged because of their high frequency in the construction. The experiencer slot is usually a pronoun, but is always animate and usually human. The final position, which can be an adjective or prepositional phrase, has a strong semantic character. Most of the fillers for this slot found in Boas' study of the BNC were synonyms with 'crazy', though there were also slightly more distantly related senses such as *to desperation,* or *to suicide.*

Certain exemplars of this construction might occur more than once. Thus we would not be surprised to find a corpus in which *it drives me crazy* (in exactly that form) occurred multiple times. Also, certain parts of the construction may occur together more often than others. Clearly, it is *drive* plus the AP or PP phrase with the appropriate meaning that expresses the lexical semantic content of the construction, but a segment of the construction, such as *drives me* might also be frequent and be chunked together, as explained in Chapter 3.

All instances of this construction that have been experienced by a language user have had some impact on the representation of the construction, though they may not all literally be lodged in memory. As with other memories, non-reinforced exemplars may become inaccessible or forgotten; both recency and frequency play a role in the maintenance of particular exemplars of constructions.

2.5.3   Evidence for an exemplar representation for constructions

In this section, I will present evidence that exemplars of constructions have an effect on cognitive representation. Some of the arguments provided here will be further developed in later chapters. The cases discussed concern idioms and prefabricated units (prefabs) as specific exemplars of constructions that require cognitive representation and the development of new constructions from specific exemplars of existing constructions, both with and without grammaticalization.

First consider the fact that idioms are instances of constructions that have their own representation. Thus *pull strings* is an instance of a VERB–OBJECT construction. The necessity of direct representation of idioms arises from their unpredictable meaning. However, there are also many conventionalized instances or exemplars of constructions that are not unpredictable in meaning or form, such as *dark night,* but are known to speakers as expressions they have experienced before. These exemplars of constructions also need to be registered in memory.

Second, consider the way new constructions arise. New constructions are specific exemplars of more general existing constructions that take on new pragmatic implications, meanings, or forms due to their use in particular contexts. Consider a construction studied by Fillmore and Kay 1999 and Johnson 1997, which they call the WXDY? construction. It is exemplified in the famous joke, shown in (10):

(10)   Diner: Waiter, *what's this fly doing in my soup?*
       Waiter: Why, madam, I believe that's the backstroke.
       (From Fillmore and Kay 1994)

The joke shows the ambiguity of the sequence in italics. The usual interpretation of 'what is X doing Y?' is one of surprise at incongruity accompanied by more than a hint of disapproval. Because it is syntactically indistinct from the construction from which it arose – a *what* question with *do* in the progressive, it gives the clever waiter license to interpret it as a literal question about what the fly is doing.

Interestingly, there is nothing in the form which explicitly suggests a meaning of incongruity, but the strong implication is nonetheless there. We can ask, then, how did an ordinary Wh-question with *doing* and a locative phrase acquire these implications? The answer must be that these implications arise from language use in context. The question of *what are you doing?* itself often has negative connotations. In a face-to-face situation – not when talking on the phone, for instance, where it is a legitimate question – such a question implies that despite a lot of visual information, if this question is asked, it must indicate that the speaker wants some explanation not just of what the addressee is doing, but why he or she is doing it. Similarly, with this construction having the locative element, as in (11), there is the possibility of ambiguity, but the first reading is probably more common.

(11) What are you doing with that knife = 'why do you have that knife?'
           or the literal meaning = 'what are you <u>doing</u> with it?'

The implication of disapproval, which is a subjective interpretation made in context, must have come from multiple instances of use with this negative nuance. As we pointed out earlier, each exemplar of a morpho-syntactic construction includes information about the contexts of use and this would include the inferences made in such contexts. Fillmore and colleagues make such implications an important part of their study of constructions (Fillmore, Kay and O'Connor 1988, Fillmore and Kay 1999). We know from studies of grammaticalization that inferences can become part of the meaning of a construction (Traugott 1989, Traugott and Dasher 2002; see below and Chapter 6). (Note that the term 'implication' refers to meaning the speaker builds into the utterance without directly expressing it, while 'inference' refers to the meanings the hearer gleans from the utterance even though they might not be directly expressed.) The only way inferences can become part of the meaning would be if language users were recording in memory the inferences in each situation, as a rich memory model would suggest. At the point at which certain inferences become strong in certain contexts, they become part of the meaning of a construction.

Specific exemplars of constructions can also become conventionalized through repetition before they take on any further nuances of meaning or changes in form. For instance, the question *What's a nice girl like you doing in a place like this?* appeared in the film *The Wild One* in 1953 (perhaps for the first time) and has been repeated until it has become something of a cliché. Spin-offs from this expression appear even in written corpora, such as the *Time Magazine* corpus, which contains the exact question (12), the question with one word changed as in (13), where it is part of the title of a cartoon, the same question in third person rather than second and with *that* instead of *this* (14), several words change as in (15). It also appears as the name of a film, as in (15) and (16), and with very specific NPs filled in as in (17).

(12) what's a nice girl like you doing in a place like this? (1974)

(13) Alice in Wonderland, or What's a Nice Kid Like You Doing in a Place Like This? (1966)

(14) What's a nice girl like her doing in a place like that? (1978)

(15) what's a nice thing like you doing in show biz. (1967)

(16) What's a Nice Girl Like You Doing in a Business Like This? (1969)

(17) What's a nice girl like Annie Hall doing in a film like Mr. Goodbar? (1977)

Note that its use in (13) and (16) in film titles suggests a conventionalization, as people often choose familiar expressions or variations on them as titles for literary or cinematic works. This expression, then, is a specific instance of the WXYD? construction in which one exemplar has become conventionalized.

The important point to note from this discussion is that new constructions arise out of specific exemplars of old constructions (Bybee 2003b, 2006a). This fact tells us much about how new constructions come to be and it also provides evidence that cognitive representations of grammar include specific information about contexts of use of exemplars and their meaning and implications in these contexts.

A similar argument can be made about grammaticalization, the process by which lexical items within constructions become grammatical morphemes (Heine et al. 1991, Bybee et al. 1994, Hopper and Traugott 2003). In grammaticalization, not only do new constructions arise out of existing constructions, but also a further step is taken in that a lexical item within this construction takes on grammatical status. A recent example in the history of English is the development of the future marker, *be going to*. This developed out of a purposive construction meaning 'to go somewhere to do something'. It is important to note that uses of *go* in other constructions do not grammaticalize into futures. This development only takes place where *go* is in the progressive and is followed by *to* plus another verb. As recently as Shakespeare's time such a construction had its literal meaning. It was just one exemplar – but the most frequent exemplar – of the more general purpose construction exemplified by these sentences from Shakespeare:

(18)   Don Alphonso,
        With other gentlemen of good esteem,
        Are journeying to salute the emperor
        And to commend their service to his will. (*Two Gentlemen of Verona*, I.3)

(19)   ...the kings
        and the princes, our kindred, are going to see the queen's picture.
        (*The Winter's Tale*, V.2)

Note that in (19) the subjects are actually moving in space. In contemporary English *we're gonna see the queen's picture* can be interpreted simply as a prediction about future time, as in a situation where the queen's picture is about to appear on a computer screen, in which case one could say, *we're going to see the queen's picture.*

As grammaticalization takes place a number of changes accrue to the new construction: phonetic reduction (as *going to* becomes *gonna*), and change in meanings and inferences, which expand the contexts of use of the new construction. For instance, the example in (20) shows both the intention and prediction meaning, while the example in (21) shows the construction with an inanimate subject.

(20) They're going to get married next spring.
(21) It's going to rain all day.

In order for these changes to become permanent, they have to be registered in the exemplar that is the source of the new construction right from the beginning. This implies that an exemplar of a construction has a memory trace to which specific phonetic, pragmatic and semantic properties can be tagged. As the new construction becomes established in the grammar, it gradually loses its associations with the construction from which it arose, as well as from other instances of the words or morphemes that comprise it.

An important argument for the network model described above is the fact that the loss of connections with other items takes place gradually (see Chapter 8). It would be very difficult to say for current English whether the *go* in the future periphrasis is considered by speakers to be a true instance of *go*. Certainly, literate speakers know the etymological source of the phrase, but it is unlikely that every use of the phrase activates other instances of *go* or *go* in other constructions.

Finally, because items that are used together frequently come to be processed together as a unit, changes in constituency and category can take place. Thus *going to* as the constant part of this construction becomes a single unit not just phonologically, but also syntactically. As the construction acquires new nuances of meaning and loses its motion sense, the following verb is taken to be the main verb. This process, known as 'reanalysis', is viewed in a usage-based perspective as being gradual, that is, as consisting of a gradual change in the exemplar cluster (Haspelmath 1998; see Chapters 7 and 8).

2.6   Conclusion

At every level of grammar evidence can be found for rich memory representations: the fact that specific phonetic details are part of a language user's knowledge of his or her language; the importance of frequency (registered by exemplar strength) to morphological structure and change; and the fact that specific instances of constructions have representations that can be accessed for analogical extensions or for the creation of new constructions.

Since exemplars provide a record of a speaker's experience with language, exemplar models allow the direct representation of both variation and gradience. Thus phonetic variation, whether lexically specific or generalized over many words or phrases, is represented directly. Such a direct representation allows a means of implementation of gradual sound change. Given exemplars and network representation, morphologically complex words can vary in frequency or strength of representation and each can have its own degrees of compositionality and analysability, depending upon how strongly each word is connected to other instances of its component parts. In syntax, differences in frequency of specific exemplars of constructions can lead to the loss of compositionality and analysability and the eventual, gradual creation of a new construction. Other implications of exemplar representation for constructions are discussed in subsequent chapters.

3   Chunking and degrees of autonomy

3.1   Introduction

In previous works I have focused attention on the role of repetition or frequency in the creation of linguistic structure through language change (see Bybee 2007). All the frequency effects I have identified work in conjunction with particular processing mechanisms. In this chapter and the next two, I examine the processing mechanisms whose repeated application gives shape to grammar, in an attempt to uncover the properties of these mechanisms. The goal, to the extent possible, is to identify the domain-general mechanisms that underlie language. These mechanisms, in conjunction with an exemplar model of linguistic representation and organization, can readily represent the ongoing modifications of the linguistic system that explain its patterning, as well as its synchronic variation and change over time.

By 'processing' I refer to the activities involved in both production of the message and the decoding of it. Thus the discussion includes in principle the set of cognitive and neuromotor mechanisms or activities that are put into use in online communication and in the mental storage of language. My hypothesis is that the particular way these processing mechanisms work determines fairly directly the facts about the nature of language. In particular, we will be examining the nature of chunking and the consequent phonetic reduction of repeated sequences, as well as the maintenance and loss of analysability and compositionality in complex expressions due to the effects of repetition. Also in this chapter, we consider once again the way the context imbues the linguistic construction with meaning especially through the inferences that the hearer makes. In the next chapter, we examine analogy, which will be defined as the use of a novel item in an existing construction, and categorization, which provides the framework of similarity upon which analogy depends.

In the previous chapter we discussed exemplar representation and networks of associations among words and parts of words. In addition to the paradigmatic relations discussed there, syntagmatic relations exist among sounds, morphemes and words. When two or more words are often used together, they also develop a sequential relation, which we will study as 'chunking' in the next section. The strength of the sequential relations is determined by the frequency with which the two words appear together. In the following sections we discuss the way the exemplar and network model helps us describe and explain chunking phenomena, including phonetic reduction, the development of autonomy in cases of extremely high frequency, and the changes in meaning brought about by use of language in context.

3.2   Chunking

The underlying cognitive basis for morphosyntax and its hierarchical organization is the chunking of sequential experiences that occurs with repetition (Miller 1956, Newell 1990, Haiman 1994, Ellis 1996, Bybee 2002a). Chunking has been identified as a process influencing all cognitive systems, based on the general organization of memory. As Newell 1990 put it:

A chunk is a unit of memory organization, formed by bringing together a set of already formed chunks in memory and welding them together into a larger unit. Chunking implies the ability to build up such structures recursively, thus leading to a hierarchical organization of memory. Chunking appears to be a ubiquitous feature of human memory. (p. 7)

The principal experience that triggers chunking is repetition. If two or more smaller chunks occur together with some degree of frequency, a larger chunk containing the smaller ones is formed. Chunking is of course a property of both production and perception and contributes significantly to fluency and ease in both modes. The longer the string that can be accessed together, the more fluent the execution and the more easily comprehension will occur. As we will see below, one effect of chunking in production is the overlap and reduction of articulatory gestures. In perception and decoding an important effect is the ability to anticipate what is coming next.

Chunking is the process behind the formation and use of formulaic or prefabricated sequences of words such as *take a break, break a habit, pick and choose* and it is also the primary mechanism leading to the formation of constructions and constituent structure (Bybee 2002a). Note that repetition is necessary, but extremely high frequency in experience is not. Chunking has been shown to be subject to the Power Law of Practice (Anderson 1982), which stipulates that performance improves with practice but the amount of improvement decreases as a function of increasing practice or frequency. Thus once chunking occurs after several repetitions, further benefits or effects of repetition accrue much more slowly.

Chunking is thought to occur in adults as readily as in children. As people get more experienced, they build additional chunks (Newell 1990). This means that rather large chunks, such as poems and proverbs, can be stored in memory, as well as other sequences that occur in rehearsed or practiced speech or writing. In general experience as well as in language, it is usually the case that the larger the chunk, the less often it will occur. The single word *break* is an item that occurs more frequently than either of the larger chunks, *take a break* and *break a habit; break a habit* is likely to occur more frequently than *break a bad habit* and so on. The greater frequency and cohesion of smaller chunks within larger ones is what gives language its hierarchical structure. The lesser usefulness and therefore lower frequency of the larger chunks slows learning after the point at which the most useful chunks have been acquired.

While language users constantly acquire more and larger chunks of language, it is not the case that in general the language acquisition process proceeds by moving from the lowest level chunks to the highest. Even if children start with single words, words themselves are composed of smaller chunks (either morphemes or phonetic sequences), which only later may be analysed by the young language user. In addition, however, children can acquire larger multi-word chunks without knowing their internal composition (Peters 1983). The acquisition process in such cases consists of the analysis of such a chunk into smaller units and a growing understanding of what parts of the chunk are substitutable or modifiable. For instance, in several studies by Lieven and colleagues, it is shown that many of the utterances of young children are initially verbatim repetitions of utterances produced by adults or utterances the children have produced themselves. As children gradually learn to make substitutions in the slots of these multi-word sequences, the sequences are gradually analysed into their component parts, allowing for greater productivity in their use (Pine and Lieven 1993, Lieven et al. 1997 and Dąbrowska and Lieven 2005). (See Chapter 4, section 4.3 for further discussion of this research.)

All sorts of conventionalized multi-word expressions, from prefabricated expressions to idioms to constructions, can be considered chunks for the purposes of processing and analysis. The tracking of exemplars and their categorization discussed in Chapter 2 leads automatically to the discovery of repeated word sequences. A multi-word expression is conventionalized if it has been established (tacitly, through repetition) as the appropriate way to say something in a particular community (Pawley and Syder 1983, Erman and Warren 2000, Wray 2002). That would include interactive expressions such as *how are you?* and *I don't know, I don't think so* as well as chunks that are part of the propositional content of utterances, such as *take a break* and *pick and choose*. Idioms are also conventionalized, and constitute a more specific sort of prefabricated expression in that they have a non-literal meaning, usually one that relies on metaphor, metonymy or hyperbole for its interpretation (Nunberg, Sag and Wasow 1994). Examples are *pull strings, lend a hand, raining cats and dogs.* I will hereafter use the term 'prefab' (prefabricated expression) to refer to any conventionalized multi-word expression. Recent studies have emphasized the pervasiveness of such multi-word expressions in natural speech and writing. Erman and Warren 2000 find that about 55 per cent of word choices are predetermined by the word's appearance in a prefab.

Just because a multi-word expression is stored and processed as a chunk does not mean that it does not have internal structure. Its internal structure is based on associations formed between the prefab and other occurrences of words that appear in the prefab, as well as associations between the prefab and the more general construction from which it arose. Thus *lend a hand* belongs in the exemplar cluster of V-NP (verbs and their direct objects), which accounts for its syntactic structure, and it is also associated with the exemplar clusters for the verb *lend* and the noun phrase *a hand* and the noun *hand*. While *lend a hand* is relatively fixed, the internal parts are still identifiable, as evidenced by the ability to add modifiers, as in *lend a helping hand* or to add an indirect object, as in *lend me a hand*. In the case of idioms, it has been shown that language users maintain a literal interpretation based on the concrete meanings of the phrase as well as the figurative interpretation (Gibbs and O'Brien 1990). The identifiability of internal parts in an expression, its analysability, will be discussed further in section 3.4.

As mentioned earlier, the status of a chunk in memory falls along a continuum. Certainly words that have never been experienced together do not constitute a chunk, but otherwise there is a continuum from words that have been experienced together only once and fairly recently, which will constitute a weak chunk whose internal parts are stronger than the whole, to more frequent chunks such as *lend a hand* or *pick and choose* which are easily accessible as wholes while still maintaining connections to their parts. Prefabs can be represented as sequential connections between one word and the next; as mentioned above, such connections can have varying strength, depending upon their frequency of co-occurrence. On the high-frequency end of the continuum, chunks such as grammaticalizing phrases or discourse markers do lose their internal structure and the identifiability of their constituent parts; see section 3.4.2 for discussion.

As discussed in Chapter 2, constructions are sequential chunks of language that are conventionally used together and that sometimes have special meanings or other properties. Their conventionalization comes about through repetition (Haiman 1994). Constructions are typically partially schematic; they come with some fixed parts and some slots that can be filled with a category of semantically defined items. Note that idioms, prefabs and constructions all demonstrate that chunks do not have to be continuous – they can be interrupted by open classes of items. For instance, the *drives X mad* construction can have a pronoun in the X position; indeed the most common word to occur there is *me*; however, it can also have a full noun phrase, as shown in Chapter 2, examples (1)–(8). As mentioned earlier, this construction can take a variety of adjectives and prepositional phrases in the position where *mad* occurs. The criterion for this position is semantic similarity to the central members, *mad* and *crazy*. These crucial properties of constructions – the fact that they involve sequences of units and also have at least one schematic category – indicate that the source of constructions is chunking plus categorization, both domain-general cognitive mechanisms.

As evidence that chunking is the mechanism behind the formation of complex units in language, from prefabs to constructions, we consider in the following sections both the phonetic effects of chunking and changes in analysability and compositionality due to chunking. Phonetic effects of chunking and repetition will be discussed in the next section. There we will see that within a construction, some elements are more fused together than others, due to their frequency of co-occurrence in the construction. Phonetic effects can be used as a diagnostic for the internal structure of constructions.

3.3 The reducing effect of frequency

3.3.1 *Reduction of words in context*

As discussed in Chapter 2, substantial evidence has recently been reported showing that phonetic reduction occurs earlier and to a greater extent in high-frequency words than in low-frequency ones. As noted there, if we postulate that reduction occurs online as words are used, then words that are used more often are exposed to reduction processes more often and thus undergo change at a faster rate. In addition, we must note that words that are used more often in a context favourable to reduction will also undergo more reduction. In general the bias towards reduction is a result of chunking: as sequences of units are repeated the articulatory gestures used tend to reduce and overlap. This generalization applies to the articulatory gestures that comprise words, but also to sequences of words. Thus further examination of relevant data has shown that it is not just the frequency of the word that determines its degree of reduction, but rather the frequency of the word in the reducing environment (Bybee 2002b). These latter findings are important for understanding how the exemplars of a word interact in categorization and storage. In addition, reduction of words in specific contexts provides important information about the properties of chunked material.

Studying the way the phonetic exemplar clusters for words change over time gives us insight into the nature of exemplar categorization. Cases where a word occurs both inside and outside the conditioning environment for a change are particularly instructive. For instance, the tendency to delete word-final [t] and [d] in American English has the potential to create two variants of words such as *hand, student, can't*, and so on, one that occurs before a consonant and thus has no final [t] or [d] (e.g. *hand me* is [hǽnmĩ] and one that occurs before vowels, which preserves the [t] or [d] (e.g. *hand it...* is [hǽndɪt]. Despite the fact the phonetic conditioning is rather clear, some words tend towards more tokens with the consonant while others tend towards more tokens without, depending upon which environment is more frequent for that word (Bybee 2002b).

Consider, for example, the negative auxiliaries in English (e.g. *don't, can't, aren't*), which have a very high probability of final [t] deletion – 86 per cent before vowels and 84 per cent before consonants (compared to figures for all words of 37 per cent before vowels and 59 per cent before consonants). Note that the deletion of the final [t] in this case occurs even before vowels. Bybee 2002b reports that the higher rate of deletion is not just due to the token frequency of the auxiliaries, but is also affected by the fact that 80 per cent of auxiliaries in the corpus occurred before words beginning with consonants (compared to 64 per cent overall). In contrast, lexical words ending in –*nt* occur before consonants only 42 per cent of the time. Their rate of deletion of final [t] is significantly less than for the auxiliaries.

The most frequent phonetic exemplars in a cluster are stronger and thus more likely to be chosen for production. The fact that negative auxiliaries occur so much more often before consonants leads to exemplar clusters in which the preconsonantal variant is the strongest; as a result this variant tends to spread to all positions. Thus the exemplar for the negative auxiliary lacking the final [t] will end up occurring even before vowels. Note that the dominance of the cluster by the most frequent exemplar, which thus has a higher likelihood of being chosen for production, leads to the tendency for words to settle on a tight range of variance or a more centred category (Pierrehumbert 2003, Wedel 2006).

These facts underscore the importance of multi-word chunks to phonetic reduction. While it is true (as we mentioned in Chapter 2) that high-frequency words reduce at a faster rate than low-frequency words, it is not the word out of context that is actually implementing the reduction. Rather as the word appears in sequence and forms chunks, the reduction can be facilitated or delayed by the particular environments in which the word occurs in continuous speech.

3.3.2   Causes of reduction

In the recent literature various factors have been invoked to explain the distribution of phonetic reduction. It is important to examine these factors and their possible interactions as we strive to determine which mechanisms are responsible for phonetic reduction and how phonetic reduction interacts with chunking. The factors identified – word frequency, frequency in context, predictability from surrounding words (to be discussed below) – reveal a subtle interplay between online accommodations and changes in stored exemplar clusters; they also provide evidence for the storage of chunks as exemplars.

Lindblom 1990 presents a theory of phonetic variation that refers to the competing tendencies operative in the speaker: the tendency of the motor system towards economy of effort and the needs of the listener to discriminate stimuli in order to identify lexical items and constructions. The speaker is subject to a general neuromotor principle that balances timing versus the degree of displacement of physical movements in such a way as to make actions more economical. Thus co-articulation or overlap as well as reduction facilitate production (1990: 425). Speakers have some degree of (perhaps not totally conscious) choice about this and can choose to allow co-articulation and reduction or they can choose to suppress these processes depending upon inferences made about the status of the listener's access to information as well as factors associated with the message the speaker intends to convey – such as the expression of emphasis or contrast. This is particularly evident in frequent phrases such as *I don't know*/*I dunno* (discussed below), which can be highly reduced or can occur in its full form, or *I'm going to*/*I'm gonna*. (The orthographic variants do not do justice to the full range of variation that is possible in such phrases.) However, some degree of choice also characterizes the phonetic variation in less frequent words and phrases: Fowler and Housum 1987 show that the second repetition of a lexical word in a discourse tends to be shorter in phonetic duration than the first instance of the same word.

Lindblom emphasizes that the listener's system is already activated, both by the categories of the language that are present in the listener's cognitive system and by the properties of the linguistic and non-linguistic context in which the utterance is embedded. The speaker, then, must judge how accessible the lexical items, phrases and constructions being used will be to the listener. Among the factors that Lindblom mentions as affecting accessibility are word frequency and neighbourhood frequency, based on the well-known effect that high-frequency words are recognized faster than low-frequency words and the related effect that words with fewer neighbours (neighbours are words that are highly similar phonetically) are recognized faster (Goldinger et al. 1989, Luce et al. 1990, Munson et al. 2004). Other factors will be mentioned below. If the speaker judges the units of the utterance to be highly accessible to the listener, then articulatory reduction and co-articulation are allowed to occur; but if the units are less accessible in the speaker's judgement, then they are articulated more carefully.

It is important to note that reduction and co-articulation in Lindblom's theory are not well described by terms such as 'ease of articulation' or 'least effort'; rather he argues that such online changes are towards a low-cost form of behaviour. There might be rather delicate timing relations (as in phrases such as *didn't you*) but what is saved is the amount of muscular displacement or activation. Browman and Goldstein 1992 and Mowrey and Pagliuca 1995 propose similar characterizations: casual speech reduction and sound change result from reduction of the magnitude of gestures and increase in the temporal overlap of consecutive gestures.

Jurafsky and colleagues have been particularly interested in the factors that facilitate the listener's task and thus allow the speaker to reduce the signal from its most explicit phonetic form. They group a series of distributional factors under the umbrella of 'predictability'. These include word frequency, the probability of the word given the preceding or following word or words, and probability of the word based on the topic of the conversation (Gregory et al. 1999, Jurafsky et al. 2001, Jurafsky et al. 2002, Bell et al. 2003). For content words the findings include word-final [t] and [d] deletion associated with word frequency (as found in other studies, see above), and with mutual information, which is the probability that the two words would occur together, given the frequency of both words. Word-final flapping of [t] or [d] is associated with mutual information (Gregory et al. 1999). Word duration is significantly associated with the predictability of the word given the following word (Bell et al. 2003). Jurafsky et al. 2002 show that many of these same factors affect function words, leading to the differential reduction in function words according to the different constructions in which they occur.

The theory that predictability is the basis of phonetic reduction emphasizes the speaker's monitoring of the listener's state of mind. However, the functioning of predictability in online processing depends upon the tendency for articulatory reduction to always be working while the speaker is controlling (largely unconsciously or automatically) the amount of reduction according to the listener's needs. It should be borne in mind in addition that the same factors that make access easier for the listener also make access easier for the speaker. Mutual information and the other measures of conditional probability relations between pairs and triplets of words measure the relative cohesion among words in prefabs or multi-word expressions. The ease of processing a sequence of words that have been accessed previously and thus have left a memory trace may account for some of the phonetic reduction. As repetition is the major factor both in chunking and in the practice that reduces neuromotor effort, reduction in predictable chunks of language may arise from mechanisms affecting the speaker even more than those benefiting the listener. Lindblom's theory, which proposes a competition between factors associated with the speaker and those associated with the listener, is thus more realistic than Jurafsky and colleagues' theory, whose predictability measures are aimed at considering only the demand on the listener.

However, even taking into account the online demands made on the speaker and listener is not enough. The probability of co-occurrence between and among words which contributes to predictability is the result of chunking. The knowledge that a sequence of words has occurred together previously is naturally represented in an exemplar model as an exemplar that includes the whole sequence. Such sequences can be weaker or stronger depending upon how often they have been experienced. Phonetic reduction may be established as part of the word sequence.

An important argument for chunking is that the online processing variables mentioned above are not enough to explain the extent of phonetic change that occurs in predictable, frequent or conventionalized word sequences. To take an extreme example, consider the reduction of *don't* in the phrase *I don't know*. Bybee and Scheibman 1999 have shown that *don't* in this phrase can have a vowel reduced to schwa, as well as an initial flap and deleted final [t]. There can even be tokens in which the initial [d] is deleted. The extent of this reduction is not likely to be due to online processing, as it rarely affects other similar words and doesn't even affect instances of *don't* in lower frequency phrases such as *I don't inhale* or *what if they don't go for your fantasy?* The fact that this 'special' reduction constitutes a continuation of the more usual reduction found across the board in online reduction suggests a cumulative effect of online reduction. Thus the shortening of the [d] to a flap has as its natural end point the complete deletion of the [d]; the shortening and reduction of the vowel, if continued, would lead to a schwa. Special reduction, then, is the accumulation of reducing effects in the memory representation of the word or phrase. *I don't know* is a highly frequent phrase and furthermore is used as a discourse marker where its literal meaning is of little relevance (Scheibman 2000). In the model discussed above, where more repetitions expose the phonetic material to more reduction, the extreme reduction of *I don't know* is due to a changed stored representation which constitutes a sort of record of previous online reductions.

Even in cases where frequency is not so high, we have evidence that change in representation occurs due to the reduction that goes on in the context of continuous speech. Recall the example of the deletion of [t] in negative auxiliaries mentioned above. Another such example is found in Brown 2004, who studies the reduction to [h] of syllable-initial, including word-initial [s], in New Mexican Spanish. The phonetic contexts favouring reduction are preceding and following non-high vowels, as shown in (1) and (2). The overall rate of word-initial reduction is only 16 per cent.

(1) Likely to reduce:
     no sabíamos 'we didn't know'   *la señora* 'the lady'
(2) Unlikely to reduce:
     el señor 'the gentleman'   *su suegra* '3s. poss. mother-in-law'

For word-initial [s], the following phonetic environment is always the same, but the preceding one changes in context. Brown found a significant difference in the reduction of word-initial [s] when taking into account how often the word

Table 3.1 *Word-initial /s/ reduction rates for words with favourable and unfavourable preceding phonological environment with low and high FFC (Brown 2004: 103)*

	FFC < 50	FFC > 50
Favourable preceding phonological environment	35/403 = 9 %	**267/741 = 36 %**
Unfavourable preceding phonological environment	33/686 = 5 %	19/344 = 6 %

Favourable: $p = 0.0000$, Chi-square = 100.4769; Unfavourable: $p = 0.6222$, Chi-square = 0.242809

occurred in a favouring environment. For instance, compare *señor* and *señora*. The latter occurs frequently after a low vowel, since it occurs after the definite and indefinite articles, both of which end in *a* in the feminine: *la señora, una señora* and this conditions the change of [s] to [h]. However, the masculine articles are *el* and *un*, both of which end in consonants and thus do not condition the reduction. Thus when *señor* occurs in a favouring environment, as in *no señor*, the reduction is much less likely to occur than if *señora* occurs in that same environment. Speakers are much more likely to say *no heñora* than they are to say *no heñor*. Table 3.1 is from Brown 2004: 103; FFC stands for 'frequency in a favourable context'. All words were rated for this measure based on their context in the corpus. In Table 3.1 words are divided between those that occurred less than 50 per cent of the time in a favourable context (FFC < 50) and those that occurred more than 50 per cent of the time in a favourable context (FFC > 50). Table 3.1 shows that words with a higher FFC had more reduction when they occurred in favourable contexts than words with a lower FFC.

This reduction, then, is not just sensitive to the hearer's needs as the predictability hypothesis would suggest, but rather to the speaker's prior experiences. Since *señora* occurs frequently in the reducing environment, the reduced exemplars for this word are much stronger than they are for *señor* and thus are more likely to be chosen for production. Interestingly, it is not just the current phonetic context that affects the word's phonetic shape, but also the other contexts in which the word usually appears. Thus despite the fact that the word occurs inside a chunk in memory, it has an effect on the general exemplar cluster for the word. This supports the point made earlier, that even though chunks are stored as units, their constituent words are still closely related to the general exemplar clusters for those words.

This is not to deny the importance of the online factors at the moment of speech: as mentioned earlier, it has been shown that the second occurrence of a word in a unit of discourse is usually shorter than the first occurrence (Fowler and Housum 1987). This shortening could be attributed to either ease of access by speaker and hearer (due to priming) or to a local practice effect. In either case, it is specific to the discourse. Similarly, the predictability effects uncovered by Jurafsky and colleagues are the original impetus for the phonetic reduction that creates new exemplars of a word or phrase. In addition, the position of the word or phrase in the linguistic string and where the prosodic prominence occurs are important: lengthening of stressed material and lengthening of material occurring before a pause are commonly observed and work against phonetic reduction. However, my point here is that the extent of reduction of a word is not just determined by online factors at the moment of speech, but also by the usage history of the word. Reduction is going to take place in frequent phrases, such as *la señora*, but also in the general exemplar cluster for the word, so that the reduced variant will show up elsewhere, too. Thus some of the predictability effects found by Jurafsky and colleagues can be traced to the presence of the reducing word within a chunk. We conclude, then, that chunking into prefabs benefits the speaker as much as the hearer and hastens phonetic reduction. Thus I have argued that both online demands on speaker and listener, and changes in stored representation affect the extent to which words are reduced or not in production.

3.3.3 *Differential reduction within high-frequency chunks*

Another source of evidence for the importance of frequency of co-occurrence in the articulatory fusion of elements can be found in the differential reduction within chunks according to how frequently the subparts occur together. For instance, the fusion of *going to* into *gonna* [gənə] is due to the fact that this sequence is invariant in the grammaticizing phrase *be going to*. The forms of *be* fuse with the subject as they do in other instances of the Progressive construction.

In our study of the reduction of *don't* in American English we found that the degree of cohesion between *don't* and the preceding vs. following word could be predicted by the frequency of their co-occurrence (Bybee and Scheibman 1999, Bybee 2001a). The reduction of the vowel of *don't* is more dependent on the subject than it is on the following verb. The reduction only occurs with *I* (and in one instance in our data with *why*), but it occurs with a variety of verbs: *know, think, have(to), want, like, mean, care* and *feel*. Moreover, the deletion of the flap occurs only with *I*, but with a variety of verbs: *know, think, like, mean* and *feel* in this corpus.

Table 3.2 shows that in the small corpus of conversation that we examined, there were 88 instances of *I don't* and a total of only fourteen types occupying the subject position. As for the position following *don't*, there are 30 distinct types and *know* occurs 39 times. Thus the frequency of *don't know* is less than the frequency of *I don't*.

Table 3.2 *Number of items preceding and following* don't *(Bybee 2001a: 163)*

Preceding *don't*:	tokens	types	Following *don't*:	tokens	types
I	88		*know*	39	
all	138	14	all	124	30

As additional evidence for the cohesion of units based on frequency of co-occurrence, we found that an adverb intervening between the subject and *don't* blocks vowel reduction, as seen in examples (3) but an adverb between *don't* and the verb does not, as in example (4).

(3) I really don't think so.
    I also don't know anyone who's tried it
(4) I don't even know if I was that hungry.

Thus even within chunks we find varying degrees of cohesion or constituency based on the frequency of the string of units.

   In this section, then, we have examined the evidence for chunking from phonetic change. Usually phonetics is not considered as a diagnostic for syntactic structure, but since our argument here is that syntactic groupings arise through chunking, phonetic change can serve as an important diagnostic for the processing units speakers use. As part of the argument, we have examined the causes of phonetic reduction, basing our discussion on Lindblom's theory that takes into account the accommodations the speaker makes to the listener and added to that the finding that permanent changes occur in cognitive representations of the phonetic shapes of words due to the contexts in which they occur. We turn now to a discussion of the effect of chunking on structure and meaning.

3.3.4   Autonomy: the structure and meaning of chunks

Some of the effects of chunking are rather subtle: small phonetic adjustments, most of which are variable; possible slight increases in accessing speed; and recognition by speakers that certain combinations are conventional. However, with increasing frequency, other more dramatic changes occur in chunks. These include changes in morphosyntactic structure, shifts in pragmatic nuances and functions, and change in semantics. In this section we discuss these changes and the mechanisms that bring them about as frequency of use increases.

   In the following discussion we distinguish semantic compositionality from analysability (Langacker 1987, Croft and Cruse 2004). While these two properties of linguistic expressions are closely related, we gain a fuller understanding of how linguistic expressions can vary if we distinguish between them. Both parameters are gradient.

Compositionality is a semantic measure and refers to the degree of predictability of the meaning of the whole from the meaning of the component parts (Langacker 1987). Derived words can be compositional or not: compare *hopeful, careful* and *watchful,* which have fairly predictable meanings based on the meanings of the noun base and suffix, to *awful* and *wonderful,* which are less compositional since *awful* indicates a negative evaluation not present in the noun *awe* and *wonderful* indicates a positive evaluation not necessarily present in *wonder.* Similarly, special constructions are often identified by their lack of compositionality vis-à-vis the construction from which they arose. For instance, as discussed in Chapter 2, the ambiguity of the famous question, *What's that fly doing in my soup?* is between the more compositional reading, to which the answer is *I believe that's the backstroke* and the special interpretation of the WXDY? construction (Fillmore and Kay 1999) in which the question is taken to be a more rhetorical expression of surprise and perhaps also disapproval. The latter is less compositional than the former.

Analysability, according to Langacker 1987: 292, is the 'recognition of the contribution that each component makes to the composite conceptualization'. Analysability would include the language user's recognition of the individual words and morphemes of an expression as well as its morphosyntactic structure. This measure is also gradient and would relate to the extent to which the parts of an expression activate the representations of these parts. As we noted in Chapter 2, an idiom such as *pull strings* is not fully compositional in that it has a metaphorical meaning, but it is analysable, in the sense that an English speaker recognizes the component words, as well as their meanings and relations to one another and perhaps activates all this in the interpretation of the idiom. Similarly, compounds such as *air conditioning* or *pipe cleaner* are analysable in that we recognize the component words; however, as is well known, the interpretation of compounds is highly context-dependent and thus they are not usually fully compositional (Downing 1977).

The examples show that compositionality can be lost while analysability is maintained, indicating that the two measures are independent. While it would seem improbable that compositionality could be maintained in the absence of analysability, there are some possible, though rare examples in inflectional suppletion. Given that members of inflectional paradigms express the same grammatical meaning with each lexical stem, suppletive forms (where suppletion is defined in the traditional way, as a form that has a different etymological stem than other members of a paradigm) are compositional though not analysable. Thus the English Past Tense forms *was, were* and *went* are predictable in their meanings as *be* + Past (for the first two) and *go* + Past, but their forms are not analysable. It is important to note here that true suppletion in inflection usually affects only the most frequent of paradigms. The following sections explore the role of repetition in the loss of analysability and compositionality.

3.4   Frequency effects and morphosyntactic change

3.4.1   *Changes in morphosyntactic analysability and semantic compositionality*

Hay 2001, 2002 discusses the effects of relative frequency on morphologically complex words. Relative frequency refers to the frequency of a complex word as compared to the base that it contains. It is often the case that the more complex or derived word is less frequent than the simpler base from which it derives, as the theory of markedness relations would predict. Thus *entice* is more frequent than *enticement*; *eternal* is more frequent than *eternally*; *top* is more frequent than *topless*. However, there are also cases where the reverse is true: *diagonally* is more frequent than *diagonal; abasement* is more frequent than *abase* and *frequently* is more frequent than *frequent*. Hay demonstrates through several experiments that the derived words that are more frequent than their bases are less compositional or less semantically transparent than complex words that are less frequent than their bases. Hay asked her subjects to compare two words – one that was more frequent than its base and one that was less frequent – and to decide which one was more 'complex'. She explained that by 'complex' she meant divisible into meaningful parts – what we would call 'analysable'. For both suffixed and prefixed forms, the subjects rated the words that were more frequent than the bases they contained as less complex than the words that were less frequent than their bases.

In a second experiment she examined the degree of semantic transparency of words according to their frequency relative to their bases. For this experiment, she consulted dictionary entries for complex words; if the entry used the base word to explain the derived word, it was judged to be more transparent. If the entry did not use the base word, it was considered less transparent. For instance, for *dishorn* the dictionary entry found was 'to deprive of horns' but for *dislocate* the definition cites displacement or putting something out of place and does not use the word *locate* at all. The results show that indeed, the complex words that are more frequent than their bases have less semantic transparency on this measure.

Hay shows that simple token frequency does not correlate with the results of either experiment, as the claim in Bybee 1985 would predict. In Bybee 1985 I proposed that loss of analysability and semantic transparency were the result of the token frequency of the derived word. Hay has improved on this claim by showing the relevant factor to be relative frequency, at least at the frequency levels she studied. My suspicion is that at extremely high token frequencies, loss of analysability and transparency will occur independently of relative frequency. In the morphosyntactic domains for instance, a grammaticalizing phrase that has shifted in meaning and pragmatics and lost some internal

Table 3.3 *Frequencies of forms of* have *and* have to *in the BNC*

have	418,175	have to	43,238
has	247,008	has to	9,859
had	394,458	had to	26,748

structure does not have to be more frequent than its component words. *Have to* with its inflected forms (with obligation meaning) is much less frequent than *have* (in other constructions) with its inflected forms, as shown in Table 3.3 with counts from the British National Corpus, and yet it has undergone semantic change (to express obligation), it has lost analysability and it has undergone special phonetic reduction (to [hæftə]).

These facts, however, do not detract from Hay's findings for less frequent words; more importantly, the cognitive processes that Hay identifies are relevant to our understanding of what happens to chunks as their frequency increases.

When a speaker or listener processes a morphologically complex word, the extent to which the component parts are activated can vary. On one extreme, the complex word could be based directly on its component morphemes, especially if it is unfamiliar, thereby activating the parts completely. Or it might be possible to access the complex word more directly as a single unit, while still activating the morphemes that make it up. On the other extreme, the complex word could be accessed without activating the component morphemes at all, which would be the case if analysability has been lost for that word. Given that activation is gradient and associations among parts of words in a network model are also gradient, there are many degrees of activation that are possible. Hay is claiming that the greater the frequency of the complex word in relation to the lexical base, the more likely it is to be accessed without a full activation of the base.

As a complex word is used, its autonomy increases, making access more efficient, just as in the chunking advantage. As soon as the more complex word or word sequence has been assembled and entered in memory, it is available for access. Hay proposes that each instance of direct access of the complex unit strengthens that path of access and weakens the access through the component parts, at the same time weakening the relations with these parts and bringing on gradual loss of analysability.

Of course, all this happens outside the controlled context of the experiment, where other factors become very important. As Bybee 1985 points out, as derived words become more frequent it is because they are used in many contexts, including those in which the basic word might not be used. Analysability is maintained in the contexts in which the base word is also primed and it is lost in contexts where the base is not primed. The same would apply to compositionality. Semantic and pragmatic shifts that reduce compositionality are aided by frequency or repetition, but their source is in the contexts in which the complex unit is used.

To sum up this discussion, Hay has presented evidence that analysability and compositionality are affected by language use: the more a sequence of morphemes or words is used together, the stronger the sequence will become as a unit and the less associated it will be to its component parts. The loss of associations with component parts leads to increasing autonomy (Bybee and Brewer 1980), which is the topic of the next section.

3.4.2   Increasing autonomy

We have already observed that the vast majority of complex units, including derived words and conventionalized word sequences such as prefabs and idioms, maintain their internal structure and their relations with the other uses of their component parts. In the network model of Bybee 1985 as well as the approach of Hay 2001, 2002, these relations, which embody analysability and compositionality, can be of varying strengths and they may even be lost entirely. Loss is particularly likely in cases of extreme frequency increases when complex units may become autonomous from their sources, losing both internal structure and transparent meaning. Thus autonomy will be defined in a gradient fashion as the loss of either compositionality or analysability or both. Three mechanisms operate either separately or together to create autonomy: repeated direct access to complex sequences, phonetic reduction and pragmatic associations arising in contexts of use.

The fact that we can document degrees of autonomy arising independently from each of these mechanisms as well as cases where two or three work together means that autonomy is an emergent property of linguistic units. The following examples are meant to distinguish among the three mechanisms to demonstrate their independence. We also examine cases where all three mechanisms are operating together, creating at the most autonomous end of the scale, grammaticalization.

Phonetic reduction can occur without any loss of semantic compositionality, as demonstrated by contractions such as *I'm, you're, he'll, I'll, you'll,* and so on. These contractions are all transparent semantically and some have clear enough internal structure, being equivalent in syntax and semantics to their uncontracted counterparts. They are autonomous in the sense that their phonetic reduction is more extreme than what would be conditioned by ordinary processes operating in connected speech. It is thus very likely that that they are accessed directly rather than composed from two parts. Similarly, the reduction of the vowel in *don't* to schwa along with the flapping of the initial and final consonants only occurs in high-frequency strings. In *I don't know* there is also a pragmatic change, but in other combinations, such as *I don't like, I don't mean* and *I don't feel* the phonetic change is not accompanied by pragmatic changes (Bybee and Scheibman 1999).

Conversely, semantic/pragmatic shifts due to frequent use in particular contexts can occur in the absence of special phonetic reduction. For instance, the Spanish construction of *andar* 'to walk' + gerund has become a minor variant of the progressive. In the process of grammaticalization, the construction has moved from meaning 'go around X+ing' to just 'be X+ing'. Thus examples (5) and (6) show progressive uses of this construction (Torres Cacoullos 2000):

(5) Yo no sabía por qué *andaba buscando* el día de San Juan.
    'I didn't realize why she was looking for the day of San Juan (in the calendar).'
(6) Ahorita *andan trabajando* en las pizcas y allá andan.
    'Right now they are working in the crops [fields] and they are there.'

Despite the semantic changes that have occurred in this construction, very little phonetic reduction is discernible, demonstrating as in the previous example that phonetic and semantic change are separate processes. Semantic change without phonetic reduction seems to be characteristic of grammaticalization in South-east Asian languages, for example (Bisang 2004).

In fact, semantic change with little or no phonetic change is quite common and occurs in the creation of new constructions, such as the WXDY? construction mentioned earlier as well as with changes in lexical items, such as *indeed*. Traugott and Dasher 2002 discuss the changes in the phrase *in dede >* *indeed*. Some analysability is retained in this expression, as we can (perhaps) recognize the two words that comprise the expression. Originally meaning 'in action', as in the expression *in word and deed*, it came to mean 'in truth' by the inference that what is observed as an action must be true. More recently it has taken on an additive function, used in discourse merely to add more information (example from the BNC):

(7) A biography is not a monograph, and, *indeed*, there are biographies of painters which do little justice to art.

Even though the erstwhile prepositional phrase is now written as one word, very little, if any, phonetic reduction is apparent.

The third mechanism that leads to autonomy – repeated direct access – is likely involved in all the preceding examples. Our question now is whether autonomy due to repeated direct access can occur without the other types of changes. As an expression reaches high frequency it becomes more difficult to find examples without phonetic reduction or semantic shift, but the examples used in an early proposal of the concept of autonomy in Bybee and Brewer 1980 appear to show the effect of direct access without other effects.

Bybee and Brewer examined verbal paradigms in Spanish and Provençal dialects. The Preterit paradigms in these related languages had, through regular sound changes, lost any consistent marker of Preterit, as each person/number form had its own expression of this aspectual meaning.[1] Some of the person/ number forms were re-made on the basis of others, which re-established a certain analysability. Thus 1st sg. *canté* 'I sang' and 1st pl. *cantámos* 'we sang' show little in common that could establish them as Preterit, but some dialects re-form the Plural on the basis of the Singular, producing *cantémos*. There are quite a variety of changes that occur in the various documented dialects of Spain and Provence, but in none of them is the 3rd sg. form ever changed. As the 3rd sg. form is the most frequent of the person/number forms, its stability is indicative of its autonomy, which in this case is due only to direct access and not to any phonetic or semantic irregularity. In support of the gradience of autonomy, it can be noted that the 1st sg. also remains unchanged most of the time. Thus relative autonomy due to repeated direct access (and lexical strength) is the factor behind the Conserving Effect of frequency.[2]

Autonomy and the mechanisms operating to create autonomy are highly correlated with token frequency. As token frequency increases, the likelihood of special phonetic reduction and semantic/pragmatic shift and autonomy in general also increases. This does not mean that frequency CAUSES phonetic reduction, or meaning changes, only that repetition is an important factor in the implementation of these changes. For phonetic reduction, repetition of the bias towards reduction leads to changed exemplar clusters, as explained above; for semantic or pragmatic shifts, repetition within certain contexts leads to new associations of the expression with a meaning, as will be discussed more below. Even autonomy in the sense of direct access is created by frequency of use only because the human brain adjusts to repeated access by creating shortcuts.

In derivational morphology and compounding we find many cases of autonomy in the sense that both analysability and compositionality have been lost. Thus derived words such as *disease, business* and *breakfast* have become disassociated from their etymological bases through semantic and phonetic changes. In grammaticalization we also find cases of complete autonomy, as we will see in the next section.

3.4.3   Grammaticalization

In cases of extreme frequency increases, as in grammaticalization, we find the most extreme cases of autonomy, cases where compositionality and analysability are completely lost (Bybee 2003b). It should be noted, however, that a certain degree of analysability remains well into the process of grammaticalization.

We discuss and explain grammaticalization more thoroughly in Chapter 6, but for now it is enough to note that in grammaticalization, a specific instance of a construction takes on new uses, gains in frequency, undergoes phonetic and semantic change and thereby begins to lose its compositionality and analysability. For instance, the English Perfect (*have done*) has its origins in a possessive verb (*have*) in a resultative construction with a Past Participle modifying an object noun (Traugott 1972, Bybee et al. 1994, Carey 1994). A modern example of the construction that gave rise to the Perfect would be *He has the letter written*. This sentence contrasts with the Present Perfect sentence *He has written the letter.* The Present Perfect with *have* is also used now in intransitive sentences (where previously the auxiliary in intransitive sentences was *be*). Thus we have *he has just arrived* in the Present Perfect (Smith 2001).

The meaning of the construction is not compositional in the sense that one cannot work strictly from possessive *have* and the participle meaning to arrive at the anterior sense of a past event with current relevance. While the writing system of English makes it clear that *have* is involved in the construction, at least some analysability has been lost, as evidenced by the fact that *have* as an auxiliary in the Perfect undergoes contraction with the subject, giving, *I've, he's, they've, you've*, while possessive *have* does not in American English. Also, auxiliary *have* is followed by the negative *not* and contracts with it, while possessive *have* does not. Thus we have *he hasn't written the letter* vs. *he doesn't have a pen.* (See Chapter 6 for a fuller discussion of grammaticalization.)

Another example of differential phonetic reduction pointing to loss of analysability is found in the grammaticalizing *be going to* construction in English. As is well-known, this construction reduces to something spelled as *gonna*, in which the erstwhile allative or infinitive marker is fused with the preceding participle. The evidence that the analysability of this sequence is being lost is the fact that *going* followed by the preposition *to*, as in *I'm going to the shop*, does not similarly reduce.

Another sort of evidence for the loss of compositionality and analysability in grammaticalization can be found in the sequences of auxiliaries *would have, could have, should have* and *might have* (Boyland 1996). These sequences of modal plus the auxiliary *have* are followed by a Past Participle and compositionally or etymologically are past modals plus the Perfect. However, the current meaning of these sequences is counterfactual, a meaning that is not compositional. Given the phonetic contraction of *have* in these common sequences, the analysability of the sequence is in doubt, as evidenced by common misspellings of *would have* as *would of*, and so on.

Even low degrees of grammaticalization can provide evidence for loss of compositionality and analysability. The expression *far be it from me to* + VERB is interesting in this regard, since the maintenance of the subjunctive form of *be* long after this mood has been lost elsewhere indicates a loss of compositionality. See examples (8) and (9). As for analysability, speakers surely recognize all the words in the expression, but there is evidence that the relationships among the words are not always grasped. Note that in the nineteen examples of this construction that occur in the BNC, the object of *from* is always first person; there are sixteen examples of *me* and three of *us*. It is thus a discourse device the speaker uses to disclaim a certain stance. While for some, the relationship between *far* and *from* might be quite transparent, it is interesting that seven of the examples in the BNC used the preposition *for* instead of the historically correct *from*. Thus examples (10) and (11):

(8) *Far be it from me to* stand in the path of true love.
(9) *Far be it from us to* condone tax evasion.
(10) But *far be it for us to* shed crocodile tears over the bruised egos
(11) That would be a good move – ; but *far be it for me to* advise the Prime Minister on that point

This change in preposition suggests that the analysability of the *far from* expression has been lost. Because the expression has an intersubjective use and refers explicitly to the speaker's stance, apparently the phrases *for me* and *for us* seem appropriate to some speakers. (*For me* occurred six times and *for us* once.)

3.4.4   Autonomy and exemplar cum network model

Frequently used phrases can be processed as single units as we noted in our discussion of chunking. This means that rather than accessing each unit separately and putting them in a construction, a whole sequence is accessed at once. This does not mean that the parts are not identifiable, but continued access as a whole contributes to the weakening of their identifiability and thus the analysability and/or compositionality of the whole expression or construction. Phonetic change further obscures the individual parts of the expression. Use in context can affect meanings and inferences, and meaning changes lead to a loss of compositionality.

We have already discussed the way phonetic change is represented in an exemplar model; semantic/pragmatic change is similarly represented. In an exemplar model, experienced utterances have a rich representation that includes many aspects of the linguistic and extra-linguistic context in which the utterance was experienced. As the utterance or ones similar to it are repeated, certain aspects of the context are reinforced while others are not. As we will see in the next section, frequently made inferences from the context can become part of the meaning of an expression or construction. This suggests no clear divide between aspects of the meaning that are derivable from context and those that are inherent to the lexical item or construction.

As representations build up that are conditioned by certain contexts, a word or expression may begin to weaken its connections to related words or expressions. This is due in part to direct access, but also to the similarity matching that goes on in categorization. When parts of an expression are no longer similar in meaning or form to their etymological bases, the strength of these connections is diminished.

In our discussion of increasing autonomy we have identified phonetic reduction and pragmatic/semantic shift as contributing factors. As mentioned, both are more likely to occur in high-frequency items. We have also mentioned direct access as a factor in diminishing a phrase's association with its component words. To some extent, we might consider autonomy to be a self-feeding process because frequent phrases are easy to access and thus continue to be frequent or even increase in frequency. *That drives me crazy* is more likely to be used than *that makes me insane* for this reason.

Finally, we should consider whether or not decreases in autonomy are also possible. As Hay has pointed out a constraining factor in developing autonomy is the frequency of the base word, or in the case of phrases, the component words. There may be some cases where a lower or decreasing frequency of a complex form leads to its becoming more analysable and compositional.

3.5   Meaning and inference

In structuralist and generativist theories, to the extent that they have dealt with meaning at all, grammatical morphemes and grammatical constructions in which they occur are thought to have an abstract, invariant meaning which is modulated in context.[3] While it is certainly true that grammatical meaning is usually abstract and general in nature, it does not follow as a theoretical principle that each morpheme or construction has only one invariant meaning. Rather it seems more realistic to assume that the meaning of forms and constructions is involved in an interesting interaction of the specific with the general. For instance, in grammaticalization we see meanings generalize and become more abstract, while some specific meanings or functions are retained.

A view of grammar as emergent from the categorization of specific experiences with language would also suggest that the categorization that leads to a working understanding of grammatical meaning does not result in classical categories of necessary and sufficient conditions. Rather, a view of meaning that is consistent with what is known about categorization of both linguistic and natural objects would propose that there would be some uses of grammatical constructions that are more central in the semantic categorization and some that are more peripheral. Indeed, considering the way that categories evolve, it would not be unexpected to find that one category had split into two, given certain contexts of use. Thus the insistence upon a single invariant meaning for each category of grammar (construction, grammatical morpheme) is antithetical to exemplar representation and the dynamic cognitive representations that emerge from experiencing language use in context.

In Chapter 10 I will examine in more detail the way grammaticalization of meaning gives us evidence about the nature of the categorization that results in grammatical meaning, but for now I would like to mention briefly the evidence supporting an exemplar view of meaning. My proposal is that a more abstract meaning is emergent from, but not a necessary consequence of, the categorization of the uses of a word or construction in context. Consider first the fact that many times the identification of an invariant meaning is not feasible. Some English examples, all of which can be replicated cross-linguistically, include the fact that the future marker *will,* which has a pure prediction meaning in many contexts (12), also has intention uses, as in (13), and willingness uses, as in (14). Examples are from Coates 1983.

(12) I think the bulk of this year's students *will* go into industry.
(13) I'*ll* put them in the post today.
(14) I don't think the bibliography should suffer because we can't find a publisher who *will* do the whole thing.

Since an invariant meaning has to be the most abstract meaning available, the more specific meanings have to be derived from the more abstract, in a reversal of the usual diachronic relation. As for the problems such a hypothesis poses, consider how one might try to derive the willingness meaning of (14) from the prediction meaning shown in (12). What in the context could be relied upon to provide that meaning?

A further question is what invariant meaning could we propose for the use of *may* in spoken language, which includes an epistemic use (15), and a permission use (16)? The root possibility use (17), which I hypothesize once united them, has mostly disappeared in spoken language (Bybee 1988b).

(15) I *may* be a few minutes late, but I don't know.
(16) *May* I read your message?

   I will wander along to your loo, if I *may*.

(17) I am afraid this is the bank's final word. I tell you this so that you *may* make arrangements elsewhere if you are able.

Consider also the use of Past Tense in hypothetical protases of conditional sentences, as in (18) and (19) (examples from the BNC).

(18) if very few people *turned* up then perhaps people might say that we didn't go around go about advertising it in the correct way
(19) if your animal *needed*, your pet *needed* treatment it would be done by the private vets

Uniting the hypothetical use of the Past Tense with its more common use, which is to signal a situation that occurred prior to the speech event, requires a very abstract meaning such as 'not now' (see Steele 1975, Langacker 1978). The problem with this is that in the past tense use, it has no such abstract meaning, but rather the more specific meaning of past.

There are various diachronic scenarios that lead to the disjoint meanings of the same morpheme and to the more specific or more abstract uses, but none of these developments could occur if speakers were limited to a single abstract meaning for each morpheme. The diachronic development that leads to the polysemy in these morphemes is discussed in Chapters 6 and 10.

To the extent that invariant meanings are proposed, they still have to be modulated in context. Most proposals for invariant meaning assume that such calculations occur online (Michaelis 2006). In an exemplar model the combinations of meaning in real utterances are registered in memory and if repeated, become conventionalized as possible interpretations. Indeed, repeated inferences made in context become part of the meaning of a word or construction and lead to its use in new contexts (Bybee 1988b, Traugott 1989, Traugott and Dasher 2002; cf. also the Law of Contiguity, James 1950, Ellis 1996: 110). Thus a rich representation of meaning that includes the inferences that have been made during use is necessary to explain the common meaning changes that occur in context.

Consider the future auxiliary *will* which has developed from a verb meaning 'want'. In Middle English *will* was still used with a sense of volition (Bybee and Pagliuca 1987), but it occurred often in contexts indicating intention, as it still does (see example 20). The intention examples are particularly common with a first person subject, but they also occur with third person, as in (20). In such a case, however, the expression of an intention of a third person implies a prediction that the predicate will be carried out. Through such implications, the *will* construction takes on prediction meaning. It then is extended to use in unambiguous predictions such as (21) and (22).

(20)   As soon as he gets a house she *will* leave home.
(21)   And I think her husband *will* probably die before she *will*.
(22)   Yeah. You better go otherwise she *will* be annoyed!

The polysemy illustrated here for *will* and *may* has developed diachronically from a richer lexical meaning that has been modulated in context; the frequent inferences made in context have been registered in memory and have become conventionalized as part of the meaning of the auxiliary. This process would not be possible if speakers and hearers always assigned one invariant meaning to a grammatical form.

The meanings developed for use in language come about because meaning is always situated in context. Context is determined both socially and cognitively. It is important to realize that our experience of the physical world and our social relations is neither uniform nor flat; it is not just a one or two dimensional conceptual space. It is vastly more varied in its topology. There are some situations that are more important and more frequently arising and referred to than others. Certain situations are conventional, such as asking permission, expressing uncertainty, getting people to do things. Time is not just two dimensional in our experience either; nor is it experienced or talked about independently of modality, both epistemic and agent-oriented. Thus the simplification of temporal or modal concepts into abstract, binary dimensions is not likely to yield a system that is sufficiently grounded or dynamic to account for language use or language change. In fact, I argue in Chapter 10 that only an analysis that takes into account the very concrete uses to which language is put will be able to explain both the similarities and differences among languages.

3.6   Conclusion

Our discussion has ranged widely over phonetics, morphosyntax and semantics, because chunking and the gradual increase in autonomy has effects at all levels of grammar. While illustrating the way an exemplar model in conjunction with network representations allows for variation, gradience and change, we have also emphasized the proposal that the domain-general process of chunking leads to many characteristics of linguistic structure. These include the following:

 (i) The formation of multi-word units such as prefabs, idioms and constructions.
 (ii) Phonetic effects within such units.
 (iii) The maintenance or loss of analysability and compositionality.
 (iv) The grouping of meaning with particular morphosyntactic constructions and with context, which at once maintains specific meanings for specific contexts and also allows new meanings to be established through inference from context.

In Chapters 5 and 8 we will see how the degrees of analysability, compositionality and autonomy lead to a view of constituent structure as gradient and capable of gradual change.

4 Analogy and similarity

4.1 Analogy and similarity in the processing of novel utterances

So far we have discussed sequential chunks of linguistic material that are stored and accessed whole. We have also mentioned the gradience in the sequential associations which depends upon how often a particular transition within the sequence occurs. Constructions are formed by chunking, but their parts are not invariant: constructions contain schematic positions that encompass sets of items that have been sorted into categories. Earlier we saw how such categories within constructions are built up from experience in an exemplar model. We will say more in Chapter 5 about what has been found through empirical investigations of the nature of these categories, but for the moment we need to consider what type of processing mechanism allows the schematic positions in constructions to be used productively – that is, with new lexical items – and consequently to grow and change.

An important source of creativity and productivity in language that allows the expression of novel concepts and the description of novel situations is the ability to expand the schematic slots in constructions to fill them with novel lexical items, phrases or other constructions. Considerable evidence indicates that this process refers to specific sets of items that have been previously experienced and stored in memory. A number of researchers have used the term 'analogy' to refer to the use of a novel item in an existing pattern, based on specific stored exemplars (Skousen 1989, Eddington 2000, Baayen 2003, Boas 2003, Krott, Baayen and Schreuder 2001, Bybee and Eddington 2006). Analogy is considered to contrast with rule-governed productivity because it is heavily based on similarity to existing items rather than on more general symbolic rules. In the present context – that of usage-based construction grammar – I will use the term in this very general way: analogy will refer to the process by which a speaker comes to use a novel item in a construction. Given the specificity of constructions and the way they are built up through experience with language, the probability and acceptability of a novel item is gradient and based on the extent of similarity to prior uses of the construction.

The definition adopted here is meant to apply at the morphosyntactic level, as when a novel utterance such as *that drives me bananas* is created using the construction discussed in Chapter 2. A comparable case on the morphological level occurs when a regularized form such as *leaped* is created using the general past tense construction. On the phonological level we could cite an example such as the pronunciation *nucular* for *nuclear*, which is very likely based on the strength of the sub-word string *–ular* as in *popular, regular*, or even more specifically, *binocular.*

In this chapter we discuss the nature of analogical processing and the evidence of item-specific extension of constructions. While we are most interested here in analogy as a processing mechanism, we also gain important insights by exploring its role in language change and child language acquisition. For linguists, analogy is often thought of as the mechanism behind morphological regularization, but here we also note its use as the primary mechanism of morphosyntactic creativity as well as a minor mechanism of phonological change.

4.2   Analogy as a domain-general process

The characterization of analogy as a domain-general process calls attention to structural similarities in two different domains despite differences in the objects that make up these domains (Gentner 1983). Historical linguistics textbooks often cite proportional analogies such as the following (see Trask 2007):

(1) talk : talked :: leap : leaped

A non-linguistic example cited by Gentner and Markman 1997 illustrates that it is the relation to the objects that is transferred and is quite independent of the properties of the objects:

(2) 1 : 3 :: 3 : 9

Thus in (2) the numeral '3' shows up in two places, but this is totally immaterial as far as the structural relationship goes.

Despite the apparent success of (1) in describing how a new form such as *leaped* could come into existence (to replace earlier *leapt*), it is very doubtful that linguistic analogies are very often of this type. First, a proportional analogy requires the language user to conjure up three forms and compare them in order to produce a new form. It is much more likely that a novel form such as *leaped* is produced by invoking the very general Past–Tense construction of English and applying it to a form which previously had an irregular Past Tense (Bybee and Moder 1983; see section 5). Second, and most important, the nature of the objects involved in the analogy is not arbitrary at all. Most analogical formations in language are based on semantic or phonological similarity with existing forms. Thus a novel utterance *drives me happy* is very unlikely because the *drives* construction goes with adjectives and phrases indicating madness or insanity. Similarly, a new verb entering the *strung* class of past tenses has to have some phonological similarity to the other verbs in that class; thus a new past tense for *dip* as *dup* would be highly unlikely (see below, section 4.5). Finally, a four-part proportional analogy implies that a single pair of items could influence another pair; however, in morphological analogy the cases in which there is only one instance of a pattern which attracts another instance are vanishingly rare (Bybee 2001a).

Gentner and Markman 1997 discuss the relationship between similarity and analogy, arguing that there is a continuum between the two.

Analogy occurs when comparisons exhibit a high degree of relational similarity with very little attribute similarity. As the amount of attribute similarity increases, the comparison shifts toward literal similarity. (p. 48)

Because of the importance of similarity or shared attributes to linguistic analogy we have to conclude that it is rarely of the purely proportional type. For this reason, the definition I used above, namely, 'the process by which a speaker comes to use a novel item in construction' seems more in keeping with the use of the term in the current linguistic literature.[1] It must be noted, however, that the use of a new item in a construction requires a lot of relational knowledge or structural alignment (Boas 2003), both of which are prerequisites for analogy (Gentner and Markman 1997).

4.3   Similarity to prior utterances

Many recent studies have demonstrated the importance of similarity to prior utterances or parts of utterances in the production of novel utterances. This has been shown in corpus studies (Boas 2003, Bybee and Eddington 2006), in language change (Israel 1996, Bybee 2003b), in child language (Lieven et al.1997, Tomasello 2003) and in experiments (Krott, Baayen and Schreuder 2001). In addition it has been shown that judgements of degree of acceptability for novel utterances are strongly based on similarity to frequent, conventionalized sequences (Bybee and Eddington 2006).[2] Such facts, which will be reviewed below, constitute powerful arguments for exemplar representation of linguistic experiences.

But before examining novel utterances more closely, it is important to point out that many utterances are not novel or at least contain parts that are not thoroughly novel. In the context of assertions about the infinite creative capacity of the human language ability and the apparent fact that humans can express any concept through language, the fact that our actual utterances contain many prepackaged word sequences comes as a bit of a surprise. Corpus studies, such as Erman and Warren 2000, have shown that even on fairly conservative counts, about 55 per cent of word choices are not 'free' but rather are determined by a larger chunk, or prefab (prefabricated unit). Other studies have produced similar results (see Pawley and Syder 1983 and Wray 2002 for discussion).

Consider the following two sentences from the Switchboard corpus where I have underlined what I consider to be the prefabs, with a space between them.[3] The two sentences have thirty-five words in all, but only twenty choices are made if each prefab is considered a single 'choice', meaning a single chunk that is accessed as a unit from cognitive storage.[4]

(3) I mean I can remember when I was
     very young, much + young + er, and I
     applied for a job
     they said, well, are + n't + you planning to
     have children? Well, I mean,
     that's none of + their + business.

     20 choices, 35 words, 25 words in prefabs

Other examples of prefabs include the chunks discussed earlier, conventionalized phrases such as resultative phrases (*drive crazy, tear apart, wipe clean* and *suck dry* [Boas 2003]), conjoined items (*black and blue, bread and butter, pick and choose,* and so on), verb–particle or verb–preposition combinations (*look up, think about*) and many, many others (see Erman and Warren 2000, Wray 2002).

Prefabs are conventional in the sense that they have been established through repetition in usage, but they do not need to be highly frequent. Just as we can learn a new word with only a few repetitions (sometimes for native speakers with only one exposure) so also can we register a prefab after experiencing only one or two tokens.

Let us return now to novel utterances. Despite the heavy use of prefabs in both speech and writing, novel utterances also occur, some highly similar to existing prefabs and some more remote. This is what endows language with its much-lauded creativity. So our question is, how exactly do speakers use language creatively? The answer to be explored here is that novel utterances are quite firmly based on prior utterances. This has been shown to be the case in early stages of language acquisition (Lieven et al. 1997, Dąbrowska and Lieven 2005; see below), and it also constitutes a rather plausible account of adult production of novel utterances at levels ranging from the morphological to the syntactic.

First, there is considerable evidence at the word level from morphology that novel formations are heavily based on similarity to existing exemplars (Bybee and Moder 1983, Koepcke 1988, Aske 1990, Eddington 2000, Baayen 2003). Bybee and Moder 1983 studied the small class of English verbs that form their Past Tense like *sing/sang/sung* or *string/strung* and found that phonological similarity to existing class members strongly influences novel formations. Thus in an experimental setting nonce verbs that had a final velar nasal were much more likely to be given a Past Tense form with the vowels [æ] or [ʌ] than nonce forms ending in other consonants. This reflects the fact that eleven out of twenty-five verbs in the *sing* and *string* classes end in velar nasals. However, a complete match of final consonants does not limit membership in the class. New extensions of the pattern are found in verbs that end in [ŋk] and also in verbs that end in a final (non-nasal) velar, such as *strike/struck, stick/stick, dig/dug*, and common, but not fully standard, *drag/drug*. There are no new extensions of this pattern except to verbs ending in velars. Note further that an initial [s] or [s] plus a consonant are also contributing factors. Thirteen of the verbs in these classes begin with [s] or [ʃ]. Thus it is not just the final consonants that determine class membership but the phonological shape of the whole verb. (See section 4.5 for further discussion.)

Other studies that demonstrate the influence of similarity to the phonological structure of existing words are studies of Spanish stress by Aske 1990, modelled in the Analogical Model of Language by Eddington 2000 and studies of phonotactics by Pierrehumbert 1994, Coleman and Pierrehumbert 1997 and Vitevich et al. 1997, among others.

A case that takes us beyond phonological similarity is a study of the linking elements in Dutch noun–noun compounds by Krott, Baayen and Schreuder 2001. There are three possibilities: no linking element, a morpheme –*en*–, or a morpheme –*s*–. It does not seem possible to formulate rules to predict which element occurs in a given compound, yet compounding is fully productive and speakers show a high degree of agreement about which element occurs in novel compounds. The authors show by experiment that speakers are comparing novel compounds to existing ones and relying on various parts of the existing compounds to establish the linking element for the new ones. The most important factor is the left-hand or modifying word of the compound. For example, if the modifying word is *lam* 'lamb' and most compounds with *lam* take –*s*–, then a novel compound with *lam* also has –*s*–. If the modifying word occurs in compounds with a variety of linking elements (as for example *schaap-en-bout* 'leg of mutton', *schaap-ø-herder* 'shepherd', *schaap-s-kooi* 'sheepfold', *schaap-en-vlees* 'mutton'), then the choices are weighted in terms of how many types use each linking element (see also Baayen 2003). The right-hand word, or the head, also has some effect, but experiments show that its effect is somewhat less than that of the modifying word. To account for the subjects' responses, Krott et al. argue for exemplar representations of compounds; when faced with the need to invent a novel compound, the family of compounds sharing the first word are activated and used as a model for forming the novel compound. Baayen 2003 notes that the analogical model used can be thought of as a formalization of the network model I proposed in a number of works (Bybee 1985, 1995, 2001). In that model, as mentioned earlier, entries sharing phonetic and semantic features are highly connected depending upon the degree of similarity. Thus in such a network, all the compounds that share words would already be connected in storage, making the application of the analogical process more direct.

The problem faced in the full elaboration of such models, however, is in specifying the relevant features upon which similarity is measured. This is a pressing empirical problem. We need to ask, why are the final consonants of the *strung* verbs more important than the initial ones? Why is the first member of the Dutch compound more important than the second member? Some possible answers to these questions are: in the case of the *strung* verbs, the vowel marking the Past Tense and the following consonants make up a phonological constituent – the rhyme – which has been shown to be an important constituent especially in English. In the case of the Dutch compounds, the linking element resembles (and derives etymologically) from a suffix – which means it is more identified with the preceding element than the following one. However, these are post hoc speculations; the pressing need is for fully elaborated substantive theories that predict which similarities will be important.

In addition, we need to ask, if the end of an English verb is the place to look for Past Tense marking, why does the beginning matter at all, as in the *strung* class? If the linking element of the Dutch compound is analysed as a suffix on the first element, why does the second element have an effect on the speakers' responses? The answer to this is that language processing seems to have a holistic component along with the more familiar linear sequencing (Bybee 2001a).

At the level of constructions the evidence also points to the importance of prior combinations in the production of novel combinations, based here on meaning. Bybee and Eddington 2006 study verbs of becoming in several large Spanish corpora to determine which verbs go with which adjectives. This case is another one in which attempts to establish rules or ferret out the relevant features of the verbs and adjectives have not been successful. There are several verbs in Spanish that are used with adjectives or prepositional phrases to signal 'entering into a state'. For instance, conventionalized combinations are as follows:

(4) *ponerse nervioso*   to get nervous
    quedarse solo   to end up alone
    quedarse sorprendido   to be surprised
    volverse loco   to go crazy

In the corpora studied, many instances of the become-verb + adjective constructions were semantically similar to the more conventionalized combinations. For example, similar to *quedarse solo*, which occurred twenty-eight times in the corpora, were the following, which occurred only once, or twice in the case of *aislado* 'isolated'.

(5) *quedarse a solas*   to end up alone
    quedarse soltera   to end up unmarried (fem.) = an old maid
    quedarse aislado   to become isolated
    quedarse sin novia   to end up without a girlfriend

Another grouping with *quedarse* centres around *quedarse sorprendido* 'to be(come) surprised'. Here are a few examples:

(6) *quedarse deslumbrado* to become dazzled
    quedarse asombrado   to become amazed
    quesdarse pasmado   to become stunned, astonished
    quedarse asustado   to become afraid

Another verb, *ponerse*, is conventionally used with *nervioso* 'nervous', a phrase that appeared seventeen times in the corpora, but it also appeared less frequently in the corpus with these adjectives related to *nervioso:*

(7) *ponerse pálido*   to become pale
    ponerse histérico   to become hysterical
    ponerse furioso   to become furious
    ponerse colorado   to turn red/become flushed

The distributions of the become-verb + adjective constructions in the data suggest that the more frequent, conventionalized phrases serve as an analogical base for the formation of new phrases. The fact that a single verb, such as *quedarse*, can occur with adjectives in different semantic groupings – 'alone' on the one hand and 'surprised' on the other – suggests that the categorization is not in terms of highly general features such as 'duration of change' or 'passive or active involvement of the subject' as has been proposed in the literature (Fente 1970, Coste and Redondo 1965), but rather is based on very local similarities of meaning to conventionalized phrases.

Acceptability judgements also support the use of item-based analogy in novel production or comprehension. Another aspect of the Bybee and Eddington 2006 study was an experiment in which subjects were asked to judge the acceptability of become-verb phrases. The stimuli were constructed to include the following: (i) higher-frequency, conventionalized phrases; (ii) low-frequency phrases that were semantically similar to the higher-frequency phrases; and (iii) phrases that were of low frequency and NOT semantically similar to existing phrases. The subjects judged the first two types of phrases as much more acceptable than the third type, suggesting that the notion of acceptability is strongly based on previously experienced tokens or similarity to previously experienced tokens. These results support the view that both production and comprehension involve similarity matching and that matching to higher-frequency exemplars is more probable than matching to lower-frequency exemplars.

Construction grammar approaches (Fillmore et al. 1988, Goldberg 1995, 2006), including Cognitive Grammar (Langacker 1987 and elsewhere), account for creativity by elaboration of the schematic slots in a construction. Two or more instantiations of a slot in a construction lead to the formulation of a more abstract node that ranges over the instantiations. Thus the adjectives in the Spanish become-verb construction illustrated in (5) might be more schematic-ally represented as 'lacking human companionship'. However, if schematicity were the only source of creativity in the formation of constructions, it would be hard to explain two types of developments: the family resemblance extension of categories and the creation of new clusters. For instance, the category in (5) also historically includes prepositional phrases with *sin* 'without'. These seem to have started with phrases indicating the loss of a family member (*sin padre* 'without a father') but now a variety of phrases are possible, for example *sin armas* 'without weapons', *sin pluma* 'without a pen' (Wilson 2009), creating what appears to be a family resemblance structure, rather than an abstract, schematic structure. In addition, new clusters arise from new prefabs, as shown by the fact that *quedarse* is also used with *sorprendido* 'surprised', which does not form a semantic class with the items in (5). Thus a goal of the current work is to understand the role of abstraction versus the role of individual exemplars in predicting novel utterances. (See Chapter 5 for more discussion.)

Some researchers have doubted whether this account of creativity or produc-tivity can ratchet up to an account of the full range of novel utterances of which human beings are capable. In fact, Pinker and colleagues (Pinker 1991, 1999) and Jackendoff (2002), while acknowledging the robust evidence for construc-tions and item-specific analogy, want to hold on to the older notion of symbolic rules – highly general (default) rules for morphology and phrase structure rules for syntax. While indeed constructions differ in their generality (see Chapter 5), there is no need to posit two distinct processing types for language. Even the most general of patterns – for example, the patterns associated with the English auxiliary and Past Tense – can be explained as the by-products of exemplar clusters that are fully schematic, and thus highly productive. The fact that they have developed gradually over time, are acquired piecemeal, and have idiosyncrasies argues against description by a symbolic rule (see Chapters 5 and 7 for a complete discussion).

4.4   Analogy in child language

Research in child language acquisition from a usage-based perspective shows great promise in explicating how a child works from specific utterances to the construction of more general patterns (Tomasello 1992, 2003, Lieven et al. 1997 and Dąbrowska and Lieven 2005). Tomasello 1992 demonstrates the close association of particular verbs with particular constructions. Pine and Lieven 1993 and Lieven et al. 1997 find evidence that young children's multi-word productions centre on certain lexical items and rote-learned expressions and do not provide evidence for generalized or abstract rules. For instance, Lieven et al. 1997 find for children aged 1;8 to 2;8 that 60 per cent of their utterances were based on twenty-five lexically based patterns (such as *There's a X, I want a Y,* and so on) while 31 per cent were fully rote-learned expressions. In another impressive study, Dąbrowska and Lieven 2005 show how the questions formulated by children aged 2 to 3 years are heavily based on questions the children have already uttered. The authors postulate two operations that can be used to produce novel utterances: juxtaposition, which is a linear concatenation of two units – words, phrases or constructions (which may themselves be internally complex from the adult's point of view) and superimposition, by which a unit elaborates or 'fills in' a schematic slot in another construction. An example of juxtaposition would be the utterance, *are you downstairs now?* or its variant *now are you downstairs?* Superimposition would involve taking the partially schematic unit *Shall I* PROCESS? and the unit *open that* to produce the novel expression *Shall I open that?*

Dąbrowska and Lieven analyse the set of questions from the later transcripts to see how many of them could be based directly on questions in the earlier transcripts using just these two operations. Their findings show a close correspondence between the earlier questions asked by the children and the later test questions. First, between 21 per cent and 75 per cent of the questions studied were direct repetitions of immediately preceding adult questions, delayed repetitions, or self-repeats by the child. More interestingly, 90 per cent of the children's other utterances could be derived from previously recorded utterances by using only the two operations described above. This picture of child language points to very specific starting points for the acquisition of constructions: children store experienced exemplars and gradually expand on these to arrive at more general patterns. The Dąbrowska and Lieven data also reveal the child's growing ability to apply the juxtaposition and superimposition operations; over the time course of the corpora, the novel utterances involve more and more operations and a greater variety of schematic material participating in superimposition.

Studies of older children begin to show evidence of greater abstractness of the patterns. Savage et al. 2003 demonstrated both lexical and structural priming of the English active and passive constructions in 6-year-old children, but only lexical priming in 3- and 4-year-old children. That is, the 6-year-olds were more likely to use an active or passive sentence depending upon which of these they had just heard; while the younger children were only influenced by the lexical items they heard. These results indicate that a high level of abstraction occurs only after considerable experience with particular lexical items and pronouns in these constructions. Does reaching this level of abstraction mean necessarily that lexical specificity is lost? Langacker 1987 argues that there is no reason to suppose that specific exemplars are discarded just because the learner has arrived at an abstraction. Indeed, it appears that some exemplars of constructions can be accessed as single units, even if the more abstract version of the construction is also available. (See Chapter 5 for further discussion and Chapter 9 on *can remember*.)

The operations proposed by Dąbrowska and Lieven – juxtaposition and superimposition – are equally available to adults producing continuous speech using constructions. Superimposition, by which the schematic slots in constructions come to be filled with lexical items or other constructions, would seem to be the major production mechanism for complex structures as well as the major source of hierarchical structure.

4.5   Analogy in language change

In historical linguistics, the term 'analogy' and its associated processes are most often invoked to describe morpho-phonemic change in morphological paradigms. Two types of change are traditionally distinguished: analogical levelling, which indicates the loss of an alternation in the paradigm and analogical extension, by which an alternation is introduced into a paradigm that did not have it before. An example of levelling would be the regularization of *leapt* to *leaped*; here the alternation between [iː] and [ɛ] is lost, thus the term 'levelling'. However, it is important to note that the mechanism of change is not best described as 'loss of an alternation'; rather what actually happens is a new, regular form is created by applying the regular construction to the base or most frequent member of the paradigm, in this case *leap*. The evidence for this mechanism for analogical levelling is first, the fact that the old form is not in fact immediately lost, but continues to compete with the new form. Thus most English dictionaries list *wept* and *weeped*, *leapt* and *leaped*, and *crept* and *creeped*. Second, analogical levelling occurs earlier in low-frequency paradigms than in high-frequency ones, for example, *keep/kept, sleep/slept* and other more frequent forms do not seem to be as susceptible to levelling. This suggests that the low accessibility of low-frequency forms leads to a situation in which a new regular form is created using the regular pattern. Third, the direction of levelling points to the same conclusion: the form on which the new form is based is usually the most frequent member of the paradigm (Mańczak 1980, Bybee 1985).

The fact that high-frequency paradigms maintain their irregularities much longer than low-frequency paradigms provides important evidence for the exemplar model. Since high-frequency exemplars have stronger representations than low-frequency ones and since high-frequency exemplar clusters have more and stronger exemplars, they are much more accessible than low-frequency exemplars. Their greater accessibility makes it much less likely that speakers would create alternate forms (such as *keeped*) that could eventually replace the irregular form. The same principle can be applied to the high-frequency exemplars of morphosyntactic constructions, as we will see below: certain exemplars of older constructions can be retained in a language despite the development of a newer, more productive construction. Such cases constitute strong evidence that specific exemplars of constructions are retained in memory representations (Bybee 2006a).

By all accounts, analogical extension in morphology is much less common than levelling. However, it does occur and the conditions under which it occurs are instructive as they indicate the determinants of productivity, even if it is limited productivity. First, extension of an irregular alternation rarely if ever occurs if the alternation exists in only one paradigm. Rather it takes a core set of paradigms to attract new members. If psycholinguistic experiments are any indication, even two paradigms sharing an alternation is not enough to spark extension (Bybee and Pardo 1981, Bybee 2001a). Thus productivity depends at least in part on type frequency: the higher the type frequency the greater the productivity or likelihood that a construction will be extended to new items.

Type frequency, however, interacts with other factors, in particular, the second important determinant of productivity, degree of schematicity (Clausner and Croft 1997). Schematicity refers to the degree of dissimilarity of the members of a class. Highly schematic classes cover a wide range of instantiations. A good example is the regular English Past Tense schema that can apply to a verb of any phonological shape. When high schematicity is combined with high type frequency, a maximally productive construction results. A morphological class with a high degree of phonological similarity will be less schematic – the phonological definition of the class will be more constrained. Low schematicity will limit productivity, since it limits the candidate items that extension could apply to. However, low schematicity combined with relatively high type frequency results in some degree of productivity.

Consider the irregular (or strong) verbs of English. They represent remnants of an older, perhaps productive system in which tense changes were signalled by internal vowel changes. In Old English one could still identify certain classes of verbs that behaved similarly to one another with respect to these vowel changes, even though the system was breaking down and the new suffixation construction was gaining in productivity (owing largely to its high degree of schematicity). Thus in the centuries between Old English and the present, many of these classes have lost members either to regularization (*helpan* 'to help' had the forms *hilpth, healp, hulpon, holpen* [3s pres., 3s past, past plu., past part.] and now has only *help/helped*) or to attrition (many of these verbs are just not used any more). However, one class of strong verbs has gained a few new members by analogical extension. This class, which was discussed earlier, is exemplified by *sing, sang, sung,* or in the case of verbs that have lost the distinction between the Past and the Past Participle, *string, strung.* Members of this class that have survived from Old English are shown in (8) sorted by their final consonants.

(8) -m	swim	swam	swum			
-n	begin	began	begun	-n	spin	spun
	run	ran	run		win	won
-ŋ	ring	rang	rung	-ŋ	cling	clung
	sing	sang	sung		swing	swung
	spring	sprang	sprung		wring	wrung
-nk	drink	drank	drunk	-ŋk	slink	slunk
	shrink	shrank	shrunk			
	stink	stank	stunk			

Members of this class that have been added since the Old English period, according to Jespersen 1942, as well as some dialectal variants are shown in (9), also sorted by final consonant.

(9) -ŋ	sling	slung
	sting	stung
	string	strung
	fling	flung
	hang	hung
	bring	brung*
-k	strike	struck
	stick	stuck
	sneak	snuck*
	shake	shuck*
-g	dig	dug
	drag	drug*

(The forms marked with an asterisk are considered non-standard.)

The new members have only two principal parts and they all have a velar consonant in their coda. Some of them also begin with a sibilant or sibilant cluster, increasing the phonetic similarity of the words as wholes. The original class members all had nasal consonants, but the new members have moved away from that requirement towards a requirement that the final coda contain a velar consonant. Thus while phonetic similarity is of supreme importance in defining this semi-productive class capable of extension, the structure of the category has changed over time. This example illustrates a low degree of schematicity because the phonetic shape of category members is quite constrained. This means that its productivity is limited; the productivity it does attain is due to a 'gang' effect: a high concentration of verbs sharing phonetic properties is more likely to attract new members than one of comparable numbers without clear phonetic definition.

Both extension and levelling occur as a construction is applied to items that previously participated in some other construction. In the examples in (9), some of the verbs are denominal and would be expected to be regularly affixed; others were already irregular but belonged to different classes, for example *bring, brought* and *strike, stroke*. Since stem alternations are in the minority in English, extension tends to apply to the expansion of a minor construction, and levelling to the expansion of a more productive construction. In historical change as in synchrony, analogy is item-specific and often described as irregular in its application. Note that in the case we have discussed here – the levelling of alternations in favor of regularly suffixed Past Tense on the one hand, and the extension of minor constructions on the other – there is a certain tension or competition that keeps systems from moving completely towards 'regularity', which means that everything would be governed by the same general rule. (See Chapter 5 for more discussion of determinants of degrees of productivity.)

4.6   Analogy and constructions

4.6.1   *Diachronic analogy in morphosyntax*

What do levelling and extension correspond to in morphosyntax? They both correspond to the productive use of a construction, whether it is a major or minor pattern. Over time it is common to observe a construction extending its domain of application or losing ground to some other more productive construction. Thus in morphosyntax as in morphology we see many examples of competing constructions and many efforts by linguists to sort out the subtle differences in function and in distribution of constructions that appear very similar. Taking a diachronic approach based on analogy and taking into account the effect of token frequency on retention of older patterns in a language helps us to understand these situations where two or more very similar constructions co-exist in a language.

Consider two types of negation in English as studied by Tottie 1991. One negation type uses *not* after the auxiliary verb or dummy verb *do* (see examples 10a and 11a), while the other uses *no* or incorporates the negation into an indefinite (examples 10b and 11b).

(10) a. ...by the time they got to summer, there wasn't any more work to do.
      b. ...by the time they got to summer, there was no more work to do
(11) a. when you just can't do a thing.
      b. when you can just do nothing.

Table 4.1 *Proportion of* no-*negation (Tottie 1991)*

	Spoken	Percentage	Written	Percentage
Existential *be*	34/38	89%	96/98	98%
Stative *have*	18/28	64%	41/42	98%
Copular *be*	12/20	60%	26/47	55%
Lexical verbs	20/76	26%	67/104	64%

Note that in (10) the two types of negation are interchangeable both semantically and pragmatically, while in (11) the two types have different meanings. Tottie chose to study just the cases where the meaning was the same, as in these cases presumably the speaker has a rather unconstrained choice about which construction to use.

The diachronic situation is as follows: the use of *no* and the negative indefinites is continuous through the documented history of English while the use of *not* has developed more recently, having its origins in a negative indefinite itself, *ne + wiht* (cf. *nought/nohht*), meaning 'not at all', which increased its sphere of usage dramatically in the Middle English and Early Modern periods (Mossé 1952, Campbell 1959; see discussion by Tottie 1991 and Chapter 7). Thus we have an older construction (the negative incorporation construction) competing with a newer and more productive construction (the *not* construction). The situation is in some ways analogous to the competition between the regular and irregular Past Tense verbs in English, where we have seen that the older pattern of inflection (using vowel changes) is retained in the more frequently used verbs while new verbs and less frequent verbs use the newer more productive pattern (Bybee 2006a).

Tottie studied these two constructions in a large corpus of spoken and written British English. She extracted only those examples in which the use of the alternate construction would have the same meaning and implications (as in 10). She found that certain constructions, especially existential *be* (as in example 10), stative *have* (as in 12) and copular *be* (as in 13), have a higher use of *no*-negation than lexical verbs do, as shown in Table 4.1. This suggests that *no*-negation, rather than being an option for all sentences, has become associated with certain constructions.

(12) the Fellowship had no funds
(13) as a nation we are not doing well enough. This is no new discovery

The existential *be*, stative *have*, and copular *be* constructions are fairly frequent, accounting together for more of the data than all the lexical verbs combined. Their frequency could help explain the fact that they preserve the older construction; much like the vowel-change verbs of English (*break, broke;*

write, wrote; and so on), their high frequency strengthens their representations and makes them less likely to be reformed on the more productive pattern. This suggests that a frequency effect might also be found among the lexical verbs.

In fact, certain frequent verbs, that is, *know, do, give* and *make*, account for many of the examples of *no*-negation in the lexical examples:

(14) no, Marilyn does no teaching I imagine she's a research assistant
(15) I've done nothing except you know bring up a family since I left school.
(16) I know nothing about his first wife.

In addition, some lexical verbs occur in conventionalized expressions or pre-fabs that are mostly used in writing:

(17) the ballads make no mention of the trapping of rabbits
(18) Make no mistake about it, the divisions are very serious.
(19) the split in the Conservative Party over Africa gives me no joy

These examples demonstrate that even after a construction has lost its productivity, specific exemplars of the construction may live on because they have accrued strength through repetition and so continue to be used. Thus such examples provide additional evidence for exemplar representations.

Similarly, the fact that existential *be*, stative *have*, and copular *be* maintain the negative incorporation construction more robustly than lexical verbs suggests a representation in which the negative is built into the construction. Thus rather than having, for example, a general stative *have* construction which combines with one or the other negative constructions in a sequence of rule applications, an English user's cognitive representation includes more specific constructions such as ... *have no...*, ...*have nothing ...*, ...*have no one...*, and so on.

To summarize: an older negative strategy using *no* or negative indefinites is being replaced by a negation construction that uses *not*, a strategy that is equally useful in sentences lacking in indefinites, giving it a distributional edge over the incorporation construction. However, the older construction is retained in combination with other high-frequency constructions and high-frequency or conventionalized lexical verbs. The spread of the newer, more productive construction thus resembles analogical levelling or regularization in that formations based on the newer construction are replacing formations based on the older construction. Other examples include the Present Perfect in English (Smith 2001).

4.6.2   *Analogy as the source of new constructions*

Finally, let us mention analogy as the source of new constructions using the example of the *quedarse* + ADJECTIVE construction in Spanish. Wilson 2009 has traced the history of this construction from when it begins in the twelfth century to the current era. The earliest examples involve the adjective *solo* 'alone' in a context in which a person is left alone due to the departure of others.

(20) <u>E el conde quando vio que de otra manera no podia ser sino como queria el comun delos romeros no quiso ay quedar solo & fa zia lo mejor & cogio sus tiendas & fue se empos delos otros.</u>

    'And when the count saw that there could be no other way than the common wishes of the pilgrims to Rome wanted it, (he) didn't want <u>to be left alone</u> and did his best and gathered his tents and went after the others.' (Gran conquista de Ultramar, anon., thirteenth century; Davies 2006)

There were three such examples in the texts studied and a few other examples of *quedarse* + ADJECTIVE in the twelfth and thirteenth centuries, but by the fourteenth century it is clear that analogies based on *quedarse solo* were filling out a category and creating a new construction. In the fourteenth and fifteenth centuries, examples such as (21) appear. Wilson argues that in this example, being left widowed or becoming a widower uses *quedar* on analogy with the earlier, entrenched expression for being left alone.

(21) <u>Enla tierra de ansaj avia vn potente rrey al qual no avia quedado sy no vna hija la qual avia avi- do de su muger que enel ora del parto murio & quedo biudo mas el rrey hjzo criar la hija muy honorable mente.</u>

    'In the land of Ansaj there was a powerful king to whom no one was left but a daughter who he had had from his woman who in the moment of birth died & (he) <u>became widowed</u>, but the king had the daughter raised honorably.' (Historia de la Linda Melosina, anon., fifteenth century; O'Neill 1999)

Also in these centuries the adjective *huerfáno* 'orphaned' is used with *quedar* as well as a series of prepositional phrases with *sin* 'without', for example *sin heredero* 'without heirs', *sin armas* 'without weapons', *sin pluma* 'without a pen' and even more abstract notions such as *sin dubda* 'without doubt' and *sin pena* 'without grief'. It appears, then, that in this period, the category of adjective or prepositional phrase that can be used with *quedar(se)* expands on analogy with the early expression with *solo,* which gives rise to expressions describing the loss of a family member, then other physical deprivations, such as lacking weapons and eventually to more abstract expressions. Thus a more general construction is formed from a beginning with a single entrenched exemplar. For a further discussion of other uses of *quedar(se)* + ADJECTIVE see Wilson 2009.

It is important to note that analogy as a type of historical linguistic change is not separate from analogy as a cognitive processing mechanism. Language change takes place as people use language and all mechanisms of change must be based on processing mechanisms. Thus when we see evidence of analogy operating over time, we infer that processing mechanisms in actual instances of language use are also operating.

4.7   Analogy vs. rules

An exemplar model directs us to examine how the specific interacts with the general. Languages certainly have many highly general patterns, but they arise diachronically and in acquisition from more local and specific patterns. Analogy as a processing mechanism enables us to examine how the specific gives rise to the more general. This perspective also relieves linguists of the duty of explaining away all exceptions. If analogy rather than symbolic rules are postulated for general patterns, exceptions from various sources are to be expected, because, for instance, particular items of high frequency may resist analogical change, or competing patterns can arise from specific instances (see discussion above). Rather than trying to make the exceptions regular (by changing their underlying structure), we might take a look at what the exceptions are telling us about the generalization.

Analogy as a processing mechanism has become more accepted recently by generative linguists for the minor, less productive patterns of language (Pinker 1991, Jackendoff 2002). These linguists, however, still hold on to the notion of symbolic rules for highly productive morphology and phrase structure rules for generalizations in syntax. Thus their models include two distinct processing types and they must argue for a discrete division between the two types of processing, with analogical processing occurring in the lexicon and symbolic processing occurring in a rules component. In contrast, analogical models (Skousen 1989, Eddington 2000) and connectionist models (Rumelhart and McClelland 1986, Bybee and McClelland 2005, McClelland and Bybee 2007) argue for a gradation between unproductive, specific patterns and the most productive, general patterns. As we have seen in this chapter, both so-called 'regular' and 'irregular' patterns are gradient in the number and similarity of items to which they apply and thus in their productivity (see also Chapter 5).

What really is the difference between these positions? In the extensive literature that has developed around the issue of the English Past Tense, the distinction between symbolic rules and analogy has been characterized as follows.

First, analogy makes reference to specific stored patterns of constructions or lexical items. Of course, similar stored exemplars are grouped together as we have seen. These groupings take a prototype structure, with a central member and more peripheral members (see Chapter 5 for more discussion). Organizational patterns, schemas or categories arise in the lexicon or what has been called the 'constructicon' (a lexicon with an inventory of constructions) and have no existence independent of the lexical units from which they emerge. In contrast, rules are postulated to exist independently of the forms to which they apply. In fact, symbolic rules are thought to belong in a component or module that is separate from the lexicon.

Second, the productivity of schemas is highly affected by the number of participant items: a schema ranging over many different verbs, for example, is more productive than one ranging over only a few. Also, in this view productivity is gradient; besides productive and unproductive patterns, there may be intermediate degrees of productivity. Rules, on the other hand, are not affected by the number of types to which they apply. Since rules are independent of the forms which they affect, there cannot be any relationship between the rule and the number of items to which it applies. Productivity of rules is determined by 'default' status. Once the child observes that a certain rule is used in 'default' situations, that is, for new formations such as verbs derived from nouns, he or she determines that this rule is the default or productive rule (Marcus et al. 1992).

Third, analogy is highly affected by the particulars of existing types. Bybee and Moder 1983 observed experimentally that the closer an English nonce verb was to the prototype or best exemplar, *strung*, the more likely the subjects would form its Past Tense by changing the vowel to /ʌ/. Similarly, Köpcke 1988 found that German subjects tended to pluralize nonce nouns that ended in full vowels with -*s*, since that is the form used in existing German nouns with full vowels, for example *Autos, Pizzas*. A symbolic rule, on the other hand, applies to a whole category, such as verb or noun, with no regard to the particular shape of individuals (Marcus et al. 1992).

Fourth, analogies are probabilistic as they are based on particular types. Individual types may be closer or farther from the best exemplars of the category. Thus speakers would exhibit probabilistic behaviour in basing a novel formation on another pattern. In contrast, rules are discrete in their behaviour: a form either is or is not subject to a rule because a form exclusively belongs or does not belong to the relevant category.

A fifth difference, which involves phrase structure rules, is that such rules are purely syntactic and have no relation with meaning. This is what is meant by autonomous syntax (Newmeyer 1998). Since constructions relate meaning to form, all syntactic relations in a construction grammar in contrast have semantic import and are grounded in the linguistic and extralinguistic contexts in which they have been used.

With a single processing mechanism, an analogical model can handle the same range of data that is handled in the dual-processing model by two mechanisms. Thus the burden of proof is on those who propose two processing mechanisms rather than one and a discrete division between the two rather than a continuum.

4.8   Analogy and frequency

Analogy as a mechanism of processing and change interacts with frequency of use in a way that is distinct from the way phonetic reduction does: high-frequency forms are less likely to undergo analogical change than low-frequency items. This can be called the Conserving Effect of high token frequency. The reason for this can be traced to what I have called 'lexical strength' (Bybee 1985). Each use of a word or construction increases the strength of its exemplar cluster, making that word or phrase more accessible lexically. In other terminology, frequency of use increases the level of resting activation of a stored instance of the construction. The greater lexical strength of such an instance makes it more likely to be accessed than a comparable yet more compositional construction.

This is quite different from the frequency effect associated with chunking, the Reducing Effect (Bybee and Thompson 2000, Bybee 2002a, 2007). The Reducing Effect is directly caused by neuromotor practice and the consequent overlapping and reduction of articulatory gestures. As it spreads through the lexicon, this mechanism of change is not analogical except perhaps in the very last stages of lexical diffusion (pace Kiparsky 1995).

4.9   Conclusion

In this chapter we have explored the nature of linguistic analogy in support of the proposal that analogical processing is the basis of the human ability to create novel utterances. In this context, it is important to note how much of speech and writing is constituted of prefabricated word sequences. These conventionalized expressions and constructions serve as the basis for the application of the domain-general process of analogy. This processing mechanism has been identified in recent studies of child language as giving rise to novel utterances and I argue that it can also be applied in adult production to account for novel utterances. This chapter also reviewed the way analogy operates in diachronic change, arguing that it is the same processing mechanism that is responsible for the changes identified traditionally as analogical. The similarities between analogical change in morphology and in syntactic constructions were also pointed out, making the case that analogy applies at both of these levels, both diachronically and in synchronic processing. The next chapter elaborates on some of the concepts presented in this chapter by reconsidering the concepts of schematicity and productivity, especially in the context of findings about the frequency distributions of instantiations of constructions in corpora.

5   Categorization and the distribution of constructions in corpora

5.1   Introduction

In the preceding three chapters we have considered some of the basic processing mechanisms that give language its structure. First we considered memory representations for language, arguing for the necessity of exemplar or rich memory representations. Then we considered sequential chunking and its importance for morphosyntactic structure. In this discussion we also saw how chunking interacts with analysability and compositionality and their loss as autonomy increases. In Chapter 4, categorization and similarity were approached in the discussion of analogy as a mechanism for extending the use of constructions with novel items. The current chapter looks at constructions in more detail, considering in particular the distribution of particular tokens and types of constructions in language use. The focus is on the nature of the categories that are created for the open slots in constructions and how both type and token frequency interact with semantic categorization to determine the properties of these categories, their degrees of schematicity and their productivity.

5.2   Why constructions?

Constructions are direct pairings of form with meaning (where meaning also includes pragmatics), often having schematic positions that range over a number of lexical items. Constructions often contain explicit lexical material, such as *way* or *what* and *be doing* as in the examples in (1). While everyone who works on constructions agrees that they cover everything from mono-morphemic words, to complex words, to idioms, all the way up to very general configurations such as 'the passive construction' (because they are all form–meaning pairings), the term is usually applied to a morphosyntactically complex structure that is partially schematic. For instance, the examples in (1) are instances of the informally expressed constructions in (2), where schematic positions are indicated by small caps or variables such as 'Y'.

(1) a. Mr. Bantam corkscrewed his way through the crowd (Israel 1996).
    b. What's that box doing up there?

(2) a. SUBJECT$_1$ VERB (MANNER OF MOTION) POSS PRO$_1$ *way* ADVERBIAL
   b. *What* BE SUBJECT *doing* Y?

Fillmore, Kay and O'Connor 1988 give the earliest explicit proposal concerning the properties of constructions. Their argument for viewing grammar
in terms of constructions is that there is much about a language that speakers
know in addition to the very general rules pertaining to subjects, objects, complement and relative clauses. There are many expressions such as those in (1)
that have a special form, meaning and pragmatic effect that cannot be captured
by more general principles of grammar that are not attached to specific lexical items or specific meanings. Thus their proposal is couched in terms of
accounting for the idiomaticity of language, which, as mentioned in the preceding chapters, comprises a large portion of actual language use. They also
demonstrate that even these idiomatic structures are productive and thus must
be considered part of the grammar of a language.[1]

Taking their argument a step further, we can note that it is not just the idiomatic
portions of language that show a strong interaction of specific lexical items with
grammatical structures. Even what must be regarded as fairly general syntactic
structures, such as clausal complements, depend heavily upon the specific verb
of the main clause. Thus *think* takes an ordinary finite clause (*I think it's going to
snow*) while *want* takes an infinitive clause (*I want it to snow*) and *see* takes a ger-
undial complement (*I saw him walking along*). The argument for constructions is
that the interaction of syntax and lexicon is much wider and deeper than the association of certain verbs with certain complements. As Langacker 1987 points out
in his discussion of the interaction of syntax and lexicon, there are thousands of
conventionalized expressions that are part of the knowledge a speaker has of his
language. Resultative expressions such as *suck dry, drive crazy,* verb + particle
phrases such as *follow up, look over, turn out,* and many others follow general
grammatical patterns but have lexically specific conventionalized combinations.
It follows, then, that one might explore the possibility that all of grammar can be
viewed in terms of constructions. Certainly, many a traditional reference grammar has been written successfully on the basis of constructions.

Croft's reasons for preferring a construction-based approach stem from serious typological work comparing morphosyntax cross-linguistically (Croft 2001).
Generative approaches are ill-equipped to specify the important, but often subtle
differences in the distribution of constructions both language-internally and in a
comparative perspective (Newmeyer 2005). By adopting constructions, which
are essentially language-specific, and then observing their variation across languages, important insights regarding the semantic spaces covered by construction
types as well as hypotheses about their development and change become available. Verhagen 2006 provides a detailed comparison of three constructions in
English and Dutch which demonstrates the utility of comparing constructions

in that this approach allows the analyst to note differences in frequency, productivity and schematicity across languages, rather than just differences in structure. As constructions appear both in very specific form, as well as at more general levels of abstraction, construction grammar provides the possibility of comparison on many levels.

Goldberg's argument for specifying grammatical relations in terms of constructions is that a given verb may appear in a number of different constructions, so that it cannot be relied upon to determine what arguments it might take. Rather, constructions carry the meaning that specifies the function of the arguments in a clause and they combine with the verb in determining the meaning of a clause (Goldberg 1995, 2006).

Tomasello, Lieven and their colleagues find constructions an appropriate construct for the description and explanation of the course of first language acquisition (Tomasello 1992, 2003, Pine and Lieven 1993, Lieven et al. 1997, Dąbrowska and Lieven 2005). As mentioned in the previous chapter, when children's utterances are tracked in detail, it is found that their new utterances are strongly based on their previous utterances with the substitution of items and phrases. It can be said, then, that they are in the process of formulating partially schematic constructions on the basis of the specific utterances they have mastered and can use.

My reasons for adopting a construction-based approach include all of the above, but in addition, include the fact that constructions are particularly appropriate units for formulating a domain-general account of the nature of grammar. First, as mentioned in the previous chapter, the formation, acquisition, and use of constructions is closely related to the domain-general process of chunking, by which bits of experience that are repeatedly associated are repackaged into a single unit. Given human sequential-learning capacities, even rather long constructions can be unified into chunks through repetition. Second, the development of the schematic portions of constructions is based on item-specific, similarity-based categorization, another domain-general cognitive ability.

Constructions are particularly appropriate for exemplar models, as they are surface based and can emerge from the categorization of experienced utterances. Exemplar models, in exchange, allow a treatment of constructions that is essential for their full understanding in that they store both specific instances of constructions and allow for the abstraction of a more generalized representation. As we will see in this chapter there are important facts about the distribution of constructions that affect their semantic and pragmatic interpretation that can only be captured if exemplars are retained in storage.

5.3   Categorization: exemplar categories

Perhaps the most important property of constructions is that they describe the relations between specific lexical items and specific grammatical structures.

The lexical items that occur in a construction contribute to the meaning of the construction and help to determine its function and distribution in discourse. As noted in Chapter 2, the distinct lexical items that occur in a slot in a construction constitute a category based primarily on semantic features. In this section we examine the principles that govern exemplar categories and in subsequent sections we discuss the way these categories manifest themselves in corpora.

Exemplar categories as built up through experience (in various domains) exhibit prototype effects. Prototype effects derive from graded category membership: some exemplars are central members of the category while others are more marginal. This property is often illustrated with natural categories such as BIRD: some birds, such as robins or sparrows are judged as more central to the category than others, for example eagles or penguins. This graded category membership has been revealed in experimental settings, using natural and cultural categories. Members of the same culture can pick out a consistent 'best exemplar' of the category, react faster when asked if a central member belongs to the category compared to a more marginal one and produce consistent rankings of degree of membership in the category (Rosch 1973, 1978, Taylor 1995, Croft and Cruse 2004).

The mechanisms of exemplar categorization give rise naturally to prototype effects (Medin and Schaffer 1978). For one thing, the fact that exemplars contain full detail of the percept (whether it be a bird or an utterance) allows for categorization by a number of features, not just those that are contrastive. For instance, a more prototypical bird is small – the size of a sparrow or a robin – while large birds are less prototypical, even though size is not a distinguishing feature of birds.

In addition, graded category membership can come about in an exemplar model by the interaction of two categorization dimensions – similarity and frequency. Rosch and colleagues argued against frequency in experience as a determinant of centrality of membership. In their experiments they control for word frequency of the names of entities and still obtain the prototype effects. However, Nosofsky 1988 has shown that increasing the frequency of a particular colour in a colour categorization task leads to a change in the categorization of marginal colours, suggesting that the centre of the category shifts towards the color whose frequency has been increased.

Given that constructions are conventional linguistic objects and not natural objects that inherently share characteristics, it seems that frequency of occurrence might significantly influence categorization in language. Considering also that using language is a matter of accessing stored representations, those that are stronger (the more frequent ones) are accessed more easily and can thus more easily be used as the basis of categorization of novel items. Because of this factor, a high-frequency exemplar classified as a member of a category is likely to be interpreted as a central member of the category, or at least its greater accessibility means that categorization can take place with reference to it. Evidence for this claim will be presented below.

Incoming exemplars are placed in semantic space closer to or farther from strong exemplars depending upon their degree of similarity. Categorization is probabilistic along the two dimensions. On some occasions categorization can be driven by similarity to a member of lesser frequency if there is greater similarity to this less frequent member (Frisch et al. 2001). However, the probabilistic interaction of frequency and similarity will result in a category whose central member is the most frequent member.

5.4   Dimensions upon which constructions vary: degree of fixedness vs. schematicity in the slots of constructions

Schematicity refers to the substantive definition of the category, which can either make reference to semantic features or phonetic features or more holistic patterns. On the low end of the schematic scale, positions in constructions can be completely fixed; higher schematicity is a function of the range of variation within the category. In this chapter our interest will be primarily in more schematic categories, but in this section we briefly take up examples illustrating the range from completely fixed to highly schematic.

In the two constructions exemplified in (1a) and (1b) at the beginning of this chapter there are some fixed elements. In (1a) *way* is fixed while the rest of the construction is more or less schematic. That is, the construction must contain *way* and it cannot be pluralized or otherwise changed. Similarly, in (1b), *what* and *do* in the Progressive are fixed elements. Both constructions also contain grammatical elements that are inflected: the possessive pronoun modifying *way* in (1a) (see (2a)) occurs in the full range of possibilities, the forms of *be* in (1b) and (2b) are inflected to agree with the subject. To the extent that these slots are schematic, they are completely grammatically determined.

Constructions can also be fairly specific in allowing only a very small range of variation in a position. Consider the adjectives that occur modified by *vanishingly*. In the *Time Magazine* corpus there are five examples of *small* and one each of *tiny, low* and *thin*. The BNC gives: *small* (20), *scarce* (1), *low* (1), *improbable* (3). While the prefab is clearly *vanishingly small*, it is interesting that a narrow degree of creativity is evidenced, creating a category around the prefab with a low degree of schematicity.

A larger, more schematic category is comprised of the adjectives that can be used with *drive someone _____*. Boas 2003 finds sixteen items in this slot in the BNC. Some examples are: *mad, crazy, insane, wild, nuts, up the wall...* Again this is a semantic class of adjectives, roughly synonymous with *crazy* (in American English) and *mad* (in British English). Other examples of classes that are schematic, but closely organized around some central members, are the class of verbs that can occur in the ditransitive construction (Goldberg 1995), the verbs that occur in the *way* construction (Israel 1996), the verbs occurring in the *into*-causative (Gries et al. 2005) and the Spanish adjectives occurring with 'become' verbs that will be discussed in the next section.

The most schematic of classes are grammatical categories at the level of NOUN or VERB. Some of the constructions we have just mentioned refer to these highly schematic and generalized categories. The *drive someone X* construction would allow almost any noun phrase as a subject. While it seems that many constructions impose some limitations on the verbs that appear in them, a highly grammaticalized construction, such as NP *be going to* VERB, allows any verb to occupy the VERB position.

As mentioned in Chapter 2, the schematic slots in constructions lead to the development of exemplar categories. In the next sections we examine the nature of these categories as established by empirical research.

5.5   Prefabs as the centres of categories

Most commonly the categories that are formed from the items that occur in the schematic slots of constructions are semantically defined. In a common distributional pattern semantically similar items are clustered around a highly frequent exemplar – an exemplar that could be considered a prefab as it represents the conventional way of expressing an idea. For instance, just taking a small sample (the 1990s and 2000s of the *Time Magazine* corpus), the adjectives and prepositional phrases occurring with *drive* and its inflected forms are as follows:

crazy	25
nuts	7
mad	4
up the wall	2
out of my mind	1
over the edge	1
Salieri-mad	1

Quite possibly most of these expressions are conventionalized, but note that in American English *drive someone crazy* is more frequent than the others. The hypothesis (following Bybee and Eddington 2006) is that the more frequent member serves as the central member of the category and that new expressions tend to be formed by analogy with the more frequent member.

Evidence for this claim can be found by looking at the numbers and uses of expressions with *drive someone* + ADJECTIVE/PREPOSITIONAL PHRASE from the 1920s to the present in the *Time Magazine* corpus. One important

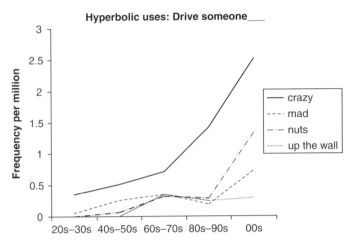

Figure 5.1 Hyperbolic uses of *drive someone crazy, mad, nuts* and *up the wall* from the 1920s to the 2000s. (*Time Magazine* corpus)

development that led to increased frequency of the set of expressions is the emergence of a hyperbolic use. Literal uses of *drive someone mad,* in which the sense of *mad* is a state of clinical insanity, occur in the 1920s and 1930s and are much more frequent than the hyperbolic uses until the 1960s. By hyperbolic I mean that the expression is used to indicate someone has become irritated or distraught, but not literally insane. *Drive someone crazy* has always been more frequent in the hyperbolic sense, which begins in the corpus in the 1930s.

The centrality of *drive someone crazy* in its hyperbolic use is shown by its steady increase in frequency from the 1930s to the present. By the 1960s the use of this expression has apparently reached a point at which it begins to attract synonymous expressions (see Figure 5.1). The hyperbolic use of *drive someone mad* peaks in the 1960s and then declines. The expression with *nuts* is documented in a literal use in the 1940s but becomes frequent in the hyperbolic use in the 1960s as well. In this corpus, when *up the wall* with *drive* first occurs in the 1960s it is in the hyperbolic use; its frequency increases in the 1970s.

Thus it appears that the increase in use of *drive someone crazy* in a subjective, hyperbolic use has served to attract other modifiers into an analogous expression, which has in turn increased the construction's schematicity. Interestingly, *drive someone mad* in its hyperbolic use does not oust its original more literal use indicating actual insanity (see Figure 5.2).

Why would *crazy* be the adjective that leads the march in this case? It is the most frequent adjective in this semantic domain. It is less serious than *mad* in

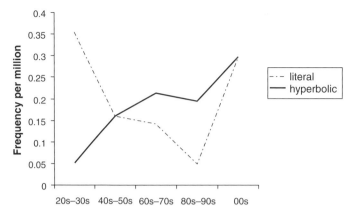

Figure 5.2 Literal vs. hyperbolic uses of *drive someone mad* from the 1920s to the 2000s

its 'insane' meaning, because for American speakers *crazy* does not necessarily indicate a clinical condition and so it is more appropriate to the hyperbolic use.

In the next section we discuss in more detail the nature of the exemplar categories that occupy schematic slots in constructions, comparing these structures with the hypothesized categories based on necessary and sufficient conditions that have been dominant in linguistics and Western thought in general. We will see once again an important role for the high-frequency member of the category and will discuss reasons for this central role.

5.6   Prototype categories: 'become' verbs in Spanish

5.6.1   *Failures of necessary and sufficient conditions*

A longstanding tradition in linguistics has been to try to identify the abstract features that characterize a category or linguistic marker. In structural and generative practice the fewer such features, the better. This leads to a search for the most abstract features possible to characterize a range of items or uses and to exclude all others. As mentioned in Chapter 2, Roman Jakobson stated quite explicitly that such abstract, indeed, binary, features were necessary to simplify the learning and usage tasks of speakers, as language is so complex (Jakobson 1990). However, specific analyses utilizing such features are invariably controversial, indicating perhaps that such features are not capturing the mechanisms that allow speakers to use their languages productively. (See discussion of the 'irrealis' category in Bybee, Perkins and Pagliuca 1994 and Bybee 1998a.)

Abstract analyses in terms of strict necessary and sufficient conditions, in which an item either belongs or does not belong to the category, stand in stark contrast to the exemplar categorization as described above in which members of categories can be graded with respect to their centrality or marginality. Categorization in this model proceeds by local comparisons of incoming items with established items, taking into account both similarity on various dimensions and frequency of occurrence. This means that items form close, local relationships wherever possible.

In our study of 'become' verbs and the adjectives they take in Spanish (Bybee and Eddington 2006), we cite various types of evidence for such local clustering of members of a constructional category. The focus of the study is four verbs that are used with animate subjects and adjectives to form 'become' expressions. These verbs are *quedarse, ponerse, volverse* and *hacerse*. A number of previous studies sought to give general characterizations of which adjectives were more felicitous with which verbs. It has been noted that not all adjectives occur with each verb, rather there appear to be conventionalized verb–adjective pairings. Attempts to characterize these in abstract terms have not been successful; possible features, such as the duration of the state entered into, or the degree of involvement of the subject, are either empirically not justifiable, or too difficult to apply in particular cases. An instance of the first problem is seen in the fact that one author (Pountain 1984) proposes that *ponerse* is used with adjectives that are also used with the copula *estar*, which indicates a temporary state, while another work (Coste and Redondo 1965) asserts that *ponerse* is not allowed with adjectives that occur with *estar*. An instance of the second problem is that *quedar(se)* is said to be used to describe passive changes initiated by an external agent (which reflects its historical source) (Fente 1970), but examples that are found in corpora exhibit a range of variation on this dimension. Some examples such as (3) imply an external cause, but others such as (4) imply internal control.

(3) y la gente cuando la vea funcionar *se* va a *quedar asustada*.
     'and people when they see it work are going to be afraid'
(4) – Como quieras, viejo. Las cosas se dan así, lo mejor es *quedarse*
     tranquilo. A mí tampoco me va tan mal.
     'As you wish, old man. Things are like this, it's better to calm down
     (become calm). To me it doesn't seem that bad.'

A third difficulty is that these features may characterize one verb's usage, but they do not necessarily distinguish it from the usage of another verb. Thus both *quedarse* and *ponerse* can be used with emotional states of short duration (*quedarse sorprendido* 'to be[come] surprised' and *ponerse nervioso* 'to get nervous') and physical states (*quedarse embarazada* 'to get pregnant' and *ponerse mal* 'to get sick'). Consider the following two examples, where *quedarse tranquilo* and *ponerse tranquilo* both occur in situations where one person is trying to calm another person:

(5) El chico se quejaba, gemía y ella lo acunaba pidiéndole que no llorase, que *se quedara tranquilo…*
'The child whined, moaned and she cradled him asking him not to cry, to calm down.'
(6) – Yo le digo "compañero" para que *se ponga tranquilo*. Calma usted…
'I called you "compañero" to calm you down. Calm down…'

Thus it has proven very difficult to characterize the group of adjectives that are used with each verb in terms of general features that include only members of the category and exclude all others.

5.6.2   *More local categorization*

The failure of general, abstract features to predict corpus uses of the 'become' verbs suggests that more local categorization governs speakers' choices of verbs to pair with adjectives. Thus Bybee and Eddington 2006 suggest for *quedarse* several clusters of semantically related adjectives, but no overarching abstract features. Based on corpus examples, we propose several categories of adjectives that occur with *quedarse* and also a set for *ponerse*. (For full details, see Bybee and Eddington 2006.)

Just to illustrate the findings of the corpus study, consider Table 5.1, which lists the adjectives that we classified as semantically related to *solo* 'alone', an adjective that occurs very frequently with *quedarse*. Note that we classified the opposite, *emparejado* 'paired with', as semantically related to 'alone' because opposites share most features while differing in only one.

We take the semantic similarity to *solo* of the less frequent adjectives as indicating that their use with the verb *quedarse* and not with any other verbs is due to analogical comparison with *quedarse solo*. The local nature of this categorization is indicated by the fact that other such clusters of adjectives around a higher-frequency exemplar (or prefab) also occur. Thus Table 5.2 shows the adjectives that are semantically similar to the more frequent *quedarse inmóvil* 'become motionless'.

Table 5.3 illustrates another such cluster – the adjectives related semantically to *quedarse sorprendido* 'to be surprised'. As mentioned earlier, it would be quite difficult to find one abstract feature that could characterize the set of adjectives that occur with this verb (to the near exclusion of the other verbs). It seems more likely that rather than accessing a highly abstract feature, speakers rely on more local comparisons. Since higher frequency means greater accessibility, the more frequent adjectives tend to serve as the basis for such analogy more often.

Table 5.1 *Number of adjectives used with* quedarse *related to* solo *in the spoken and written corpus*

Adjective	Spoken	Written
solo 'alone'	7	21
soltera 'single, unmarried'	1	2
aislado 'isolated'	2	0
a solas 'alone'	1	0
sin novia 'without a girlfriend'	1	0
Opposite:		
emparejado 'paired with'	1	0

Table 5.2 *Adjectives with* quedarse *grouped with* inmóvil *indicating motionlessness*

Adjective	Spoken	Written
inmóvil 'motionless'	0	17
parado 'stopped, standing'	2	0
tieso 'stiff'	0	3
duro 'hard'	0	2
petrificado 'turned to stone'	0	1
de piedra 'made of stone'	1	0
paralizado 'paralyzed'	0	1
seco 'dry'	0	1
clavado al suelo 'nailed to the ground'	0	1
inoperante 'inoperative'	1	0
encerrado 'closed in'	0	1

5.6.3   Similarity in categorization

Expansion of categories by adding similar members can take different shapes because similarity can be assessed differently in different instances of language use in context. In the data on Spanish 'become' expressions, we find several types of semantic similarity manifested in categories, four of which can be illustrated with examples from the *inmóvil* cluster shown in Table 5.2.

First, as one might expect, synonyms or near-synonyms can be attracted into a category. Thus, *parado* 'stopped, standing' is used with *quedarse* just as *inmóvil* is. Second, metaphors that result in similar meanings will also occur in the same category, for example *de piedra* 'of stone' with the interpretation of motionless. Third, hyperbolic expressions such as *paralizado* 'paralyzed' with the meaning 'motionless' are also used with *quedarse*. Fourth, there are items

Table 5.3 *Adjectives with* quedarse *grouped with* sorprendido

Adjective	Spoken	Written
sorprendido 'surprised'	4	3
deslumbrado 'dazzled'	1	0
fascinado 'fascinated'	0	1
asombrado 'amazed'	0	1
asustado 'frightened'	1	0
seco 'dry, frightened'	1	0
acojonado 'impressed'	1	0
trastornado 'disturbed'	0	1
alucinado 'amazed'	3	0
loco 'crazy'	1	0
frío 'surprised'	1	1
perplejo 'perplexed'	0	1
pasmado 'stunned'	0	1
estupefacto 'stupified'	0	2
atónito 'astounded'	0	1
preocupado 'worried'	0	1
frustrado 'frustrated'	1	0
colgado 'disappointed'	1	0

that share a feature (motionlessness) but add other features, such as *atrapado* 'trapped', which indicates motionlessness attributed to some restraining entity. Finally, much to our surprise, in an experiment that asked subjects to judge the similarity between pairs of adjectives, the following adjectives were rated as highly similar: *bueno* 'good', *rico* 'rich', *famoso* 'famous', and *fuerte* 'strong'. These ratings, which are not of the type that a linguist's semantic analysis would yield, suggest that socially-informed inferential associations may also be at work in language user's categorizations. These adjectives all occur in the data with the verb *hacerse*.

5.6.4   Multiple clusters in constructional categories

It is not unusual to find local distributions within constructional categories. A number of examples of two or more categories filling a position in the construction have been discussed in the literature. For instance, the *way*-construction is said to take two kinds of verbs – manner of motion and creation of a path (Goldberg 1995, Israel 1996). Example (7) illustrates the manner-of-motion type and example (8) illustrates the creation-of-path type (examples from the *Time Magazine* corpus).

(7) Annabel *wormed her way* into the circle around Kezia...
(8) A skier *carves his way* down a pristine slope of powder...

Early examples with the ancestor of the modal verb *can* (*cunnan*) in Old English show three types of complement verbs, each having evolved in their own way (Bybee 2003b, see also Goosens 1990). The earlier meaning of *can* was 'to know' and the three uses reflect this meaning. The complement verbs in one set deal with knowledge and understanding and as such, simply bolster the fading meaning of *can* as it becomes more frequent. Another set are verbs of saying, which, when combined with *can* indicate that the subject has the knowledge to assert his proposition truthfully. The third type is used with verbs indicating skills. Earlier, one could say 'X can (knows) the harp' meaning that X plays the harp. Later another verb is added to such sentences: 'X can (knows) the harp play'.

Goldberg 1995 also identifies a number of clusters of verbs used in the ditransitive construction. These include, for example, those signifying acts of giving: *give, hand, pass, sell, trade, lend, serve, feed;* verbs of sending: *send, mail, ship;* verbs of communicating a message: *tell, show, ask, teach, write;* verbs of creation: *bake, sew, make, build, knit,* and so on. In this case, there may be some links among the categories, but there is no overarching abstract meaning that reliably tells a speaker of English which verbs can be used in this construction and which cannot.

Thus the situation of finding several clusters of lexical items that are used in a position in a construction is quite common and apparently poses no anomaly for language users, as would be suggested by an analysis that tries to find a single abstract meaning or contrast to characterize the entire class of items that occurs in a certain position in the construction. Instead, the distributions discussed here suggest categorization on the basis of specific, concrete semantic properties of the lexical items, which creates categories (sometimes several) with graded membership.

5.7   The role of the most frequent member of the category

In Adele Goldberg's studies of argument structure constructions, she has also noted frequency skewings among the verbs that occur in such constructions and considered their role in the acquisition of constructions. The corpus of mothers' speech to children analysed by Goldberg, Casenheiser and Sethuraman 2004 reveals that each of three constructions has one verb that is more frequent than all the others. Table 5.4 is reproduced from Goldberg 2006.

Goldberg argues that the verbs *go, put* and *give* are frequent in these constructions, not just because they are frequent in the language, but because they are semantically general and can be applied to a wide range of arguments. She also argues that each of these verbs 'designates a basic pattern of experience' and thus have meanings that are readily accessible to children (2006: 77). Further she notes that the verbs themselves have meanings that strongly resemble the meanings posited for the constructions they occur in. Thus the use of

Table 5.4 *Fifteen mothers' most frequent verbs and number of verb types for three constructions in Bates et al. (1988) corpus*

Construction	Mothers	Number of verb types
SUBJ − VERB − OBLIQUE	39% *go* (136/353)	39
SUBJ − VERB − OBJ − OBLIQUE	38% *put* (99/256)	43
SUBJ − VERB − OBJ − OBJ$_2$	20% *give* (11/54)	13

the construction with these verbs that provide no additional meaning helps the child establish the meaning of the construction. Presumably from this basis, the child (and adult) can go on to use the construction with other verbs that may add other meanings to the whole utterance.

Casenheiser and Goldberg 2005 tested the effect of skewed input on learning in an experiment with children aged 5 to 7 years and on adults. They designed an experiment to test the contribution of type and token frequency in which both children and adults were taught a nonce argument construction in English. The construction had a nonce verb (with a suffix in some of the conditions) and the verb appeared at the end of the clause, making it like no other construction in English. The meaning of the construction was taught through a video presentation that accompanied the linguistic stimuli. In one condition nonce verbs appeared in the stimuli with relatively low token frequency: three novel verbs occurred four times and two occurred twice (4-4-4-2-2). In the other condition the same number of verbs were presented, but one had a higher token frequency than all the others, occurring eight times, while the other four occurred twice (8-2-2-2-2).

In previous literature, type frequency has been found to be an important determinant of productivity, while no such role has been found for token frequency (MacWhinney 1978, Bybee 1985, Hay and Baayen 2002). On this basis, it would be expected that subjects might respond similarly in both conditions. However, the results showed that both the adults and children learned the construction better in the more skewed condition, in which one verb type was presented eight times, in that they responded correctly more often to novel instances of the construction.

Casenheiser and Goldberg 2005 and Goldberg 2006 propose that the repetition of a particular verb in a particular construction helps to establish the correlation between the meaning of the construction and its formal expression. Goldberg 2006 goes on to argue that in category learning in general a centred, or low variance, category is easier to learn. The condition with one instance of higher token frequency is just such a category.

One might add a reference here to domain-general work on analogies. Kotovsky and Gentner 1996 show that familiarity with a fixed set of relations is necessary before those relations can be extended to other objects. Holding as many parts as constant as possible helps with the internalization of the relationships. Thus having an instance of a construction that is fixed over a few repetitions may aid in learning the parts of the construction and how they produce the overall meaning.

As for adult language users, it is also important to note that conventionalized uses of linguistic forms reflect conventionalized situations one refers to frequently. Thus both the form and meaning are easily accessible and set up good models for novel analogical formations, which fill out the category space around the central or frequent member.

Finally, as we mentioned in the previous chapter, diachronic development seems to emanate outwardly from the central member of a category. It appears that conventionalized expressions can develop through a few repetitions and set up a conventionalized way to talk about a situation. Then variations on this theme begin to create a category. As mentioned in Chapter 4, Wilson 2009 discusses the development of the *quedarse* + ADJ construction, which seems to have begun with *quedarse solo* 'to be (left) alone'. Soon this expression was joined by other uses of *quedarse* in this sense, such as: *quedarse sin padre* 'without a father', *quedarse viuda* 'widow', *quedarse huérfano* 'orphan' and *quedarse sin herederos* 'without heirs'.

Graded category membership and the central role of the frequent member thus pervade linguistic dimensions, playing a role in synchronic language use (as reflected in corpus distributions), in child language acquisition and in diachronic expansion of categories.

5.8   Family resemblance structure

Given the interaction of the two factors I am proposing account for category structure – frequency and similarity – and the proposal that their application to any given situation is probabilistic, analogies may be based on a member of lesser frequency if that member shows greater similarity to the novel situation. Such situations lead to the creative expansion of categories and to what Wittgenstein 1953 called 'family resemblance structure'.

For instance, going back to the adjectives used with *quedarse*, one of the most frequent ones is *quieto* which means 'quiet/still'. This relates to another frequent adjective with *quedarse, inmóvil*, which refers to motionlessness, but not necessarily quiet. On the other side, *tranquilo* 'tranquil' indicates stillness with positive connotations of peacefulness. Related to *tranquil*, then, is *conforme* 'satisfied', which then leads to the adjective, *a gusto* 'pleased'. Now *a gusto* shares no features with *inmóvil* directly – one means 'pleased' and the other 'motionless' – yet they participate in the same extended category by virtue of this chain of family resemblances, as shown in (9). Family resemblance chains are compatible with the mechanism of local analogies that allow for novel combinations.

(9) *inmóvil –   quieto – tranquilo – conforme – a gusto*
     'motionless', 'still', 'tranquil', 'satisfied', 'pleased'

The local analogies also allow for creativity and nonce-creation. In the *Time Magazine* corpus there is a use of the *drive* construction with the nonce creation *Salieri-mad*. This seems to indicate a type of madness that was manifested in the composer Salieri, who was so jealous of Mozart's success that he allegedly poisoned him and was responsible for the latter composer's death. Here is the passage from the corpus:

(10) …for the rest of your life, knowing that if you had just not slept in that one morning or skipped your kid's stupid school play, you could have made it? Wouldn't that <u>drive you Salieri-mad</u>? That's why I needed to call someone who just missed the TIME 100 and let him know. It was the only way I could feel better about myself. There were several candidates who just missed the list…

Family resemblance structure is, then, a consequence of the way categories expand by analogy. Chains of local analogies create family resemblance chains. Such chains can span a broad portion of semantic space, leading to highly schematic categories. They can also be narrowly centred on a high-frequency member in cases of lower schematicity. In the next section we consider more schematic categories that appear to be less centred than the ones discussed so far.

5.9   Categories which are more schematic

So far we have examined highly focused categories that are organized around a central member and show high degrees of similarity among the members. These would be less schematic categories, due to their narrow range. But other relationships among the items that occur in a position in a construction are possible as well. Exemplar learning allows categories of various sorts. Some categories are much more schematic and do not have a central high-frequency member. Others do have a high-frequency member but do not show expansion on the basis of that member.

   In our study of the adjectives that occur with *quedarse* we found that one group of adjectives – those indicating bodily conditions – seemed much more schematic than the other categories we had uncovered. See the list of adjectives in Table 5.5. The conventionalized way of saying that a woman is pregnant is *quedarse embarazada* and the conventional way of saying the same about an animal is *quedarse preñada*. The other adjectives are not especially closely

Table 5.5 *Adjectives with* quedarse *indicating bodily states*

Adjective	Spoken	Written
embarazada 'pregnant'	4	0
preñada 'pregnant'	3	1
desnutrido 'malnourished'	1	0
en bolas 'naked'	1	0
ciego 'blind'	0	4
asfixiado 'suffocated'	1	0
calvo 'bald'	2	0
encogido 'cringing'	0	1
mejor 'better'	1	0
viejo 'old'	1	0
pelado 'shaved'	0	1
toruno 'castrated'	0	1
delgado 'thin'	0	1
estéril 'sterile'	0	1

related to these in any of the similarity relations we have found in the data for the more focused categories. Despite these more distant similarity relations, these items may constitute a category, but a much more schematic one than the categories we have examined so far.

Another example of a highly schematic, though small, category is found with the verb *volverse*. The conventional way of saying 'to go crazy' in Spanish is *volverse loco* and it occurs frequently in both the spoken and written data. One might expect that such an expression would give rise to synonymous expressions the way *drive someone crazy* in English has spawned a whole set of expressions. However, the Spanish data yielded the adjectives with *volverse* listed in Table 5.6. Except for *idiota* 'idiotic' and *llena de furia* 'full of fury', the adjectives used with *volverse* do not show any special resemblance to *loco*. We were not able to explain this unexpected result. We can only observe that such patterns exist in language use.

Another highly schematic category occurs with *hacerse*, the other Spanish verb that is used with animate subjects and adjectives to mean 'become'. This verb has many uses with inanimate subjects and with nouns as well, including conventionalized expressions such as *hacerse tarde* 'to become late' and *hacerse amigos* 'to become friends'. However, with animate subjects and adjectives it occurred only twenty-four times with sixteen different adjectives. As Table 5.7 shows, these were quite diverse in their meaning. Earlier, we noted that subjects in a similarity-rating experiment found *bueno, fuerte, rico* and *famoso* to be related. The only other adjectives we tested were *aburrido* 'boring' and *presente* 'present' and these were rated as quite dissimilar to each other and to the other adjectives tested.

Table 5.6 *Adjectives with* volverse

Adjective	Spoken	Written
loco 'crazy'	6	10
idiota 'idiotic'	0	1
llena de furia 'full of fury'	0	1
mística 'mystical'	0	1
pesado 'annoying'	0	1
raquítico 'rickety, weak'	0	1
fino 'fine'	0	1
exquisito 'exquisite'	1	0
esquivo 'shy'	0	1
ensimismado 'introverted'	0	1
sumiso 'submissive'	0	1
susceptible 'susceptible'	0	1
mieles 'sweet (lit. honeys)'	0	1
negro 'black'	0	1
viejo 'old'	0	1

Table 5.7 *Adjectives with* hacerse

Adjective	Spoken	Written
aburrido 'boring'	1	0
cursi 'tacky'	1	0
consciente 'aware of'	1	2
realista 'realistic'	0	1
responsable 'responsible'	0	1
mayor 'grown up'	1	1
viejo 'old'	0	2
duro 'hard'	0	1
fuerte 'strong'	1	1
invulnerable 'invulnerable'	0	1
no inferior 'not inferior'	1	0
digno 'dignified'	0	1
bueno 'good'	1	0
famoso 'famous'	1	1
rico 'rich'	0	2
visible 'visible'	0	2
presente 'present'	0	3

The groups in Tables 5.6 and 5.7 – the adjectives used with *volverse* and *hacerse* – constitute quite schematic groups, as their meanings cover a wide territory. Despite this schematicity, the data show that the constructions with these verbs are not nearly as productive as those with the other two verbs – *quedarse* and *ponerse*. The difference in productivity can be observed in Table 5.8, which

Table 5.8 *Number of occurrences and number of types with a human subject and an adjective in a spoken corpus of 1.1 million words and a written corpus of about one million words (Marcos Marín 1992; Eddington 1999)*

| | Spoken | | Written | | Total |
	Tokens	Types	Tokens	Types	Types^2
quedarse	68	40	181	54	69
ponerse	36	23	85	45	62
hacerse	8	8	16	11	16
volverse	7	2	22	13	14
Total	119		304		147

shows the token and type frequencies for each verb in the corpora. *Quedarse* and *ponerse* account for the majority of the tokens as well as a majority of the types found in the data. In the next section we discuss what is known about the factors that determine productivity.

While the categories of adjectives used with *volverse* and *hacerse* are small and not very productive, they are highly schematic, in that they cover a wide range of semantic features. It is also common for a category within a construction to be highly schematic and also highly productive. Such well-studied categories as the English regular Past Tense are both highly schematic (applying to any phonological or semantic type of verb) and highly productive (applying easily to new verbs). Similarly, constructions that are highly grammaticalized become both highly schematic and productive. For instance, although the verbs used with *can* were once restricted, favouring verbs of speaking and cognitive verbs, now any semantic type of verb can be used with *can*. The fact that the more centred and less schematic classes of the *quedarse* and *ponerse* constructions are highly productive (given the semantic categorization) shows that schematicity and productivity are independent dimensions along which constructions vary.

5.10   Productivity

Productivity is the likelihood that a construction will apply to a new item. It is thus a property of the category or categories formed by the open positions in a construction. Each lexical slot in a construction has its own degree of productivity. Thus in the construction exemplified by *drive someone crazy* the verb slot is found to be occupied by the verbs *drive, send, make* (Boas 2003), while the adjective slot, as we have noted earlier, is found with a larger number of types and is thus more productive. Note, however, that the verb slot is less well-defined semantically and thus more schematic than the adjective slot, another demonstration that schematicity and productivity are independent.

Productivity has been studied in the morphological domain more than any other and some of the factors that determine productivity in morphology can be applied to morphosyntactic constructions as well. As mentioned just above, type frequency is an important determinant of productivity, with higher type frequency leading to greater productivity. The effect of type frequency can be constrained in various ways. One must take into account the fact that types of extremely high token frequency contribute less to productivity because of their autonomy and loss of analysability. In addition, schematicity constrains productivity: the highly focused nature of the class of adjectives occurring in the *drive someone* ___ construction constrains its ability to expand.

There have been several explanations for the importance of type frequency proposed in the literature. Baayen 1993 emphasizes the number of types that occur in a single token in a corpus as indicative of productivity. Because these 'hapax legomena' are less familiar, perhaps novel, they require parsing, which activates the component parts renewing the analysability of the construction. In the case of derivational morphology, this protects the activation levels of the affixes against decay. In the case of morpho-syntactic constructions, the use of low-frequency exemplars activates the whole construction and strengthens its representation more than the use of a high-frequency exemplar of the construction.

While agreeing with the explanation for productivity just mentioned – that parsing contributes to the activation of the construction (see also Hay 2001, Hay and Baayen 2002) – we may also recognize that in an exemplar model, the number of stored exemplars of a constructional slot with high type frequency will be much greater than the number for a slot with low type frequency. Given that the mechanism behind productivity is item-specific analogy, a construction with a high type frequency slot will be more likely to be used to form a novel utterance than one with lower type frequency, simply because there are more candidates on which to base the analogy.

As Baayen points out, parsing is necessary for low-frequency tokens and contributes to productivity. At the other end of the spectrum, the relative autonomy of high-frequency tokens does not contribute to the productivity of the general construction (as pointed out in Bybee 1985 and elsewhere). As an exemplar of a construction reaches high token frequency, it is processed without activating the other exemplars of the construction and begins to lose analysability and compositionality. Thus constructions represented primarily by high-frequency members or formulaic expressions will tend not to be productive. Consider the example of the two types of negation discussed in Chapter 3. *No* negation has a token frequency of 314 in the corpus Tottie 1991 studied and *not* negation has a token frequency of 139. As the latter is more productive, clearly token frequency is not the determinant of productivity. The high token count for *no* negation is due to its high level of use with some very frequent verbs – existential and copular *be* and stative *have*. *No* negation is also used with some lexical verbs but many of these are in formulaic expressions. Thus the type/token ratio for *no* negation in the spoken corpus is much lower (0.45) than that of *not* negation (0.57), as it is in the written corpus, where the ratio is 0.63 for *no* negation and 0.86 for *not* negation (Tottie 1991: 449).

Thus high token frequency detracts from productivity in morphology and also in morphosyntax if a certain level of autonomy is reached. The next section contains a brief discussion of autonomy.

5.11   Centrality of membership is not autonomy

In this chapter we have seen that the relatively high-frequency exemplars of a construction are central members and serve to attract new members to a construction. In Chapter 3 we argued that at extremely high-frequency levels exemplars may become autonomous, thereby creating a new construction. Autonomous members do not contribute to categorization or productivity because they have formed their own construction. Thus there are two different types of behaviour depending upon degrees of frequency of use.

Increasing autonomy, which creates a new construction, has been discussed in Bybee 2003b and 2006a. Of relevance for the current discussion is the fact that when a particular instance of a construction – that is, a construction with a particular lexical item – becomes highly frequent, it is processed as a unit. As we saw in Chapter 3, the more often a sequence is processed directly as a unit, the less likely it is to activate other units or the construction to which it belongs and the more likely it is to lose its analysability. At the same time, use in particular contexts contributes to shifts in meaning, which decrease compositionality and make the former exemplar of a construction move away from its source. For example, the *be going to* construction arose from a purpose clause construction in which any verb could occupy the position *go* now occupies. Because of the semantic generality of *go,* it happened to be the most frequent movement verb in the purpose construction. Because of its use in context, one could infer a sense of intention to do something from it, and this became part of its meaning. As a result of its frequent access as a unit and the semantic change due to inferences in context, SUBJECT *be going to* VERB has become a new construction independent of the purpose construction from which it arose.

Note in contrast that exemplars of constructions such as *quedarse solo* 'to end up alone', do not exhibit autonomy, nor is the verb on its way to becoming a grammatical morpheme. The exemplar remains semantically compositional and fully analysable; it is conventionalized and is used as a reference point for analogical extensions of the construction.

5.12   Problems with Collostructional Analysis

Collostructional Analysis, another method for analysing the distribution of lexemes in constructions for the purpose of addressing the meaning of constructions, has been developed recently. Collostructional Analysis (Stefanowitsch and Gries 2003) is particularly concerned with using computational methods to determine which lexemes are most 'attracted' to constructions and which are 'repelled' by constructions. The researchers developing this method feel that it is important to take into account the overall token frequency of a lexeme in determining how expected it is in a construction, as well as the lexeme's frequency in the construction. Thus a lexeme with an overall high token count will be judged as less attracted to a construction than one with a low frequency, all other things being equal. In addition, the calculation takes into account the lexeme's frequency in the construction relative to other lexemes that appear in the construction. The final and fourth factor is the frequency of all the constructions in the corpus. Because all four factors are used to calculate collostructional strength, the method allows no way to determine if all four factors are significant. I suggest for reasons to be outlined below that the frequency of the lexeme L in the construction is the most important factor with perhaps the frequency relative to the overall frequency of the construction playing a role.

Consider first the question of whether or not the overall frequency of a lexeme detracts from its attraction to a construction. Stefanowitsch and Gries 2003 and Gries et al. 2005 explain that attraction refers to the strength of the association between the lexeme and the construction. Given that Gries et al. claim that Collostructional Analysis can help determine the meaning of a construction, 'attraction' or Collostructional Strength would correspond to how prototypical or central the lexeme is to the meaning and usage of the construction. In the calculation, high overall token frequency of a lexeme detracts from its Collostructional Strength. The stated reasoning is to control for general frequency effects: in order for a lexeme to have high Collostructional Strength it must occur in the construction more often than would be predicted by pure chance (Gries et al. 2005: 646).

The problem with this line of reasoning is that lexemes do not occur in corpora by pure chance. Every lexeme was chosen by a speaker in a particular context for a particular reason. Furthermore, it is entirely possible that the factors that make a lexeme high frequency in a corpus are precisely the factors that make it a central and defining member of the category of lexemes that occurs in a slot in a construction (see sections 5.7 and 5.11). Consider for example, the Spanish adjective *solo*, which is one of the most frequent adjectives to occur in the *quedarse* expression in Spanish. Its meaning is 'alone', a highly general meaning compared to *aislado* 'isolated', *soltera* 'unmarried (fem.)', and so on. Its highly general meaning makes it frequent in the corpora and it is also this general meaning that makes it a central member of the category of adjectives occurring in this construction. So in this case, Collostructional Analysis may give the wrong results, because a high overall frequency will give the word *solo* a lower degree of attraction to the construction according to this formula.

Gries et al. 2005 disparage the use of 'mere frequency' (presumably they mean token frequency) in usage-based analysis. They say:

> We, therefore, wish to emphasize again that arguing and theorizing on the basis of mere frequency data alone runs a considerable risk of producing results which might not only be completely due to the random distribution of words [in a corpus], but which may also be much less usage-based than the analysis purports to be. (p. 665)

Since Bybee and Eddington 2006 use 'mere frequency' or token frequency of an adjective in a construction to examine the nature of the categories of adjectives used with each 'become' verb in Spanish, a comparison can be made between the results obtained in that way with the results of Collostructional Analysis. To calculate Collostructional Strength, we used overall token frequency counts for all the adjectives (in all their inflected forms) in the written corpus used in Bybee and Eddington[3]. Unfortunately, there is some uncertainty about the fourth factor mentioned above – the number of constructions that occur in the corpus. There is no known way to count the number of constructions in a corpus because a given clause may instantiate multiple constructions. Stefanowitsch and Gries 2003 and Gries et al. 2005 use a count of the number of verbs in the corpus. Because we were not using a tagged corpus, such a count was not available to us. Instead, we used the size of the corpus as the fourth factor and calculated Collostructional Strength in using several different corpus sizes. The results reported here take the corpus size to be two million words, although other corpus sizes yield similar results.

The corpus-based analysis of Bybee and Eddington takes the most frequent adjectives occurring with each of four 'become' verbs as the centres of categories, with semantically related adjectives surrounding these central adjectives depending on their semantic similarity, as discussed above. Thus our analysis uses both frequency and semantics. Proponents of Collostructional Analysis hope to arrive at a semantic analysis, but do not include any semantic factors in their method. Since no semantic considerations go into the analysis, it seems plausible that no semantic analysis can emerge from it.

The Bybee and Eddington analysis was corroborated by two experiments. One was a semantic similarity judgement task whose results showed that over a large number of speakers, there was considerable agreement with our proposals of degree of similarity among adjectives. The second experiment asked for acceptability judgements on sentences largely taken from the corpus. Thus all the stimuli sentences were well-formed grammatically, but even so, speakers were able to rate them on a five-point scale according to whether they sounded 'perfectly fine' on one pole, or 'strange' on the other. These judgements should tell us how prototypical or central an adjective is to the construction it occurred in in the stimuli sentences. Our hypothesis was that adjectives that occurred frequently in the construction would be rated the highest, those that were of low frequency in the construction but semantically related to the high-frequency adjectives would be the next highest in acceptability rating, and those that occurred infrequently in the construction and were not semantically related to adjectives that occurred with high frequency in the construction would have the lowest acceptability ratings. These findings were strongly upheld by the results of the experiment.

A good way to compare Collostructional Analysis to a mere frequency analysis is to see how Collostructional Analysis fares in predicting the results of the acceptability experiment – the higher the Collostructional Strength of the adjective in the construction, the more acceptable the sentence should be.

In Tables 5.9 and 5.10 we compare the Collostructional Strength and the frequency in the construction to the subjects' acceptability judgements. (Forty-eight subjects completed the task.) In the first column are the adjectives that occurred in the stimuli. The second column shows the total number of subjects' responses that put the sentence in the two highest categories of acceptability. The third column shows the Collostructional Strength calculation, the fourth column the frequency of the adjective in the construction and the fifth column shows the corpus frequency of the adjective. The corpus frequency lowers the Collostructional Strength, so this number helps explain the third column values. The adjectives are divided into three groups: high frequency in the construction, low frequency in the construction, but semantically related to the high-frequency exemplars, and low frequency, not semantically related to the high-frequency exemplars. (*Convencido* and *redondo* have a Frequency in Construction of '0' because they did not actually occur in the corpus; since the low-frequency unrelated adjectives were rare in the corpus Bybee and Eddington had to make up some stimuli for the experiment.)

First, observe that the adjectives that occurred in the constructions with the highest frequency have the highest Collostructional Strength and also have high ratings for acceptability. For these cases, Collostructional Strength and mere frequency make the same predictions.

For the low-frequency adjectives, however, the experiment revealed, as Bybee and Eddington had predicted, a difference between low-frequency adjectives that were semantically similar to the high-frequency ones and

Table 5.9 *Comparison of acceptability judgements, Collostructional Strength and frequency in construction for adjectives with* quedarse[4]

	High Acceptability	Collostructional Strength	Frequency in Construction	Corpus frequency
High frequency				
dormido 'asleep'	42	79.34	28	161
sorpendido 'surprised'	42	17.57	7	92
quieto 'still/calm'	39	85.76	29	129
solo 'alone'	29	56.25	28	1000
Low frequency related				
perplejo 'perplexed'	40	2.62	1	20
paralizado 'paralyzed/at a standstill'	35	2.49	1	1
pasmado 'amazed'	30	2.72	1	16
clavado al suelo 'riveted'	29	3.92	1	1
Low frequency unrelated				
convencido 'convinced'	31	0	0	87
desnutrido 'undernourished'	17	3.23	1	5
redondo 'round'	10	0.01	0	128
orgullosísmo 'proud', 'arrogant'	6	3.92	1	1

those that were not. This turned out to be quite significant in the experiment with the low-frequency, semantically related adjectives garnering judgements almost as high as the high-frequency adjectives. In contrast, Collostructional Analysis treats all of the adjectives that occurred with low frequency in the construction the same, giving them very low scores. Of course, the Collostructional Analysis cannot make the distinction between semantically related and unrelated since it works only with numbers and not with meaning. Thus, for determining what lexemes are the best fit or the most central to a construction, a simple frequency analysis with semantic similarity produces the best results.

A reasonable interpretation of the results of the Bybee and Eddington corpus study and experiment is that lexemes with relatively high frequency in a construction are central to defining the meaning of the construction (Goldberg 2006) and serve as a reference point for novel uses of the construction. If this interpretation is correct, then the frequency of the lexeme in other uses is not important. Gries and colleagues argue for their statistical method but do not propose a cognitive mechanism that corresponds to their analysis. By what cognitive mechanism does a language user devalue a lexeme in

Table 5.10 *Comparison of acceptability judgements, Collostructional Strength and frequency in construction for adjectives with* ponerse

	High Acceptability	Collostructional Strength	Frequency in Construction	Corpus frequency
High frequency				
nervioso 'nervous'	37	50.06	17	159
enfermo 'sick'	32	8.82	4	243
furioso 'furious'	24	14.49	5	60
pesado 'heavy'	22	15.83	6	124
Low frequency related				
agresivo 'aggressive'	34	2.55	1	49
inaguantable 'intolerable'	27	3.54	1	5
negro 'nasty/cross'	22	1.20	1	1129
revoltoso 'rebellious'	6	3.46	1	6
Low frequency unrelated				
sentimental 'sentimental'	19	2.58	1	45
viejo 'old'	11	1.07	1	1551
maternal 'motherly'	11	2.94	1	20
putona 'promiscuous'	2	3.54	1	5

a construction if it is of high frequency generally? This is the question Collostructional Analysis must address.

One further comment about the results of Collostructional Analysis: lexemes that occur only once in a construction within a corpus are treated in two ways by Collostructional Analysis: if they are frequent throughout the corpus, then they are said to be repelled by the construction and if they are infrequent in the corpus, then they are likely to be attracted to the construction. We have already noted that without consulting the meaning of the lexemes such results may make no sense. In addition, in many such analyses – see for example many of the tables in Stefanowitsch and Gries 2003 – low-frequency lexemes are ignored. The problem with this is that the low-frequency lexemes often show the productive expansion of the category of lexemes used in the construction (Baayen 1993). Without knowing what the range of low frequency, semantically related lexemes is, one cannot define the semantic category of lexemes that can be used in a construction.

5.13   Greater degrees of abstraction

Most linguistic theories assume a priori that grammars contain very broad generalizations and highly abstract categories such as SUBJECT, OBJECT,

ADJECTIVE, and so forth. In our discussion so far we have focused on many small constructions which form local generalizations over groups of lexical items. The focus has been on these lower-level generalizations because they have been so neglected in other theories. In addition, it seems possible that empirical evidence about these local generalizations will help us eventually to understand the mechanisms that create grammar. But now the time has come to ask what status more abstract categories and generalizations have in a usage-based grammar.

The first question to be posed concerns the evidence for more abstract categories and constructions. The reason that structural and generative theories assume the existence of abstractions is the fact that language users can produce novel utterances that are well formed in that they follow the patterns of the other utterances in the language. These theories assume that speakers apply general rules to accomplish this feat. However, the evidence brought forward in usage-based work, including this chapter, shows that productivity (the ability to apply existing structure to new utterances) can be accomplished through local analogies to existing exemplars, without reference to higher-level or more abstract generalizations. Thus rather than simply assuming that speakers form more abstract generalizations, it is preferable to look for explicit evidence that this is the case.

There are various reasons not to just assume that higher-level abstractions exist in cognition for language. The fact that many constructions share characteristics, such as reference to a subject, verb, or NP, is covered in Construction Grammar by the notion of 'inheritance' which relates constructions in a synchronic grammar and allows them to share properties. However, the fact that constructions share properties does not necessarily mean that generalizations over constructions are made by speakers. A diachronic explanation is also possible: since new constructions develop out of existing constructions, the properties of existing constructions are carried over into new ones over time. Thus the category of SUBJECT will be the same across a large set of constructions in a language. Because this diachronic relation is in itself a sufficient explanation for the sharing of properties, proposals about generalizations that speakers make must be explicitly tested.

Both evidence and counter-evidence has been found. On a domain-general level, Bowdle and Gentner (2005: 198) argue that people can match situation types to form an abstract problem schema – this could be similar to the more abstract categories of grammar. However, more research would be needed to see if this type of situation matching can be applied to language. In research tied directly to language, Savage et al. 2003 found that 3- and 4-year-olds were affected by lexical priming in a task in which they described a picture after having heard a description of another picture. In contrast, 6-year-olds were affected by both lexical and structural priming (having been primed with active transitive or passive sentences). This study suggests that younger children are acquiring constructions in very specific lexical contexts, but older children are beginning to form more abstract constructions which range over many exemplars. Studies showing structural priming with adults, using such general constructions as the ditransitive and the passive, also suggest a level of abstraction can be reached.

Because linguists have assumed the generality of linguistic rules, very little research has seriously considered the question of how general such rules can actually be and how the general interacts with the specific. Some reasons for doubting maximal generality have arisen in recent work. For instance, Goldberg's experiment in which she taught English-speaking children and adults a verb-final construction shows that people can learn constructions with word order that does not match any other construction in the language. In fact, the situation in German where main clauses have verb-second word order and subordinate clauses have verb-final order shows that there is no necessity for the maximal generalization of word order. Bybee 2001b points out many cases where main and subordinate clauses have different properties, which calls into question the generalized notion of CLAUSE at least on a universal basis.

The strength of certain linguistic generalizations, such as the high productivity of the English regular Past Tense suffix or the ubiquity and the regularity of the patterns for the English auxiliary, suggest abstractions in the form of rules. However, the fact that high type frequency leads to even higher type frequency (and thus regularity or generality) does not necessarily point to abstract, symbolic rules; the availability of a pattern as a model for the analogical formation of novel exemplars of the pattern can provide a much more concrete explanation for generality without resorting to abstractions. Even accepting this conclusion, many questions still remain as to the interaction of the more general, schematic and productive constructions with specific instances of these constructions.

5.14   Conclusion

This chapter has explored some of the usage properties of constructions that affect their internal structure, their productivity, schematicity and analysability by focusing on the structure of the categories that constitute the schematic slots in constructions. Evidence that usage affects the structure of the categories in constructions is found in the fact that items with high token frequency in constructions constitute the centre of the constructional categories and that high type frequency correlates with productivity. Semantic categorization of the lexemes that occur in constructions is also shown to be a determining factor in how a construction can spread to new items. The data presented here argue for rich memory representations because such representations provide for the strengthening of particular exemplars with use and the registration of details of the meaning of lexemes used in constructions which can be referred to in producing analogical innovations.

6   Where do constructions come from? Synchrony and diachrony in a usage-based theory

6.1   Diachrony as part of linguistic theory

Returning now to our discussion of language as a complex adaptive or self-organizing system, this chapter addresses directly the processes of change that create emergent structures, for these processes or mechanisms of change are the ultimate basis for the explanation of why language is the way it is. The importance of diachrony for understanding grammar, especially in a typological context, but also for understanding cognitive processes, has been emphasized by a number of linguists over the decades; for instance Greenberg 1963, 1969, 1978, Givón 1979 and elsewhere, Heine et al. 1991, Haiman 2002, as well as in my own work – Bybee 1985, 1988c and Bybee et al. 1994 and elsewhere. Language change is not just a peripheral phenomenon that can be tacked on to a synchronic theory; synchrony and diachrony have to be viewed as an integrated whole. Change is both a window into cognitive representations and a creator of linguistic patterns. Moreover, if we view language in the manner described in this book, as both variable and having gradient categories, then change becomes an integral part of the complete picture.

This chapter and the next two deal directly with diachrony. We begin our discussion in sections 6.2–6.5 with the diachronic phenomenon of grammaticalization, which has been intensely studied over the last few decades. In my view, the empirical research into grammaticalization has contributed more to our understanding of grammar than any other empirical work during the same period. The perspective afforded by studies of grammaticalization is one of grammar ever evolving through the natural everyday process of language use; it views language as part of our general perceptual, neuromotor and cognitive experience (Bybee 2002a). Seeing how grammaticalization operates demystifies grammar and shows it to be derivable through domain-general processes. The new view of grammar that emerges from grammaticalization work also shows that the assumption that child language acquisition is a potential source of major linguistic changes is undoubtedly in error. A comparison of usage vs. acquisition as the source of linguistic change is laid out in section 6.6.

Grammaticalization itself derives from a collection of concurrent processes that affect every level involved in an utterance from phonology to morphosyntax to semantics and pragmatics. In view of the priority awarded to morphosyntax in many current theories, Chapter 7 examines the way an important morphosyntactic category of English – the category of auxiliary – developed over time. The patterns associated with this category are shown to have developed gradually and in line with the factors affecting constructions that were discussed in the previous chapters. Chapter 8 discusses the issue of syntactic reanalysis, arguing that constituent structure shows gradience that allows for reanalysis of syntactic structures to also be gradient.

Further considering the interaction of diachrony with synchrony, Chapter 10 discusses the implications of grammaticalization and usage-based grammar for the understanding of grammatical meaning. As in other areas, we find an interesting interplay between the very general and the specific. I argue as I have in other work that the structuralist view of grammatical meaning as consisting of a set of abstract oppositions does not square with either the synchronic evidence of usage or the diachronic evidence of how such meanings evolve.

6.2   Grammaticalization

The most pervasive process by which grammatical items and structures are created is the process of grammaticalization. Grammaticalization is usually defined as the process by which a lexical item or a sequence of items becomes a grammatical morpheme, changing its distribution and function in the process (Meillet 1912, Lehmann 1982, Heine and Reh 1984, Heine, Claudi and Hünnemeyer 1991, Hopper and Traugott 2003). Thus English *going to* (with a finite form of *be)* becomes the intention/future marker *gonna.* However, more recently it has been observed that it is important to add that grammaticalization of lexical items takes place within PARTICULAR CONSTRUCTIONS and further that grammaticalization creates new constructions (Bybee 2003b, Traugott, 2003). Thus *going to* does not grammaticalize in the construction exemplified by *I'm going to the gym* but only in the construction in which a verb follows *to,* as in *I'm going to help you.*

The construction that gave rise to the *be going to* future was a more general purpose clause construction as in *they are going to Windsor to see the king,* or *they are journeying to see the queen's picture.* As the *be going to* future has a different function today from the earlier purpose construction and the verb *go* has lost its movement sense in this usage, we can say that [SUBJ *be going to* VERB] is a construction distinct from the purpose-clause construction. New grammatical morphemes are created by grammaticalization but since grammatical morphemes are defined in terms of the construction in which they occur, both a new grammatical morpheme and a new construction result from the process.

Historical linguists have long been aware of grammaticalization as a way to create new grammatical morphemes, but it was research in the 1980s and 1990s that revealed the ubiquity of grammaticalization. Cross-linguistic and historical documentation make it clear that grammaticalization is going on in all languages at all times, and further that all aspects of grammar are affected. In addition, there is the remarkable fact that across unrelated languages lexical items with very similar meanings enter into the process and give rise to grammatical morphemes which also have very similar meanings. Bybee, Perkins and Pagliuca 1994 studied such correspondences in tense, aspect and modality in a sample of seventy-six languages representing the major linguistic groups of the world. In that work it was found that future markers evolve from movement verbs in a wide range of unrelated languages; future markers also derive from verbs of volition (e.g. English *will*); progressives commonly come from locative expressions ('be located doing something'); progressives can further evolve into imperfectives or presents; past tenses and perfectives come from resultative expressions ('have something done') or from verbs meaning 'finish'. Examples in this domain can be found in Bybee et al. 1994 and a wider range of examples can be found in Heine and Kuteva 2002. The significance of these cross-linguistic correspondences will be further discussed in Chapter 11.

6.3 How grammaticalization occurs

A fairly intense examination of the grammaticalization process in texts, in ongoing change and across languages leads to the conclusion that the process occurs during language use (Bybee and Pagliuca 1987, Bybee 1988b, Bybee, Perkins and Pagliuca 1994, Bybee 2003b). A number of factors come into play and these factors have been discussed in the literature cited above and many of them have already been discussed in the previous chapters of this book. As mentioned above, grammaticalization involves the creation of a new construction out of an existing construction. It thus involves the process by which a particular lexical instance of a construction (*go* in the purpose construction) becomes autonomous from the other instances of the construction. This process of course includes the loss of analysability and compositionality (see Chapters 3 and 8). It involves making new chunks, with the concomitant phonetic changes triggered by increased frequency. Semantic and pragmatic changes occur as a result of the contexts in which the emerging construction is used.

Let us now examine these parts of the grammaticalization process one by one. We will see that an increase in token frequency plays an important role in the changes that occur, while at the same time some of the changes in return lead to increases in token frequency. This self-feeding effect explains the momentum that pushes a grammaticalization change forward.

With repetition, the particular instance of a construction becomes a chunk. As we mentioned in Chapter 3, the sequences involved in the chunk undergo phonetic reduction. Because they eventually can attain extremely high frequency of occurrence, grammaticalizing constructions can undergo rather radical reduction. The extent of reduction is one measure of the degree of grammaticalization (Bybee et al. 1994, Chapter 4). As examples, I have already mentioned *going to* reducing to *gonna*. There is also ongoing reduction in phrases such as *want to, have to,* and *supposed to.* Looking back to the past, we find that English *–ed* is the reduction of *dyde* 'did'; the Spanish first person singular future suffix *–é* is the reduced form of the Latin auxiliary *habeo.* Such reduction is due to the automatization of the articulatory gestures in these sequences; as these strings are repeated they become more fluent with more overlap and reduction of gestures (see the discussion in Chapter 3).

Also as a result of chunking, the internal units of the grammaticalizing expression become less transparently analysable and more independent of other instances of the same units (see Boyland 1996). Thus the *have* in *have to* becomes more distant from the *have* in another grammatical expression, the Perfect. The forms of *have* in the Perfect contract with the subject (*I've seen, he's taken,* and so on) but the forms of *have* in *have to* do not (**I've to go*). Of course, this is driven in part by the semantic changes that occur.

Semantic change occurs gradually and involves various types of change. For instance, components of meaning appear to be lost. Thus *gonna* no longer indicates movement in space; *will* no longer indicates 'wanting to'; *can* no longer means 'know' or 'know how to' in all instances; *a/an* is still singular, but does not explicitly specify 'one'. This type of change has been called 'bleaching'. It comes about as these expressions increase the contexts in which they are used. Even though *can* still indicates that the subject has the knowledge to tell truthfully in (1), it does not indicate anything at all about knowledge in the more generalized (2).

(1) I can tell you that she has gone with her uncle.
(2) Walk as quietly as you can.

As a new construction (such as [SUBJECT + *be going to* VERB]) spreads to use with more and more subjects and main verbs its meaning also generalizes. It can be noted additionally that frequent use leads to habituation, by which a repeated element loses some of its semantic force (Haiman 1994). As generalization and habituation weaken the meaning of a grammaticalizing construction, it can then apply to more and more cases, causing an increase in frequency.

However, not all semantic change involves loss of meaning, as Traugott has pointed out in many publications (Traugott 1989, Traugott and Dasher 2002 and others). As mentioned in earlier chapters, acts of communication are never totally explicit and require a high use of inference – cases where the hearer reads in more than is expressed. That is, an utterance implies certain things and the hearer reaps this information by inference. In change by pragmatic inference, meanings that are frequently implied by a construction within the accompanying context can be conventionalized as part of the meaning of the expression. Frequent contexts of use for *be going to* such as *I am going to deliver this letter* imply intention and as a result intention to act has become an important part of the meaning of the *be going to* expression.

The fact that grammaticalization is manifest in phonetics, morphosyntax, semantics and pragmatics points to constructions as an appropriate unit for describing and explaining this process, as constructions provide the locus for connecting these aspects of the linguistic sign. The additional fact that grammaticalization creates variation in usage makes exemplars appropriate for modelling the cognitive representations that allow grammaticalization to occur. Many constructions involving grammaticalizing morphemes have a range of usage from very specific meanings (usually reflecting older usage, but see Chapter 10) to very general meanings, as in examples (1) and (2). An exemplar model of successive stages would represent the changing relative frequencies of the different uses of a construction. In addition, an exemplar representation includes much information about the context in which an utterance occurred and what meanings were extracted from its use as the inferences that go along with the use of constructions are also recorded in cognitive representation (see Chapters 2, 3 and 8). If specific inferences commonly occur with a construction, their representation will be strengthened and eventually they can be activated automatically when the construction occurs, making them, in essence, part of the meaning of the construction. The range of phonetic variation that occurs in grammatical morphemes within constructions is also naturally represented in an exemplar model (Bybee 2001a).

The description of grammaticalization presented here has emphasized the mechanisms that operate to cause the changes whose cumulative effect is the creation of new grammatical morphemes. All of these mechanisms of change require repetition and are driven by increased usage: chunking, phonetic reduction, increasing autonomy, generalization to new contexts (via analogy), habituation, and pragmatic inference. These are the basic mechanisms of change that can act on any grammaticalizing material. The same processes are at work in very common grammaticalizations, such as the 'go' futures and also in the rarer ones, such as futures from temporal adverbs (e.g. Tok Pisin *bai < by and by*). While these processes explain similarities across language, they also allow for and create differences: a future grammaticalized from 'go' will have different semantic nuances than a future from 'want'; a future that has recently grammaticalized will have a strong intention reading, while a future that has undergone more development may have no intention uses at all

(Bybee, Perkins and Pagliuca 1994). Thus grammaticalization has great potential for explaining the similarities as well as the differences among languages (Bybee and Dahl 1989).

Through grammaticalization we see how the grammar of a language can arise just as structure arises in a complex adaptive system. The mechanisms operating in real time as speakers and listeners use language, repeated over and over again in multiple speech events, lead to gradual change by which grammatical morphemes and their associated constructions emerge. The lexical material which consists of both form and meaning is molded into constructions which are conventionalized, repeated and undergo further change in both form and meaning.

6.4   The explanatory power of grammaticalization

Understanding how structures arise in grammars provides us with possibilities for explanation not available in purely synchronic descriptions. Because morphosyntactic patterns are the result of long trajectories of change, they may be synchronically arbitrary; thus the only source of explaining their properties may be diachronic.

For instance, because new constructions are specific instances of old constructions many of their properties, such as element ordering, are determined by the construction from which they arose. If we ask, why does English *not* come after rather than before the first auxiliary or copula element in the verb phrase, we have to turn to diachrony for an answer. That answer is that the element *not* derived in Middle English from a negative element *nā* or *nō* plus an indefinite pronoun *wiht* meaning 'someone, something' when the latter pronoun was the object of the verb. Being the direct object of the verb, at a stage when VO was the normal order, the negative followed the verb. It actually followed all verbs, including main finite verbs, but was later restricted to following auxiliaries and copulas in the way described in Chapter 7.

The same development set up a competition between this newer negative *not* and the older means of negating using 'negative incorporation' phrases such as *no longer, nothing, no one,* and so on. As mentioned in Chapter 4, this competition continues today in the synonymous pairs such as:

(3) I know nothing.   vs.   I don't know anything.
(4) There were no funds.   vs.   There weren't any funds.

The explanation for the fact that English has two sentence negation constructions, as well as the explanation for the properties of each, depends upon our understanding of the particular grammaticalization changes that took place and what properties constructions had during the period of time in which grammaticalization occurred (see Chapter 7 for more discussion).

Another role that diachrony plays is in the explanation of typological patterns, such as the correlations between word order in different constituents, known as 'word order universals' (Greenberg 1963, Dryer 1988). These patterns have straightforward explanations through grammaticalization (Givón 1984). For instance, consider the fact that auxiliary verbs (verbs which take another verb as complement and share the same arguments as the other verb) occur after the main verb in OV languages but before the main verb in VO languages. Auxiliary verbs develop from main verbs themselves, main verbs that take other verbs as complements. In OV languages such complements precede the finite verb (the one that will become the auxiliary) while in VO languages the complements follow the finite verb. Thus the order V-AUX will be characteristic of OV languages while the opposite order will be characteristic of VO languages. In addition, if such auxiliaries become affixes, they will be suffixes in OV languages and prefixes in VO languages. For this case, no synchronic principles (such as Cross-Category Harmony (Hawkins 1983)) are necessary; grammaticalization gives us the correct orders for free. Consider the following examples from Givón 1984: 231:

Swahili: VO word order

(5) a-li-soma kitabu   li 'be' > PAST
     he-PAST-read book
     'he read a book'

(6) a-ta-soma kitabu   taka 'want' > FUTURE
     he-FUT-read book
     'he will read a book'

(7) a-me-soma kitabu   *mála 'finish' > ANTERIOR
     he-ANT-read book
     'he has read a book'

Ute: OV word order

(8) wúųka-xa   have / be > ANTERIOR
     work-ANT
     'he has worked'

(9) wúųka -vaa(ni)   *páa 'go/pass' > FUTURE
     work-FUT
     'he will work'

The occurrence of exceptions to the usual ordering correlations supports this interpretation. For instance in Swahili and other languages, where a perfect or perfective derives from a verb meaning 'finish' (in this case from Proto-Bantu *gid 'finish'), it becomes a suffix even though the Bantu languages are classified as VO. The reason is that when a sequence of verbs that grammaticalizes involves the verb 'to finish', that verb tends to occur in iconic order – after the verb describing what is finished. Here is an example from Ewe (Heine and Reh 1984: 127).

(10) é-du   nu   vɔ   vɔ 'finish' > ANTERIOR
     he-eat thing finish
     'he has eaten'

Similar explanations for word order correlations are available for the ordering of adpositions, genitives and other constructions. Thus grammaticalization
provides a powerful source of explanation for language-specific facts as well
as cross-linguistic generalizations.

6.5   Criticisms of grammaticalization: unidirectionality and grammaticalization theory

After observing the process of grammaticalization and the mechanisms that
propel the process, as well as the gradualness of change and variability of grammatical constructions, my view of the nature of grammar changed completely
from what I had been taught. The structuralist and generativist view of discrete,
abstract structures and rules is simply not compatible with the dynamic and
variable facts of grammaticalization. In contrast, a grammatical theory based
on constructions and allowing for usage-based variability among the instances
of constructions (as proposed here and in Bybee 2006a), is well suited to the
representation of ongoing grammaticalization.

Many of the criticisms of grammaticalization come from generative linguists who see this incompatibility and conclude that there must be something
wrong with accounts of grammaticalization rather than concluding that there
must be something wrong with a structural or generative theory of grammar.
It is not coincidental that most of the research on grammaticalization in the
1980s and 1990s was done by functionalist linguists who do not accept generative assumptions. This work is therefore difficult to reconcile with generative
theory. The following are some of the criticisms of grammaticalization raised
by critics.

(1) Grammaticalization is epiphenomenal in that it involves the co-
occurrence of various types of change that also occur independently: that is
phonetic reduction, inference-making, and semantic bleaching (Campbell 2001,
Newmeyer 1998). There is no question that this statement is correct. In fact it
is a point explicitly made by Hopper 1991, a distinctly functional grammaticalization researcher. Hopper demonstrates that all the best-known principles
of grammaticalization are also operative in what must be regarded as lexical
change. Indeed, if grammar is a complex adaptive system and if it is based on
domain-general processes, then the implication is that grammar itself is epiphenomenal. However, it is important to note that the common co-occurrence of the
set of processes leading to grammar still needs an explanation. I have hinted at
this explanation in the preceding account: because all the processes depend in

one way or another upon repetition, increases in frequency trigger their operation, while at the same time the output of these processes (semantically more generalized meanings or a wider applicability due to inferences) leads to further frequency increases (Bybee 2009a). Thus we can agree that grammaticalization is a set of processes rather than a single monolithic process.

(2) A more basic criticism and one that reflects deep theoretical differences among generativists and usage-based linguists is the claim that there cannot be any diachronic processes at all (Newmeyer 1998: 238):

> But I feel that the term 'process' is dangerous when applied to a set of *diachronic* developments. The reason for the danger is that it invites one to conceive of such developments as being subject to a distinct set of laws that are independent of the minds and behaviours of individual language users. However, nothing transgenerational can be situated in *any* human faculty. Children are not born with racial memories that fill them in with the details of the history of forms that they hear.

The problem for generativists, then, lies in understanding how a process can proceed in the same direction across individuals and generations. This is indeed a problem if one assumes that language change can only take place during language acquisition (but see section 6.6). However, if the diachronic processes are continually pushed forward by mechanisms that occur when language is used by all speakers of all generations, then subsuming the repeated application of mechanisms under the rubric of a 'process' contains no danger. On the contrary, it is quite revealing provided that we always search for the mechanisms behind the process.

It is also important to note that functionalist grammaticalization researchers have never considered the processes involved to be 'independent of the minds and behaviours of individual language users'. Traugott's many studies of inference refer directly to language users and their cognitive frameworks. Similarly the proposals of Heine and colleagues concerning the role of metaphor and metonymy in semantic change also consider these to be real time cognitive processes. In Bybee, Perkins and Pagliuca 1994, the last chapter is dedicated to the discussion of the mechanisms of change that occur in grammaticalization, all of which operate in individual language users as they use language.

(3) The notion of unidirectionality has raised similar criticisms (Janda 2001). One fascinating aspect of grammaticalization is that once begun, it is quite common for the process to continue in the same direction – changing forms from less to more grammatical. Changes going in the opposite direction are quite rare and tend to move only one step in the backwards direction rather than reversing systematically (Norde 2001). The most common sort are cases of lexicalization (Brinton and Traugott 2005), such as using a preposition or adverb as a verb, as in *to up the ante,* but other interesting cases exist as well. Such changes, however, constitute a very small minority of grammatical

changes, while the vast majority go from less to more grammatical. Thus the changes are not at all random. Janda assumes that change only occurs in acquisition; he supports this assumption by citing authors who have made similar assumptions, but he provides no empirical evidence that this is the case. Based on this assumption, he points out that children cannot know in which direction a change is proceeding.

The problem here is of course that the assumption that language can only change during acquisition is incorrect. It is worth noting that this claim is frequently made by researchers whose empirical research does not actually address this question (Janda, Newmeyer). In the next section we address the issue of child-based language change directly. For now note that it is the generativist view of grammar as discrete and unchanging in the adult, that makes this assumption necessary and which thus denies the striking unidirectionality of grammaticalization change. In contrast, if usage is the basis of grammar and change in the grammar, then there is no a priori reason why change cannot occur over an adult's lifetime. Given that the mechanisms that propel the changes encompassed by grammaticalization are operative in all generations, there is no reason to doubt that change can be unidirectional.

(4) Finally, there is criticism that there is no such thing as a grammaticalization theory (Newmeyer 1998: 240). Again the problem rests in the assumptions made by generativists. As I mentioned earlier, grammaticalization requires that we give up many of the assumptions of generative grammar and replace them with other assumptions or hypotheses. For instance, the notion that grammars are abstract, discrete and unchanging within the individual and that all variation and gradience is tacked on to the end of the grammar or is owing to performance is abandoned as a result of the study of grammaticalization. Rather grammaticalization leads us directly to usage-based theory: the term 'grammaticalization theory' refers both to the synchronic and diachronic dimensions. In this theory the two are not opposed but must be considered together as we strive to understand language. This theory not only makes strong diachronic predictions, but also has profound consequences for synchronic analysis and description, as demonstrated in this book. That makes it a theory.

6.6   The source of change: language acquisition or language use?

Empirical studies show clearly that change occurs gradually, with long periods of variation in which statistical tendencies become more pronounced leading at times to almost categorical distributions (Kroch 1989a and 1989b, Hook 1991, Torres-Cacoullos 2000). The gradualness of change has always been a problem for structural theories, because if underlying structures are discrete and non-variable, it must follow that change is abrupt. In usage-based theories change occurs as language is used, and it can be implemented by means of small changes in distributional probabilities over time. There is no need to postulate massive restructuring taking place in the space of one generation (see the examples in Chapters 7 and 8).

Given that in structural and generative theories grammatical structures are discrete and independent of meaning and use, change must be regarded as an anomaly. The source of change cannot reside in usage or the grammar itself, and thus it has been proposed in these theories that change in the grammar can only come about during its transmission across generations. While many writers assume that the child language acquisition process changes language (Halle 1962, Kiparsky 1968, Lightfoot 1979 and many others both earlier and later; see Janda 2001 for more references), empirical evidence that this is actually the case is still lacking (Croft 2000).

Indeed, the few studies that compare language change with child language come up with as many differences as similarities. In phonology, Drachman (1978) and Vihman (1980) compare phonological alterations common in child language to sound changes found in the languages of the world and find great dissimilarities. For instance, while consonant harmony is common in child language (that is, children tend to use the same consonant twice in a word, e.g. *dadi* for *doggie*), consonant harmony does not occur in the (adult) languages of the world. In contrast, vowel harmony occurs in many languages, but not in child language. Hooper (1979) and Bybee and Slobin (1982) find both similarities and differences between the acquisition of morphology and morphological change. On the one hand, Hooper finds that children do learn basic or unmarked forms first and use them to make more complex forms, which mirrors some analogical changes. On the other hand, Bybee and Slobin report that some formations produced by young children are not continued by older children and adults.

In her 1977 study, Naomi Baron compares the development of periphrastic causatives in child language and in the history of English. Her results show some similarities and some differences: (a) Comparing periphrastic causatives with *make, have* and *get,* she finds that *get* is the last to develop historically, but the first to develop in contemporary child language. This demonstrates that the factors influencing diachronic development are probably not always the same as those that influence child language development. (b) In contrast, *get* + noun + locative (*did you get some clay on your nose?*) is the earliest development both in children and in history. The concreteness of this construction compared to the causative with an adjective (*I get my boots muddy*), past participle (*he will get hitten by a bus, won't he?*) and infinitive (*Let's get her to send a cable*) (examples from Baron 1977: 138–47) probably accounts for its earlier development in both diachrony and ontogeny. (c) The spread of the *get* causatives to infinitival complements happens rapidly but it is very late in children, perhaps due to the fact that infinitives are rarely used in speech to children;[1]

(d) Children generalize from *get* + noun + locative, to adjectives and then to past participles. In history, the *get* periphrasis begins with locatives, goes to infinitives, then past participles and adjectives. This study, then, shows that child language and diachronic development have some similarities and some differences, but clearly supports the claim that not all language change can be attributed to the acquisition process.

Also taking into account changes that occur in the grammaticalization of meaning, Slobin (1997b) argues that the semantic/pragmatic senses – such as epistemic meanings – produced by the grammaticalization process are not available to very young children. The type of inferencing that is necessary for semantic change to proceed in grammaticalization is something that children learn later in development. These studies, then, do not show the close correspondence between child language acquisition and language change that one would expect if the former were the vehicle for language change.

Where there are similarities, as in the order of acquisition of the senses of the English Present Perfect and its development diachronically, it seems to be the case that similarities arise not because children are responsible for changing language but because children are responding to the same factors as adults. Slobin 1994 demonstrates that the discourse contexts in which children discover the functions of the Present Perfect show some parallels with the contexts in which the Present Perfect historically develops its present-day functions. In addition, the order in which uses of the Present Perfect develop for children is similar to the diachronic order: for instance, children use the resulting state meaning of the Present Perfect before the perfect of experience and the continuative perfect, which reflects the order of development diachronically. However, Slobin notes that children start with the concrete notions and those most anchored in the present because these notions are cognitively the most simple, natural and accessible. Similarly, in diachrony, the most concrete notions often constitute the starting points for grammaticalization because the material the process works on comes from the basic lexicon – concrete nouns such as body parts and highly generalized verbs such as *be, have* and *go*. Thus the parallel here between ontogeny and phylogeny is the correspondence between two processes that may be only superficially similar.

A usage-based approach would predict that a child's grammar, while naturally separate from the adults' – in the sense that the child's grammar is lodged in the child's cognition which is separate from the adult's cognition – would nonetheless be based on the child's experience filtered through his or her limited abilities. Thus the child's cognitive representations would reflect the variation found in the input language. This is what studies of current variation and ongoing changes reveal: we do not find gaps or abrupt changes across generations as the child-based change hypothesis would predict, but rather that even fairly young children produce variants of linguistic forms that are good reflections of the adult variation.

In studies of the acquisition of phonological variation, it is consistently observed that children produce variants with probabilities reflecting those found in adult speech first for phonological constraints (as early as ages 3 and 7 years) and then later social constraints (Patterson 1992, J. Roberts 1997, Chevrot et al. 2000). There are no reports of categorical productions followed by the acquisition of variation, as one might expect if children's grammars represent discrete changes from the adult grammar. J. Roberts 1997 finds that 3- and 4-year-old American English-speaking children have the same phonological constraints on t/d deletion that adults do. They also have similar morphological constraints. Patterson 1992 and J. Roberts 1994 find that 3- and 4-year-old children used the same stylistic and grammatical constraints as adults in using the variants of –ing. Foulkes and Docherty 2006, in a study of subphonemic variation of stops in the speech of Newcastle adults and children, find that pre-school children had preaspirated stop variants that reflected those found in their mothers' speech, with some producing even more preaspiration than their mothers. As the children grew older, however, their stop articulations began to differentiate, with girls maintaining preaspiration, which is characteristic of the speech of young women, and boys losing it.

Just as in adult language, Chevrot et al. 2000 proposed that variation is situated in the lexical entries of particular words. Díaz-Campos 2004 finds that Spanish-speaking children aged 42–71 months (3;6 to 5;11) acquire the deletion of medial /d/ in an adult-like fashion, not so much with a variable rule but in terms of particular lexical items: high-frequency words have more deletion than low-frequency words just as in the adult data. It thus appears that children are sensitive to probabilities in the input and acquire specific words and structures in a detailed fashion that mirrors the usage found around them.

Fewer studies have addressed morphosyntactic variants in child language, but studies of the creole language Tok Pisin strongly support the more continuous view of language change, as well as showing that first-language learners are not the only ones that can change language. In a massive study of the use of the morpheme *bai* as a future marker (from English *by and by*), Romaine 1995 studies the placement of this morpheme directly before the verb as an indicator of its having reached an advanced stage of grammaticalization. Romaine compares data from first language users of Tok Pisin with those who use it as a second language. She finds that pre-verbal use of *bai* occurs at the same rate in both groups of speakers. In other words, the first language users of Tok Pisin are not making substantial changes in the use of the forms of the language. All the users are moving the language in the same direction (see also Smith 2002 for similar results for other constructions in Tok Pisin).

These studies strongly support a usage-based perspective on language change. Child data are variable in many of the same ways that adult data are. Moreover, there is a continuous flow from one generation to another; the very notion of generation, in fact, is too simplistic a notion since children receive input from speakers of all ages. Any language user can change language when language change is viewed as gradual changes in distributional patterns of usage. Of course, being a type of routinized behaviour, linguistic behaviour is not likely to undergo major changes in either phonology or morphosyntax in adulthood. But as argued here, even in adulthood, certain changes can occur. Sankoff and Blondeau 2007 study a change in the place of articulation of /r/ in Montreal French in the same cohort of speakers over time and find that indeed, the rate at which they produce an innovative variant – the dorsal [R] – increases in some speakers in adulthood.

It is generally agreed that phonological patterns are particularly resistant to change in adulthood, but that lexical choice and morphosyntactic patterns are more flexible. Indeed there is no reason to suppose that quantitative changes in construction use cannot occur in adults. Certainly, adults can adopt new forms as they become more frequent in the input. An excellent example is the spread of *you guys* as the second-person-plural pronoun in American English. Many people of my generation have experienced the rapid increase in frequency of this form and its spread across dialect areas. Because of its frequency in experience, no matter how much one objects to using the form (especially for female addressees), we end up adopting it. In addition, it is reasonable to assume that adults can generalize constructions by using them creatively with novel lexical items. Indeed, this is quite normal in everyday production and accounts for the ability to express thoughts not previously given linguistic form. Recall from the previous chapter the rapid increase in the use of the [*drive someone* ADJ] construction in the 1960s and 1970s. Presumably adults were extending this construction to express a hyperbolic meaning and to increase its type frequency with expressions such as *drive someone up the wall*. The next chapter will also show that the gradual extension of periphrastic *do* in questions and *not*-negatives in the sixteenth century took place in adult language rather than in inter-generational transmission (Warner 2004).

Of course, new generations do contribute to changes in distribution and may contribute to the loss of constructions. Younger generations may be freer to extend the use of constructions. Also, variants of linguistic forms or particular constructions that are of very low frequency may not find their way into the younger speaker's repertoire of forms. An example would be the gradual attrition of *shall* as an auxiliary. In American English it had become restricted to certain kinds of questions (*Shall I let him go?*) and fixed expressions (*shall we say*), but even in these contexts it has become rarer. One doubts whether many young speakers ever use the form at all. The availability of alternate constructions for the same function increases the likelihood of loss.

Finally, considerations of the sociolinguistic situation young children find themselves in strongly suggests that they would adjust their utterances and thus their cognitive representations to the older speakers around them rather than insisting upon their own creations, as the generative view of language suggests. Young children simply do not have the social clout to create language change across large groups of adult speakers. Labov 1982 presents the finding that changes are most advanced in adolescents and pre-adolescents rather than in children in the midst of the acquisition process, as these older language users may be expressing some defiance of the norms and creating their own cohesive social group.

6.7   Conclusions

While it is certainly necessary to understand the separate roles of synchrony and diachrony in both description and theory, it is also important to bear in mind that language is a conventional cultural object that has evolved over time and continues to evolve. A linguistic theory is not complete if it does not embrace the contribution of language change to the understanding of language structure.

Given the recent empirical research on grammaticalization, it can be confidently said that we understand much more about the origins of grammar than we did before. Having identified the domain-general processes that work together to create grammar, we can also postulate a plausible scenario for the first origins of grammar. As discussed further in Chapter 11, as soon as two words can be put together and used in context the potential exists for conventionalization of word order and the automatization, habituation and categorization that go into creating grammatical morphemes and constructions.

7   Reanalysis or the gradual creation of new categories? The English Auxiliary

7.1   Approaches to reanalysis

The study of grammaticalization has shown that new grammatical markers and constructions come into being gradually over time, through the operation of various reductive processes, as well as processes of inference in context. These gradual changes have the effect of creating new grammatical categories or new members of categories, and what could be viewed as new 'rules' or conventions of grammar. The creation of new grammatical structures is often called 'reanalysis'. Reanalysis is usually viewed as an abrupt, but covert, change in the grammar that may not have any immediate overt effects (Langacker 1978, Lightfoot 1979, Kroch 1989a, Harris and Campbell 1995, Haspelmath 1998, Janda 2001, Roberts and Roussou 2003, Van Gelderen 2004). It is this view that requires a discontinuity in the transmission of language across generations (Andersen 1973); the child has access only to the surface forms of the language and not to the adult grammar and may therefore formulate a grammar that differs in structure from the adult grammar. As mentioned in Chapter 6, Janda 2001 argues that the discontinuity between generations makes some aspects of grammaticalization – such as unidirectionality – implausible and unexplainable.

The gradual nature of grammaticalization and the lack of evidence for abrupt reanalysis suggest that rather than postulate covert, inherently unobservable changes, we revise our conception of synchronic grammar so that it is more in line with the facts of grammatical change. Haspelmath 1998 points out that reanalysis would not have to be considered abrupt if grammatical categories and constituents themselves were viewed as fluid, gradient and variable. Thus the gradient facts of usage, synchronic variation and gradual diachronic change could be taken as principal evidence that grammars themselves incorporate the gradience and variability seen in the data.

This chapter examines the development of the category 'auxiliary' in English. I chose this example because it is an excellent example of a closed class of items with a particular set of morphosyntactic properties. Most theories of grammar would claim that a language either has such a category or it does not. Within such theories it is difficult to imagine how such a category might develop gradually. Yet the available data show a period of some fluctuation in the manifestation of this category. The response to this situation has been to propose that there was an abrupt change that created this category, but the surface forms only changed very gradually (Lightfoot 1979, 1991, Kroch 1989a, 1989b, Harris and Campbell 1995).

A contrasting approach would be to revise our notions of synchronic grammar in such a way that gradience in categories, gradual change and quantitative factors are directly represented in the grammar. Under such a view, grammatical change, whether described as grammaticalization or reanalysis, could take place gradually. In the analysis presented here, the development of the category of auxiliary is seen as the development and gradual spread of some new constructions – the modal auxiliary construction and the negative *not* – and the restriction of an older construction – subject–verb inversion – to high-frequency items. A grammar that takes constructions as the basic unit for the pairing of sound and meaning, and which contains representations of exemplars of constructions as well as generalized constructions, can account for the gradual process of grammaticalization as well as the creation of new categories, which is often described as 'reanalysis'.

The other important issue in the reanalysis debate concerns changes in constituent structure, in particular the creation of new constituents and the loss of internal structure in grammaticalizing constructions. This issue will be dealt with in the next chapter in the context of an examination of how constituent structure emerges in a usage-based grammar.

7.2   Auxiliaries in English

Fischer 2007 has called the development of the English auxiliary a paradigm case of morphosyntactic change, partly because it has been the focus of treatment from various perspectives, starting in the generative era with Lightfoot 1979, a work which stimulated much discussion (Warner 1983, Plank 1984, Goossen 1987, Nagle 1989, Denison 1993). Because the auxiliary develops through grammaticalization, there are changes in both the semantic/pragmatic and morphosyntactic domains. While functionalist studies of grammaticalization including my own have focused on the former types of change, the discussion here is intended to shed light on how the morphosyntactic category and related constructions developed.[1] Important evidence for achieving this goal concerns the rise and spread of the use of *do* in questions and negatives, because the use of *do* is necessary for the constructions marking questions and negation, in which the auxiliary plays a special role, to apply to all clauses. However, most studies of the auxiliary have concentrated on the modals and not included the development of *do* (Lightfoot 1979, Plank 1984, Fischer 2007).

Conversely, studies of the spread of *do* have not usually included factors relating to the grammaticalization of the modals (Ogura 1993, Kroch 1989a). While Lightfoot 1979, I. Roberts 1985, and Kroch 1989a relate the rise of periphrastic *do* to the development of the category 'auxiliary verb' in English, they do not regard it as instrumental in the development of this category.

I will argue that the motivation for the rise of *do* in questions and negatives is the increased frequency of use of the modal auxiliaries which led to the establishment of competing constructions for the expression of interrogation and negation. Through the study of the spread of *do* in these contexts, we see that the new constructions increased their productivity at the expense of the older ones, which tended to be used for a longer time with main verbs of higher frequency. The central claim made here is that quantitative distributions matter and are part of the grammar. The discussion will refer to many of the mechanisms of change and the effects of frequency outlined earlier in this book.

I will use the term 'auxiliary' in reference to English to include all of the items that can invert with the subject in questions and that are followed directly by the negative in main clause negation. Note that this is appropriate because closed classes are directly defined by the positions in the constructions in which they occur (Croft 2001). Our investigation involves a formal class and how it evolved over time. It is of interest because it is a fairly rigid and small class, and it participates in several constructions. However, it is important to note that it is not semantically coherent, as it includes modal auxiliaries, two tense/aspect constructions – the Perfect and the Progressive, the copula, and until recently, possessive *have*. Furthermore, these members of the class did not develop simultaneously; rather each one has had its own trajectory and rate of semantic change (Plank 1984).

7.3   Grammaticalization of the modals and other auxiliaries

The constructions that define the category of auxiliary developed through a set of grammaticalization changes that were not necessarily related to one another. We consider here the development of the modal auxiliaries, the periphrastic Perfect and Progressive and the grammaticalization of the negative element *not*.

The modal auxiliaries that have survived into Present Day English are *will, would, shall, should, may, might, can, could,* and *must*. In addition, two verbs (*dare* and *need*) are used both as main verbs and modal auxiliaries throughout their histories. The defining features of modal auxiliaries are that they invert with the subject in questions and a few other contexts, they take the negative directly after them and they have no 3rd singular inflection in the present tense. Their history has been discussed in a large number of works (Lightfoot 1979, Plank 1984, Denison 1993, Fischer 2007) and will only be briefly recounted here.

The modals listed above all derive historically from verbs, but by the time Old English is documented they had already developed some properties that distinguished them from the rest of the verbs. All of them except for *will* were Preterit–Present verbs, a term which refers to the conjugational pattern in which the Present tense actually has the pattern of a Strong verb Past (or Preterit) tense and the Past tense is based on the Weak verb pattern (involving *–d–*). This inflectional pattern probably indicates an earlier semantic change by which the Past form implied present meaning and this implication became part of the new meaning (Bybee et al. 1994: 74–8). Many of the Preterit–Present verbs had meanings that commonly enter grammaticalization paths that lead to modal or future meanings: *sceal* 'be obligated, owe', *mæg* 'have power', *cann* 'know', *dearr* 'dare' and *moste* 'can, must'. In Old English they could be used as the main finite verb of the clause or with another main verb. Over time, the latter use became more frequent and their ability to occur as main verbs was lost. However, it is important to note that this happened at different times for each modal and was related to the gradual loss of lexical meaning, that is, the grammaticalization of each modal (Plank 1984). Differences in the timing of grammaticalization can be seen in *shall* and *will*, for though they both eventually express future meaning, *shall* grammaticalized much earlier than *will* (Bybee and Pagliuca 1987). *May* and *can* are also in the same semantic domain (of ability and possibility), but *may* takes on epistemic meaning by Early Modern English, while *can* has yet to reach that stage (Bybee 1988b).

As mentioned earlier, increased grammaticalization is always accompanied by increases in the frequency of use, which means in this case that clauses containing a modal auxiliary and a main verb increased gradually in frequency from the Old English period right up to the present. We will see in the next section that by the middle of the sixteenth century, about one third of all finite clauses had a modal in them.

In addition, the periphrastic Perfect, which had its origins in a resultative construction in Old English (Carey 1994, Hopper and Traugott 2003), continued its grammaticalization through Middle English. Although in Early Modern English it occurred in only about 5 per cent of clauses, it still contributes to the number of clauses that have an auxiliary element in addition to a main verb. The Progressive also had begun a process of grammaticalization, but in the century we are focused on it was still quite infrequent. Thus the grammaticalization of the modals and the Perfect led to a situation in which more and more clauses had an auxiliary element.

7.4   A new negative construction

Another newly grammaticalized construction, in which a new negative element, *not,* followed the verb, also comes into play. In Old English and Early

Middle English, sentence negation was accomplished with a preverbal particle *ne* or *na*. In Middle English a reinforcing element consisting of *nā* or *nō* + *wiht* 'someone, something' became *noht* (with many other variant spellings) and later *not*. At first *not* occurred along with the preverbal *ne* (as in (1)) but later that marker was lost and *not* alone served as the negator (2). Since it was derived from a negative plus a noun in direct object position, it followed the verb, first as the direct object, then in addition to a direct object (Mossé 1968, Denison 1993).

(1) he ne   edstont nawt as foles   doð ah...
     he not stops   not   as fools   do but...
(2) my wife rose nott

Thus a new construction for negation arose out of a specific case of the VO construction. Note that since *not* occurred after the finite verb, it would also occur just after the developing modal and other auxiliary verbs, since they were still treated largely as verbs in this early Middle English period. Examples from the Early Modern period of Shakespeare are in (3):

(3) a. you lack not folly to commit them
     b. I do not all believe
     c. The Count Rousillon cannot be my brother
        (Shakespeare, *All's Well That Ends Well*, I.3)

7.5   An old construction for questions

The last construction we are going to consider here is the one that has the subject and verb inverted from their usual positions. This ordering in questions and other constructions existed from the Old English period and could be used with all verbs (Traugott 1972: 73, 119, 160). Both yes–no questions and wh-questions had the verb before the subject. The modern inverted order of the subject and the auxiliary constitutes a special case of this older construction. Since the order with the verb before the subject persisted into Early Modern English, the illustrations in (4) from Shakespeare show one with the main verb before the subject and the other with a developing modal auxiliary:

(4) a. what say you of this gentlewoman?
     b. may the world know them?
        (Shakespeare, *All's Well That Ends Well*, I.3)

In English up to the Early Modern period, the general construction for questions has the finite verb occurring before the subject. It might be represented as:

(5) [(WH-WORD)   MAIN VERB   SUBJECT]$_{question}$

Table 7.1 *Increase in frequency of auxiliaries (modals,* be *in passive and perfect,* have *in perfect) compared to finite main verbs (with or without* do*) and* be *as a main verb. All clause types*[2]

Dates	Finite verb	*Be*	Auxiliaries	Percentage *do* periphrasis
1460–80	118 (50%)	63 (27%)	55 (23%)	0
1550–70	102 (47%)	44 (20%)	73 (33%)	17%
1594–1602	349 (36%)	263 (27%)	352 (37%)	54%
1630–1707	136 (44%)	76 (25%)	98 (32%)	53%
Present Day English[3]	83 (41%)	39 (19%)	50 (25%)	100%

Before the modals grammaticalized and increased in frequency, the slot in this construction labeled MAIN VERB would include any verb, including those that later became modals or auxiliaries. This construction will be referred to in what follows as 'Q-MAIN VERB'.

7.6   A second pattern emerges

In both questions and negatives, then, the emerging auxiliaries were treated just like main verbs in English preceding the sixteenth century. The fact that the modals were grammaticalizing (along with the Perfect and Progressive) means that they were increasing markedly in frequency of occurrence. Table 7.1 shows how the auxiliaries (primarily the modals and a few instances of Perfects) compare in frequency to copular *be* and finite main verbs.

Note that by Shakespeare's time (1594–1602) 37 per cent of clauses had auxiliaries in them. Because so many clauses have copular *be* (27 per cent), the number of clauses with finite main verbs was down to 36 per cent.

A similar situation holds in questions (Table 7.1 shows clauses of all types). Table 7.2 shows the relative frequency of auxiliaries in questions in the period of interest here. Again, due to the frequency of copular *be* and the modals, finite main verbs constitute only about a third of the tokens.

As mentioned in the earlier discussion of chunking, the fact that a sequence is frequent enough to establish it as a processing unit means that it constitutes a construction. *Will* and *shall* take the lead in questions; in a sampling of 118 questions from *All's Well That Ends Well* 32 have modals and of these 18 have *will* and 6 have *shall*.[4] This pattern in the experience of the speakers would give rise to the question constructions shown in (6) and (7).

(6) [(WH-WORD)   *will*   SUBJECT   MAIN VERB   X]$_{\text{question}}$
(7) [(WH-WORD)   *shall*   SUBJECT   MAIN VERB   X]$_{\text{question}}$

Table 7.2 *Questions occurring with a main verb (whether used with* do *or the main verb inverted), forms of* be *and the modals and perfects. (Possessive* have *was not included.)*

Play	Date	Main verb w/ or w/o *do*	*be*	Modals + perfects	N
Udall	1566	11 (17%)	28 (44%)	24 (43%)	63
Stevenson	1550	25 (33%)	24 (27%)	26 (38%)	75
Shakespeare*	1599–1602	131 (34%)	149 (39%)	107 (28%)	387

* Sampled from *All's Well That Ends Well* and *As You Like It*.

The other modals – *can, must, would, should*, and so on – also occur often enough to give rise to processing chunks of the same shape. If these separate constructions were to be grouped together under a single abstraction, the following would result:

(8) [(WH WORD) $\left\{\begin{array}{l} \textit{will} \\ \textit{shall} \\ \textit{would} \\ \textit{can} \\ \textit{must} \\ \textit{may} \\ \textit{could} \\ \textit{should} \\ \textit{might} \end{array}\right\}$ SUBJECT   MAIN VERB]$_{\text{question}}$

As linguists we are tempted to use a category term such as 'modal' or 'grammaticalizing verb' to describe the list of elements that go in a construction. However, it is important to remember that the very fact that these words are allowed in this construction defines them as a class (Croft 2001); no abstract term is necessarily indicated, especially given exemplar representation. We do, however, need a name for this construction for our discussion; we will refer to it as 'Q-AUX'.

The emergence of this construction from the earlier construction that inverted all verbs is due to the increased frequency of the modals. There is no reanalysis because a set of verbs did not change their status from verb to auxiliary. Rather a new construction emerged gradually from the older one (Q-MAIN VERB) as the modals came to be used more. Both constructions (Q-MAIN VERB and Q-AUX) continue to be used in the language; the older construction continues with certain main verbs into the seventeenth century. Both constructions are lexically specific, though the new construction is much more restricted.

As many have noted (Kroch 1989a, Warner 2004) in the Q-AUX construction in (8) the subject appears before the main verb, which is, of course, its position in declarative affirmatives and other constructions. Given that constructions are part of a network in which similar items and orderings are related to one another, the affirmative word order of SUBJECT – MAIN VERB could reinforce this part of the construction, giving it priority over the older construction (Q-MAIN VERB) in which the order is MAIN VERB – SUBJECT. Kroch et al. 1982 and Warner 2004 talk about this as a processing strategy which aids in comprehension. As they are working with a model that has phrase structure rules and movement rules rather than constructions, their appeal to this similarity has to be in terms of a processing strategy, a device needed over and above the grammatical rules. In contrast, in a construction grammar, the representation of this advantage is quite straightforward since parts of different constructions can be related directly to one another. Diessel and Tomasello 2005 find that children's responses to relative clauses in an experimental setting show that the preference for relatives formed on subjects and agents is at least in part owing to the maintenance in these relatives of main clause word order. Thus in the competition that has been set up between the two constructions, the newer construction (8) might be favoured because of its similarity to main clause structure.

In addition to the two ways of forming questions that we have just discussed, it is reasonable to assume that because of the high frequency of the verb *to be*, it would have its own question construction. It of course continued the practice of inverting with the subject:

(9) [(WH-WORD)   *be*   SUBJECT ...]$_{\text{question}}$

Another main verb with high frequency was *have*; one might also postulate a separate construction for questions with *have*.

(10) [(WH-WORD)   *have*   SUBJECT ...]$_{\text{question}}$

Leaving aside *be* and *have* for the moment, the competition that is set up is between the construction Q-MAIN VERB and Q-AUX; the first positions the main verb before the subject, while the second positions an auxiliary before the subject leaving the main verb to follow it. Note that the new construction cannot reach full generality as it cannot apply to unmodified, finite main verbs.

7.7   Two patterns for negatives with *not*

For negatives with *not* a similar set of constructions arises. *Not* occurred after the finite verb (and sometimes after the pronominal object as well) so that the original construction for *not* was as in (11), to be called NEG-MAIN VERB:

(11) [SUBJ   MAIN VERB   *not* ...]$_{\text{negative}}$

Table 7.3 *Negatives with* not, *numbers showing main verbs (whether used with* do *or not), forms of* be *and the modals and perfects. (Possessive* have *was not included.)*

Play	Date	Main verb w/ or w/o *do*	*be*	Modals + perfects	N
Udall	1566	19 (28%)	8 (12%)	42 (61%)	69
Stevenson	1575	25 (30%)	27 (32%)	31 (37%)	84
Shakespeare**	1595–1602	58 (21%)	85 (30%)	137 (49%)	280

**Sampled from *All's Well That Ends Well* and *A Midsummer Night's Dream.*

But again, the increase in frequency of the developing modals led to the development of a new construction. Table 7.3 shows the frequency of auxiliaries in negative sentences with *not* compared to those with finite main verbs and *be*.

It appears that modals in negative clauses are even more frequent than in questions and affirmatives. The construction in (12) shows the list of modal verbs occurring in the new construction (in descending order of frequency).[5] Again *will* is the most frequent. Note that in the text counted the list of modals in negatives differs from the list given above for questions. The negative list includes *dare* and *need* and omits *might* as shown in (12). Of course, a complete account of the construction would include all attested auxiliaries. This construction will be referred to as NEG-AUX.

(12)   [SUBJECT $\left\{ \begin{array}{l} \textit{will} \\ \textit{would} \\ \textit{dare} \\ \textit{could} \\ \textit{must} \\ \textit{shall} \\ \textit{should} \\ \textit{can} \\ \textit{may} \\ \textit{need} \end{array} \right\}$ *not*   MAIN VERB...]$_{\text{NEGATIVE}}$

There were several ways of putting negation into a clause in the Early Modern period: an older construction using Neg-incorporation (see the discussion in Chapter 4) competed against the newer construction with *not*, so that not all negative clauses were candidates for periphrastic *do*.

However, as with questions, the surge in frequency of the modals and Perfects, along with the continuing frequency of *be*, left only 20–30 per cent of clauses negated with *not* with unmodified main verbs. Given the availability of *do* as an auxiliary to parallel the modals, and the perfect with *have* or *be* (and the passive with the latter), the construction shown above could spread to be used with all verbs through the spread of *do*.

As with questions, one might consider the other auxiliaries (*have* of the Perfect, *be* of the Passive and Progressive) to fit into this construction at least in general. Also, as in the case of questions, the two constructions exist simultaneously in the language. Their competition will be a subject of sections 7.9–7.11.

7.8   Infinitive with *to*

Another defining property of the modal auxiliaries is that they take the infinitive form of the main verb without the infinitival marker *to*. The modals have been used with main verb complements since the Old English period, when infinitives were marked by a suffix *–an*. The use of *to* as a purpose-clause marker occurred in Old English, but the gradual spread (via grammaticalization) of *to* to more and more infinitive contexts had only just begun. The constructions of modal + main verb relevant here were already conventionalized without *to* and have never been re-formed on the newer pattern because of their high frequency of use. (Haspelmath 1989 shows that infinitives develop out of purpose-clause markers cross-linguistically; see Los 2005 for the English *to* infinitive).

7.9   Periphrastic *do*

As noted above, the newer constructions that are beginning to define a class of auxiliaries cannot apply to clauses that have a finite main verb rather than an emerging auxiliary. The constructions Q-AUX and NEG-AUX cannot generalize to sentences without auxiliaries. However, there was also a periphrastic construction using *do* in which *do* had lost most (or all) of its earlier, probably causative, meaning (Ellegård 1953, Denison 1985, Kroch 1989a).

(13) Thou dost the truth tell. (Udall, *Roister Doister* 1566)

The literature on the source of the auxiliary *do* seems to favour the view that it arose from a causative construction in which an infinitive followed *do* (Ellegård 1953, Denison 1985). According to Ellegård, there are only a few examples in Old English of such a use, but *do* in a causative meaning became common in Middle English in the Eastern dialects. In ME the periphrastic *do* (said to be empty of meaning) co-existed with the causative *do* in some dialects. Ziegeler 2004 and others also note a perfective use of *do* as it expands beyond the causative and begins to be used as an 'empty' auxiliary.

As *do* comes to be used in the question and negative constructions, the auxiliary construction type can spread to main verbs. This happens gradually and at a different rate in questions and negatives. Since the use of periphrastic *do* is diagnostic for the spread of the new auxiliary constructions, the following sections document the expansion of *do* to support the hypothesis that the development of the modern auxiliary came about gradually through the extension of the constructions that defined this category, rather than abruptly by reanalysis in the process of language acquisition.

7.10   Two hypotheses

The current account rests on two hypotheses: First, a major trigger for the spread of the auxiliary constructions was the increased frequency of use of the modals; and second, that the spread of *do* in these constructions is best accounted for by the postulation of two competing constructions, one of which gains in type frequency and productivity at the expense of the other, which holds on mainly in high-frequency exemplars.

Consider the first hypothesis. The constructions Q-AUX and NEG-AUX were used more frequently than Q-MAIN VERB and NEG-MAIN VERB by this period because of the increased usage of modals, as shown in Tables 7.1, 7.2 and 7.3. The counts for the sixteenth century show roughly one-third main finite verbs, one-third copulas and one-third modals and other auxiliaries overall, as well as in questions and negatives. Thus clauses with finite main verbs were not in the majority at this time. The hypothesis, then, is that the Q-AUX and NEG-AUX constructions spread to clauses with finite main verbs through the use of *do*.

Ellegård 1953: 154–5 argues against an earlier proposal that the use of *do* developed on analogy with the developing auxiliaries (Bradley 1904, Curme 1931) because the use of *do* did not spread also to affirmative declarative sentences. Table 7.4 shows that questions and negatives constitute a small minority of all finite clauses. The high frequency of affirmative declaratives means that they could resist change on the basis of these minor patterns. Also the fact that the two constructions under discussion had specific functions – signalling questions in one case and negatives in the other – means there was no motivation for *do* to spread to affirmative declaratives.

Furthermore, as Table 7.5 shows (in comparison to Tables 7.1 and 7.2), there is a tendency to have more finite main verbs (without auxiliaries) in affirmative declaratives than in questions and negatives. Thus there is no reason to predict that *do* as an auxiliary would spread to declarative affirmative contexts.

The second (related) hypothesis is that the spread of *do* constituted the spread of the two new question and negative auxiliary constructions at the expense of the older constructions. The mechanism for this change was analogy, the process by which a speaker comes to use a novel item in a construction (see Chapter 4). The increasing application of analogy is expressed in a corpus as an increase in type frequency – as more items are used with the construction.

Table 7.4 *Negative declaratives and questions are much less frequent than affirmative declaratives*

Play	Date	Finite clauses counted	Negatives	Questions
Udall	1566	128	21 (16%)	17 (13%)
Stevenson	1575	122	12 (10%)	12 (10%)
Shakespeare	1601/1602	131	21 (16%)	19 (15%)
MWW	Act I	305	20 (6%)	38 (10%)
Middleton	1630	127	13 (10%)	10 (8%)

Table 7.5 *Distribution of finite main verbs, forms of* be, *modals and perfects in affirmative declarative clauses*

Play	Date	Finite main verb	be	Modals + perfect	N
Udall	1566	62 (50%)	20 (16%)	30 (24%)	124
Stevenson	1575	37 (43%)	19 (22%)	29 (34%)	85
Shakespeare*	1601/1602	103 (34%)	105 (34%)	97 (32%)	305

*Act I of the *The Merry Wives of Windsor*.

At the same time, items with high token frequency resist change by analogy. Thus we expect that the use of *do* will occur in early stages with main verbs of lower token frequency.

Since more frequent verbs will occur in the older construction longer, finite main verb inversion will involve fewer types and more tokens at first. In Tables 7.6 and 7.7, note that the type/token ratio for inverted finite main verbs is always lower than for *do*. Note also that the percentages of tokens using *do* goes up gradually.

Though the use of *do* in *not*-negatives lags behind its use in questions, Table 7.6 shows the same relation between the type/token ratios for the use of *do* versus its absence: in each time period, the type/token ratio is lower for *not* following a finite main verb than for *not* following an auxiliary element. This means that the higher frequency verbs were maintaining the older pattern longer, as we would predict if the change were based on analogy to the auxiliary constructions.

Tables 7.6 and 7.7 also show that *do* in questions advanced more rapidly than *do* in negation. This chronology cannot be attributed to a difference in the frequency of questions vs. negation in the texts. In all probability the trend is related to the fact that there were alternate ways of expressing negation, that is, through negative incorporation, where *do* was not used.

Table 7.6 *Type/token ratios for questions with main verb inverted and questions with* do *inverted*[6]

Dates	Main verb	Type/token ratio	*do*	Type/token ratio	Percentage *do*
1566–88	31/50	0.62	24/32	0.75	39%
1599–1602	18/53	0.34	42/61	0.69	54%
1621–49	20/32	0.63	47/53	0.89	62%
1663–97	10/17	0.59	51/83	0.61	83%

Table 7.7 *Type/token ratios for negatives with* not *appearing after a finite main verb, and with* do *(or* don't*)*

Dates	Main verb	Type/token ratio	*do*	Type/token ratio	Percentage *do*
1566–88	48/65	0.74	15/15	1.00	23%
1599–1602	56/110	0.51	20/27	0.74	20%
1621–49	84/115	0.73	43/48	0.90	29%
1663–97	10/31	0.32	57/80	0.71	72%

7.11   Lexical diffusion

The type/token ratios of Tables 7.6 and 7.7 bring up the question of exactly which verbs were maintained in the older constructions longer. The studies of lexical diffusion of the use of periphrastic *do* by Ellegård 1953 and Ogura 1993 show both high-frequency verbs and verbs in fixed expressions being retained in the old constructions longer. Not surprisingly, the verbs are different for questions than for negative declaratives.

(14) For affirmative object questions, the verbs used without *do* the longest are as follows:
      say, mean, do, think

(15) For negative declaratives, the verbs used without *do* the longest are as follows:
      know, do, doubt, care, fear

In addition, for negative declaratives *list, skill, trow* and *boot* are conservative because they appear in fixed expressions.

(16) It boots thee not to be compassionate. (*Richard II*, I.3)
      It skills not much when they are delivered. (*Twelfth Night*, V.1)
      I list not prophesy. (*The Winter's Tale*, IV.1)

The fact that the verbs that resist the introduction of *do* are different in the two constructions suggests strongly that while the two constructions were developing in parallel and obviously have had some connection, they are nonetheless *two* constructions, not one 'rule' (e.g. '*do*-support').

Possessive *have,* which is the least frequent of the items participating in the negative and question constructions has more recently begun to take *do,* especially in American English. Note that Perfect *have* does not take *do,* indicating a split between these uses of *have.*

While I originally took up the study of the English auxiliaries and the constructions they occur in because the behaviour of these items seemed to be so rule-like, the gradual lexical diffusion of the *do* constructions indicates that these 'rules' leak as much as any others. The fact that possessive *have* has recently succumbed to use with *do,* as well as the fact that some older residual uses of subject-verb inversion remain in the language, indicates that the constructions spread gradually but do not necessarily become completely general. An example of the retention of the older construction occurs in *How goes it?*

Another problem that is solved by the construction-based analysis is the ambivalent behaviour of *dare* and *need,* which have always occurred in both types of constructions (Traugott 2001, also see Beths 1999 and Taeymans 2004, 2006). Rather than having to decide whether they are main verbs or auxiliaries, the construction grammar approach allows a construction to assign membership to the items that occur in its slots. Thus when *dare* and *need* occur in the auxiliary position, they are auxiliaries. These two verbs have for centuries occurred in both main verb and auxiliary positions, as shown in examples (17) and (18) from Sienicki (2008).

(17) Main verb:
    a. In two or three years a Tarpawlin shall not dare to look after being better then a Boatswain (Pepys, 1666–1667)
    b. that we shall nede to be purefyed (In die Innocencium, 1497)

(18) Auxiliary:
    a. Now I dare swear he thinks you had 'em at great Command, they obey'd you so readily. (Vanbrugh, 1696)
    b. If it need be, adde therto abstynence and other manere turmentynge of thy flesshe. (Malory, 1470)

One might ask why other verbs do not have as much freedom as *dare* and *need.* Of course, earlier some did: *have* in its possessive sense has gradually changed from use in the auxiliary constructions to use in the main verb position. The other modals and auxiliaries, being much more frequent, have become more entrenched in their constructions. Also, since they are semantically changed, they can no longer be used as main verbs.

7.12   Conclusions: constructions and adult-based change

Both grammaticalization and gradual reanalysis take place through the development of a new construction out of a particular instance of an old construction.

This explains the behaviour of infinitives, in particular why there is no *to* used with the modals and why the newer developing modals, *gonna, have to, want to,* and so on do have *to.* Since the modals developed in a period in which *to* had not yet become the infinitive marker, it is absent; since the newer modals are developing in a period when *to* is the infinitive marker, it is present in these phrases.

In the present analysis of the spread of the auxiliary constructions, we have appealed to the effects of both type and token frequency. As high type frequency correlates with productivity, we have been able to trace the spread of the auxiliary constructions with the use of *do* with more and more verb types. High token frequency of particular exemplars of constructions explains the resistance to change by the modals, Perfect *have* and copular *be.* As the most frequent verbal elements in the language, they maintain the old means of forming questions and negatives, by inverting or by taking the negative directly after them. This hypothesis is supported by the fact that commonly used main verbs in the negative and in questions were the last to change and the least frequent modals, *dare* and *need,* and possessive *have* changed after main verbs did.

Thus we have been able to show how so-called 'reanalysis' can be gradual: if we view grammar in terms of constructions, and further acknowledge that exemplars of constructions occur in cognitive representation and are strengthened by language use, then gradual change in frequency distributions can be represented directly in the grammar. As these change over time, then the grammar can also gradually change over time.

Further evidence that the creation of the category of 'auxiliary' occurs in gradual change even in adult lifetimes and not as a result of the transmission of language across generations (as claimed by Lightfoot 1979, 1991, Roberts and Roussou 2003, Van Gelderen 2004) is presented in Warner 2004. Using several measures and data from a number of authors in the sixteenth and seventeenth centuries, Warner tested the hypothesis of generational change. Tracing the use of *do* by authors in the seventeenth century he found some evidence that individual authors (Samuel Johnson and William Shakespeare) increased their use of *do* over time. Tracking the use of *do* by age of the authors, Warner finds no pattern that suggests generational change. Rather the usage patterns are more individual, suggesting what he calls 'communal change' or change in individual adult usage.

Finally, the analysis presented here does not privilege the class of items that invert with the subject and take a following *not.* The claim is that these items happened to be quite frequent in the older constructions and have resisted change. Of course, not all of the modal auxiliaries were of extreme high frequency, so it is necessary to invoke analogy in the creation of this grammatical class. But the analysis does emphasize the heterogeneity of the class, both structurally and semantically. As pointed out in Chapter 1, even the modal auxiliaries are rather diverse semantically, covering modality, tense and aspect. The Perfect, Progressive and copular *be* are structurally diverse, each of the first two taking a different form of the main verb, and the copula functioning in some ways as a main verb itself. This illustrates how the structure of a language is the product of its history. Since conventionalization relies more on repetition than on meaning or structure, languages may contain patterns for which a synchronic explanation cannot be found. This point is further illustrated in the next chapter, where gradual reanalysis is discussed in the context of apparent changes in constituent structure.

8   Gradient constituency and gradual reanalysis

8.1   Introduction

In previous chapters we have discussed the cognitive processes that interact to create the linguistic structure we think of as grammar. This chapter and the next argue further for these hypotheses by showing (i) how domain-general processes can create the cohesion among units that linguists regard as constituent structure and also account for gradual reanalysis (this chapter), and (ii) how conventionalization can create local patterns that might be considered 'subgrammatical' because they link properties that are not characteristic of grammar as traditionally defined (Chapter 9).

8.2   Chunking and constituency

In Chapter 3 we saw that the domain-general process of chunking could account for the conventionalization and cohesion (both phonetic and semantic) that is found in word groups that recur in experience. In Bybee 2002a I argued that constituent structure is derivable from the sequential chunking of material that tends to occur together. The main determinant of co-occurrence is of course meaning: units that are semantically relevant to one another tend to occur adjacent to one another in discourse (Haiman 1985). Thus demonstratives and determiners occur next to nouns, markers of aspect and tense occur near verbs, and so on. Semantically coherent sequences of units that have been chunked through repetition are then considered constituents.

The evidence that constituent structure itself is not a given but derivable from more basic processes is that these processes also apply in cases where traditional constituents do not emerge. In Bybee 2002a I discussed the case of the English auxiliary, which can contract with the subject, especially in cases where the subject is a pronoun. As Krug 1998 has pointed out, the most frequent element to follow *I* is *am*; *I am* is also the most frequent pair of words to contract.

Bybee 2002a considers the auxiliary *will* and the elements that precede and follow it. As a tense auxiliary, one might expect a greater cohesion with

Table 8.1 *The ten most frequent items occurring before and after* will *and* 'll. *(Switchboard corpus; N = 3195)*

Preceding		Following	
I	918	*be*	466
they	471	,	244
we	368	*have*	199
it	256	*get*	130
you	200	*go*	119
that	183	*do*	103
he	122	*probably*	90
she	53	*just*	81
,	47	*tell*	75
people	38	.	42

the following verb than with the preceding subject of the clause. What then accounts for its contraction with the subject? Table 8.1 (reproduced from Bybee 2002a, Table 5) shows the ten most frequent items to precede and follow *will,* or its contracted form in the Switchboard corpus. (The comma and period/full stop stand for pauses.) Here it is clear that the pairings of subject and auxiliary are more frequent than the pairings of auxiliary and verb. That is, in the Switchboard corpus, *I will* (or *I'll*) occurred nearly twice as often as the most frequent *will* + VERB combination, which was *will be*. Since the subject and auxiliary are traditionally assigned to different constituents and since their combination evinces no semantic coherence or relevance, it is only their frequency of co-occurrence that drives them to fuse into a single phonological unit.

Of course, the frequency of the two-word strings is not the whole story, as some of the pronoun + *will* or *'ll* combinations (e.g. with *she*) are less frequent than some of the *will/'ll* + verb combinations. It appears that the contraction has extended from the more frequent pronouns to the less frequent ones and possibly to some full noun phrases, although in the Switchboard corpus, the contracted form is only found with pronouns.

As mentioned in Chapter 3, frequency of co-occurrence is important for the phrase *I don't know*: there is more fusion between *I* and *don't* than between *don't* and *know*. *Don't* is the second most frequent item to follow *I*, right after *am*, and although a number of verbs follow *don't*, none do so with as great a frequency as *I* preceding *don't*.

It is interesting that the extreme high frequency of certain auxiliary + VERB combinations also allows fusion in some cases. For instance, *don't know* is often used alone, as in *dunno*. In addition, certain phrases such as *maybe, wanna be,* and *would-be* have become adjectives or adverbs.

The examples of subject–auxiliary contraction demonstrate that one of the basic mechanisms for the creation of constituent structure is chunking. This is the Linear Fusion Hypothesis of Bybee 2002a. The other requirement is some semantic coherence of the whole unit. Subject–auxiliary contraction shows that these two requirements are independent, but because they often coincide, a resulting epiphenomenon is constituent structure.

Because chunking is a gradient process, constituent structure can also be gradient, as argued in Bybee and Scheibman 1999. In fact, changes that occur gradually in grammaticalization also show that constituent structure is a gradient phenomenon. While languages often display excellent examples of constituents, such as NPs, there are many cases where a discrete constituent analysis cannot be supported strongly by the data.

8.3   Categorization and constituency

The other factor that is essential for determining constituent structure is categorization, which results in network connections which underlie analysability, as discussed in Chapter 3. Consider as an example the debate on the status of complex prepositions such as *on top of*, *in front of* and *in spite of*. English has quite a number of such phrases which in many ways function in the same way as simple prepositions. They obviously originate in a sequence of two prepositional phrases, but the first noun in the phrase is often a relational one that tends to lose its nominal status, as it loses the ability to be inflected and take determiners or adjective modifiers. The full constituent analysis of the original phrase is shown in (1), with one PP embedded under an NP which is itself the object of a preposition.

(1) [in [spite [of [the king] $_{NP}$] $_{PP}$] $_{NP}$] $_{PP}$

As we argue in Beckner and Bybee (2009), arriving at this structural analysis requires identification of the elements within the phrase as occurring elsewhere in the lexicon, that is, it requires categorization. In the network model discussed earlier, this would mean forming associations with the exemplars of the particular prepositions and nouns in the phrase. Repetition of the phrase also sets it up as an exemplar in its own right (because it is a chunk) and allows meanings, inferences and contextual factors to be assigned directly to it.

Figure 8.1 shows the network relations of the phrase *in spite of*. Each word of this phrase is related to the 'same' word in other contexts in the lexicon. However, the degrees of relatedness are gradient as we shall see below. The word *spite* of the phrase can be related to the noun *spite* which has its own meaning, and is in turn related to the verb *spite*. The two prepositions can be identified with other instances of the same prepositions. In Figure 8.1, no meanings have been assigned to these highly general prepositions. We assume

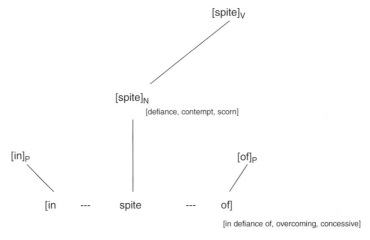

Figure 8.1 Network of connections between *in spite of* and its component words

rather that each of them is situated in a large network of contexts of use which include both specific and generalized meanings.

As we just mentioned, as a string of words that often occur together, *in spite of* has its own exemplar representation which includes information about its contexts of use, its meaning and inferences. The degree to which *in spite of* is an autonomous phrase and the degree to which it is analysable depends upon the strength of the activation of the whole vs. the component parts in usage. In the representation in Figure 8.1, the lines connecting the parts of the phrase to other exemplars of these parts can become weaker as the phrase is increasingly accessed as a whole. In this sense, the analysability decreases, as does the internal constituent structure (see Hay 2001 and the discussion in Chapter 3). In terms of constructions, *in spite of* + NP has become a construction through repetition. In the current context our discussion will involve how the fixed sequence in the construction evolved and became autonomous.

8.4   Constituent structure of complex prepositions

The problem of the constituency of complex prepositions is twofold: given a starting point as in (1) where a constituent boundary exists between [*in spite*] and [*of* NP] is there first, some point at which the first noun loses its autonomy and categoriality, and second, does the phrase *in spite of* become a single constituent with the NP as its object, in which case *of* is no longer a preposition in this phrase? The arguments for and against viewing such phrases as constituents or complex prepositions rather than a sequence of two prepositional phrases involve the extent to which the individual parts (the prepositions and the noun) can be identified as such, in other words, their analysability.

Consider the 'indicators of syntactic separateness' listed by Quirk et al. 1985. Four of these have to do with the analysability of the noun: can the noun take a range of determiners (2), can it take premodifying adjectives (3) and can it be replaced by another noun (4)? Their examples compare *on the shelf by (the door)* to *in spite of.* The former phrase meets the conditions for two prepositional phrases, while the second meets the criteria for a complex preposition:

(2) on a shelf by (the door)   *in a/the spite of
(3) on the low shelf by...   *in evident spite of
(4) on the ledge by...   *in malice of

Quirk et al. also use the ability of the noun in the complex preposition to be pluralized as a criterion. Since *spite* is a mass noun, not a count noun, we have to resort to a different example. Thus we find that the plural in (5) has a different meaning than its singular:

(5) a. in the neighborhood of Boston
    b. in the neighborhoods of Boston

These criteria all depend upon the analysis of the word (*shelf* or *spite*) as a noun with a full set of nominal properties. If the phrase has become unanalysable to some degree, the identification of the erstwhile noun as such has become weaker, making these modification and replacement operations inapplicable.

Another set of criteria concerns whether or not the second preposition and its object can be omitted, as in (6), or replaced by a possessive pronoun, as in (7) without altogether changing the meaning:

(6) on the shelf   *in spite
(7) on its shelf   *in its spite

These indicators also depend upon the extent to which the noun in the phrase is still identifiable as a noun.

The final set of indicators has to do with the prepositions and whether or not they can be varied. This criterion shows how analysable the prepositions are as prepositions as well as how analysable the noun is.

(8) on the shelf at (the door)   *in spite for
(9) under the shelf by...   *for spite of

It appears, then, that the criteria for constituency proposed by Quirk et al. have to do with the extent to which the parts of the phrase are still analysed as prepositions and nouns, that is, associated with other exemplars of the same prepositions and nouns. This is, of course, a matter or degree, and within the same phrase one could have some parts that are less identifiable (e.g. *dint* in *by dint of*) and some that are more identifiable (e.g. *by* in *by dint of*).

Of course, what we are witnessing here is the gradual grammaticalization of sequences of prepositional phrases into complex prepositions, which eventually can become simple prepositions (Hoffman 2005, Hopper and Traugott 2003). Such is the source of the prepositions *before, behind, inside* and so on. Since the process is gradual, the loss of analysability is also gradual. Since each phrase is undergoing its own development, there is no necessity of the same behaviour across the entire set of candidate complex prepositions. The gradience of the synchronic situation leaves open the possibility for grammarians to argue about whether or not one should recognize a category of complex prepositions. While Quirk et al. argue explicitly for gradience and possibly multiple overlapping analyses, more generative-minded researchers want to maintain the position that complex prepositions do not exist as a category of the grammar of English (Seppänen et al. 1994, Huddleston and Pullum 2002).

Seppänen et al. 1994 propose four other criteria for determining the constituent structure of complex prepositions: Fronting, Coordination, Ellipsis and Interpolation. One of their main concerns is determining the status of the final preposition in the phrases, that is, *of* in *in front of, inside of* and *in spite of*. Here is how they apply these tests to *in spite of*:

(10) Fronting
      Of what obstacles did he say he would do it *in spite?*
(11) Coordination
      In spite of your objections and *of* the point raised by Dr Andersson, we feel confident that we can proceed with the project.
(12) Ellipsis
      Speaker A: He did it *in spite of* John and the auditor.
      Speaker B: *Of* what auditor? I didn't know they had one in this firm.
(13) Interpolation
      The morning air was clear and clean, *in spite,* one might add, *of* the traffic and crowds.

Even though *in spite of* fails one of the tests (the Fronting test), the fact that it passes all the others in these made-up sentences is enough evidence to satisfy Seppänen et al. of the prepositional status of *of* in this phrase. Working with a discrete notion of constituent structure, they have no explanation for why one test fails while the others appear to succeed.

Consider now the nature of the data used by Seppänen et al. These made-up sentences all sound very literary and stilted. Of course, we can make up sentences such as these, but do people really use Coordination, Ellipsis and Interpolation as these sentences suggest? Beckner and Bybee report that a search of the 385 million-word Corpus of Contemporary American English (COCA) turned up only seven comparable examples of coordination, all of them from written sources. Here are three examples:

(14) Last July after she beat out a field of 67 applicants in a nationwide search, President Anderson feels that she was chosen for the job, not *because* or *in spite of* the fact that she is Black and a woman, but simply because she was the most qualified applicant. (1992)

(15) The prime minister remains unable to reap the credit for economic success, which is perceived to have occurred *in spite*, not *because*, *of* his policies; he is unable to unify his party or even his cabinet because he does not have the authority (1995)

(16) a lesson in how Congress makes politically expedient decisions *at the expense* (or *in spite*) *of* the constitutional implications of their actions (2002)

However, in cases of coordination of *in spite of* with another similar expression, we find even more cases in which *of* is repeated, arguing for the fixed nature of this phrase. In the Corpus of Contemporary American English, Beckner and Bybee located thirty-five such instances. Two examples are given below:

(17) the dogma of self-expression says that the gifted child can flower *in the absence of* or *in spite of* art education. (1995)

(18) in this allegedly anti-American country Sarkozy would be elected (as early as the spring of 2007) either *because of* or *in spite of* the public perception that he is somehow 'American'. (2005)

Also providing evidence for the fixed nature of this phrase are usage patterns with respect to multiple instances of *in spite of* that are conjoined. English speakers strongly prefer to present multiple instances of *in spite of* as an uninterrupted sequence; (19) is one characteristic example:

(19) *In spite of* motorbikes, *in spite of* karaoke music, *in spite of* the stink of gasoline fumes that seeps into each kitchen. (2005)

In the Corpus of Contemporary American English, there are forty-three examples of this type, with no counter-examples in which only sub-parts of *in spite of* are conjoined.

In addition, the fact that *in spite of* can be conjoined with simple prepositions as in (20) and (21) suggests that it is functioning as a unit.

(20) Scorsese's strongest works are fictions of formation, in which a religious conviction comes *with* or *in spite of* a vocation. (1991)

(21) Commitment is healthiest when it is not *without* doubt, but *in spite of* doubt. (1991)

Seppänen et al. (1994) further argue that *in spite of* retains an internal constituent structure because it can be interrupted in speech, as in their constructed example (13). Beckner and Bybee searched the *Time* Corpus and the Corpus of Contemporary American English for such usages, and located just one such corpus example (from 1999, quoting Robert Ingersoll from 1877):

(22) The religionists of our time are occupying about the same ground occupied by heretics and infidels of one hundred years ago. The church has advanced *in spite*, as it were, *of* itself.

In example (22) Ingersoll's obvious intention is to revive the original semantics of *spite*, and he thus interrupts *in spite of* to call attention to the component words in the sequence. Seppänen et al.'s other criterion, Ellipsis, based on rather unrealistic, made-up dialogs, seems to have no support in natural corpus data.

The evidence then points to the possibility of multiple, gradient analyses of the complex preposition *in spite of*. Figure 8.1 is consistent with the corpus data. While the connecting lines between the parts of the phrase and their counterpart exemplars in other contexts are weakening, they are still to some extent viable, allowing speakers some degree of freedom, especially in writing, to manipulate the parts of the phrase.

8.5   Semantic change: *in spite of*

The syntactic analyses of Seppänen et al. 1994 and Huddleston and Pullum 2002, unlike that of Quirk et al., rule out the use of semantics in determining constituent structure. These authors regard semantics as an unreliable guide to syntactic structure. Quirk et al.'s point that complex prepositions function like simple prepositions thus does not count as evidence for constituent status in the generativists' analysis. In contrast, a usage-based approach would consider meaning to be at least as important as the syntactic criteria in determining the analysis that speakers are likely come up with. The fact that semantically, *on top of* functions as the opposite of *under* (a simpler preposition), or that *in spite of* is paraphrasable by *despite* are indicators that these originally complex expressions have taken on a unitary status.

Especially in the common case in Present Day English where *in spite of* has concessive meaning, its internal parts are of little or no consequence. In its earliest uses (from the fifteenth century), the phrase was used in cases where the noun, *spite*, rang true with its nominal meaning of 'scorn, contempt or defiance' with an object that was an enemy or an authority that was defied. (For a similar evolution of Spanish *a pesar de* 'in spite of', see Torres Cacoullos and Schwenter 2005, Tornes Cacoullos 2006.)

(23) The Erle þen, with his pepill, drove ouer þe havon of Gravenyng thaire pray of bestes, att lowe water, *in spite of* al þe Flemmynges, and brought hem with al thaire prisoners to Caleis, and lost neuer a man; thonket be God! (*The Brut,* 1400–82)

'Then the Earl, with his people, drove over their herd of animals, the inlet at Gravening at low water, in spite of the Flemish, and brought them with all their prisoners to Calais, and never lost a man; thanks be to God!'

Later examples (from the sixteenth to the nineteenth century) have generalized the object of *in spite of* to some force or obstacle that has to be overcome. Now the meaning of *spite* in this phrase no longer points to its meaning as a noun.

(24)   The benefits of innoculation have established the practice *in spight of* all opposition. (*Gentl. Mag.*, 1762. XXXII. 217/2)

(25)   The tears, *in spite of* her, forced their way between her fingers. (SCOTT *Br. Lamm.* 1818, xx)

The further semantic change in this phrase comes about through inference (Traugott 1989, Traugott and Dasher 2002, Hoffmann 2005). If a situation is attained even when there were opposing forces or obstacles, the inference is that one would not have expected the situation under those circumstances. The concessive meaning, which is often found today, indicates that something was done counter to expectation. Modern corpora reveal examples that are ambiguous between the counter forces and counter-expectation readings, as in (26), as well as examples that have only the counter-expectation readings, as in (27).

(26)   *In spite of* the rough conditions, travel advisories and the war on terrorism, scores of older Americans are uprooting their lives to help needy nations improve their living conditions. (*Time Magazine* 2003)

(27)   Yet *in spite of* music's remarkable influence on the human psyche, scientists have spent little time attempting to understand why it possesses such potency. (*Time Magazine* 2000)

Examples such as (27), which are common today, show that no internal analysis of the meanings of the parts of the expression are accessed when it is used. There is simply no direct way to get from the meanings of the parts, especially the meaning of the erstwhile noun, to the concessive interpretation. In my view, this is as clear an indication of constituent status as one would hope to find.

8.6   Decategorialization as a result of the loss of analysability

An important indicator of the grammaticalization of a noun or verb within a construction is decategorialization. Hopper 1991 bases his discussion of this phenomenon on the relative notion of lexical category described in Hopper and Thompson 1984. The extent to which a noun, for instance, is capable of being 'decked out' in characteristically noun-like attributes, such as number or case inflection, determiners and other modifiers, is a matter of degree and depends crucially upon that element's use in discourse. Given that a noun within a grammaticalizing phrase such as a complex preposition is not performing the referential functions typical of nouns, it follows that it would lose its noun-like attributes.

Using just the processes already examined in this book, the Exemplar cum Network model allows us to give a formal account of the diachronic process of decategorialization. This analysis is inherent in the diagram in Figure 8.1 and the processes of change this representation will undergo as the expression *in spite of* is used. Referring back now to the proposals of Hay 2001, as explained in Chapter 3, we can illustrate how usage impacts this representation and moves it from being analysable and compositional to being autonomous. (See Torres Cacoullos 2006 for a comparable treatment of the grammaticalization of *a pesar de* 'in spite of' in Spanish.)

After a few repetitions of a sequence of words in experience, the brain sets up a representation (or exemplar) for that sequence as a shortcut. The words in the sequence still activate other exemplars of the same word strongly at first. The evidence Hay 2001 presents, and the evidence from grammaticalization, suggest that subsequently access to this sequence is through the shortcut, with varying degrees of activation of the component words. Each instance of access of the whole unit further strengthens the whole unit. Each instance of access through or by activating the component words strengthens the relations with the component words.

The compositionality of the phrase might be maintained at first through use in contexts in which the meanings of the component parts are emphasized. But as the meaning of *spite* weakens through use in contexts in which it is not to be taken literally, the relation with the noun *spite* continues to weaken, and this word in the phrase *in spite of* loses its noun properties.

Consider some examples. In the comedies of William Shakespeare the noun *spite* occurs twenty times, but only six of these occurrences are in the phrase *in spite of*. It is interesting that in two of these examples, the relation with the noun *spite* is quite transparent. In (28) *spite* is modified by *very*, which in this usage meant 'true' when modifying a noun. In (29) Beatrice continues by using *spite* as a verb, thus conjuring up its full lexical meaning.

(28) *Troilus and Cressida* (Shakespeare) c. 1600
     Ajax hath lost a friend
     And foams at mouth, and he is arm'd and at it,
     Roaring for Troilus, who hath done to-day
     Mad and fantastic execution,
     Engaging and redeeming of himself
     With such a careless force and forceless care
     As if that luck, *in* very *spite of* cunning,
     Bade him win all.

(29) *Much Ado About Nothing*
      BENEDICK Suffer love! a good epithet! I do suffer love
      indeed, for I love thee against my will.
      BEATRICE *In spite of* your heart, I think; alas, poor heart!
      If you *spite* it for my sake, I will *spite* it for
      yours; for I will never love that which my friend hates.

Other seventeenth-century examples show more analysability than is possible now, as (30) shows *spite* with the definite article and (31) shows a replacement of the first preposition.

(30) *In the spight of* so many enemies. (SANDERSON, *Serm.* 546,1632)
(31) *For spight of* his Tarbox he died of the Scab. (OSBORN, *King James* Wks. 1658 [1673])

Such examples are rare these days, if they occur at all, as the relation of *in spite of* to *spite* is semantically more remote, especially when the former has the concessive reading. Hay 2001 predicts that the loss of analysability and compositionality would come about most readily when the base form (in this case *spite*) grows less frequent than the derived form (in this case *in spite of*). In Shakespeare's comedies, as we have said, out of twenty tokens of *spite,* only six occurred in our phrase. In the present day language, however, 90 per cent of the tokens of *spite* occur in *in spite of.* Torres Cacoullos 2006 finds a similar decrease in the frequency of *pesar* as compared to the phrase *a pesar de* 'in spite of' in Spanish.

Thus as the noun in the grammaticalizing phrase grows more remote from other noun instances because it is locked in a phrase, and as it loses its earlier meaning that would have linked it to the independent noun, it loses its categoriality. A consequence of the loss of categoriality is the loss of some of the internal structure of the phrase. From two prepositional phrases, we get one multi-word preposition. It appears that grammaticalization always results in the loss of internal constituent structure. This loss of complexity is an instance of one of the principles of Hawkins 2004: frequency reduces complexity.

8.7   Reanalysis as gradual

Some writers on grammaticalization seem to equate such a complexity reduction process with reanalysis, making statements such as, grammaticalization is the process by which a lexical item is reanalysed as a grammatical morpheme (Lord 1976, Marchese 1986, Harris and Campbell 1995, Roberts and Roussou 2003). It is often not clear, however, whether such statements are intended to describe the outcome of the process – before grammaticalization item X was a lexical item and now it is grammatical – or the actual mechanism of change whereby speakers/learners apply a different analysis to a string than it had before. In the case of the latter interpretation, a theory with discrete constituent and category structure has difficulty dealing with the fact that grammaticalization takes place gradually. (See the discussion in Chapter 7.)

We have already seen that the network representations that give rise to constituency can change gradually, resulting in gradual changes in the degrees of analysability and compositionality of grammaticalizing constructions. There are two other ways in which reanalysis may be considered gradual and we will deal with them in the remainder of this chapter.[1]

First, not all members of a grammaticalizing class change at the same rate. We mentioned this with regard to the modal auxiliaries in Chapter 7: *shall* becomes a future marker before *will* does; *may* attains status for marking root possibility before *can* does, and has already moved to epistemic possibility (Bybee and Pagliuca 1987, Bybee 1988b). There are many other examples. Lichtenberk 1991, for instance, mentions that the verbs that become prepositions in To'aba'ita do so at different rates, losing verbal properties at different times. He points out that one important predictor of the rate of change is the token frequency of the preposition. A similar point can be made about the complex prepositions of English – they are becoming less analysable at different rates according to the tests applied by Quirk et al. 1985, Seppänen et al. 1994 and Huddleston and Pullum 2002.

Second, some exemplars of grammaticalizing constructions lose analysability (= undergo reanalysis) before others do. In the next section we discuss the data from Bybee and Torres Cacoullos 2009 on the development of the progressive in Spanish. Here we find that instances of the same construction with different verbs behave differently with respect to various syntactic and semantic criteria. For examples of the same phenomenon in the expression of the English future, see Torres Cacoullos and Walker 2009.

8.8   The Spanish Progressive: advanced grammaticalization in prefabs

In Bybee and Torres Cacoullos 2009 we explore the effect of higher frequency, prefabricated uses of constructions on the progress of the grammaticalization of the generalized construction. The case study is of Progressives in Spanish, which have developed from locational-postural verbs, such as *estar* 'to be located', or from movement verbs, such as *andar* 'to go around' and *ir* 'to go', plus a gerund (whose suffix is *–ndo*). At first the finite verb is an independent lexical item with full spatial meaning, as shown in the following thirteenth-century examples, (32)–(34). The evidence of locative meaning in these examples is a locative phrase, which is underlined. The grammaticalizing phrase is shown in small capital letters.

(32) Et alli ESTAUA el puerco <u>en aquella llaguna</u> BOLCANDO se (XIII, GE.II)
     'And <u>there</u> WAS the pig <u>in that pond</u> TURNING itself '
(33) YUASSE ANDANDO <u>por la carrera</u> que ua al pozo (XIII, GE.I)
     'He WENT WALKING <u>along the road</u> that goes to the well'
(34) Et ANDANDO BUSCANDO los. encontrosse con un omne quel pregunto
     como <u>andaua</u> o que <u>buscaua</u>. (XIII, GE.I)
     'And GOING AROUND LOOKING for them he met a man who asked him
     how he was <u>going</u> or what he was <u>looking</u> for'

While the locative meaning is clearly discernible in these examples, in Modern
Spanish expressions with *estar* (35)*, andar* (36) and *ir* (37) with a gerund usu-
ally express the aspectual meaning of progressive, as in these examples from
Torres Cacoullos 1999, 2001:

(35) Pero ESTÁS HABLANDO de una forma de vida, Gordo.
     'But you are talking about a way of life, Gordo.'
(36) ANDO BUSCANDO unas tijeras, porque se me rompió una uña.
     'I am looking for some scissors, because I broke a nail.'
(37) Pero ya VA SALIENDO la cosecha así, por partes.
     'But the harvest now is coming out this way, bit by bit.'

However, as is common in grammaticalization, there is a great deal of overlap in the uses of these constructions; some aspectual instances occur very
early, while some recent uses still reveal the locative source.

The reanalysis involved in the grammaticalization of these constructions
takes a main verb with a gerund complement and converts that sequence into
a periphrastic or compound verb form in which the finite verb functions as an
auxiliary and the verb in gerund form is taken to be the main verb.

(38) $[estar]_{verb}$ $[\text{VERB} + ndo]_{comp} \rightarrow [estar + \text{VERB} + ndo]_{verb\ progressive}$

Diagnostics of the change in constituency are (i) the gradual diminution of
elements intervening between the emerging auxiliary and the gerund (39), (ii)
loss of the ability to put more than one gerund with the same emerging auxiliary (40), and (iii) the placement of object clitic pronouns before the whole
complex rather than attached to the gerund (41).

(39) ESTÁ <u>Melibea muy affligida</u> HABLANDO con Lucrecia sobre la tardança de
     Calisto
     '[Stage instructions] IS <u>Melibea, deeply distressed,</u> TALKING to Lucrecia
     about the tardiness of Calisto'
(40) le YVAN MENGUANDO los bastimentos <u>e</u> CRECIENDO las necesidades
     'Supplies WERE [lit: went] SHRINKING <u>and</u> needs GROWING'
(41) ESTÁ DIZIÉNDOla allá su corazón
     'His heart there IS TELLING her'

Table 8.2 *Prefabs (as percentage of aux and of gerund; all time periods combined)*

		Percentage 'auxiliary'	Percentage gerund
ESTAR	*aguardando* 'waiting'	2% (14/672)	93% (14/15)
	diciendo 'saying'	3% (22/672)	44% (22/50)
	durmiendo 'sleeping'	2% (14/672)	93% (14/15)
	escuchando 'listening'	3% (23/672)	96% (23/24)
	esperando 'waiting'	7% (48/672)	89% (48/54)
	hablando 'talking'	5% (32/672)	71% (32/45)
	mirando 'looking'	7% (49/672)	84% (49/58)
	oyendo 'hearing'	2% (15/672)	94% (15/16)
	pensando 'thinking'	2% (13/672)	62% (13/21)

As examples such as these begin to disappear, we have an indication of the unithood of the new progressive constructions. A quantitative study of the number of examples of these types shows increasing grammaticalization or unithood over the centuries from the thirteenth through to the nineteenth (Bybee and Torres Cacoullos 2009).

These emerging progressive constructions have spawned a number of prefabs, which here we define with reference to the relative frequency of the auxiliary-gerund combination compared to the total number of tokens of the auxiliary and the total number of tokens of the gerund. If a certain combination, for example *estar aguardando* 'to be waiting', makes up 2 per cent or more of the auxiliary data (the total use of *estar*) and 50 per cent or more of the gerund data (that is, *aguardando* is used with *estar* more than with any other auxiliary), then it is considered to be a prefab. Table 8.2 shows the prefabs identified for the auxiliary *estar.*

Two of these prefabs are attested from the earliest period, *estar hablando* 'to be talking' and *estar esperando* 'to be waiting'. Others have become prefabs from the seventeenth to the nineteenth century. Using the three diagnostics for constituency or unithood mentioned above, we show that these prefabs are ahead of the general construction in attaining unithood status. That is, they have fewer elements intervening between the auxiliary and the gerund, they have fewer conjoined gerunds and they have more clitics placed in front of the whole complex in each century examined.

As these prefabs are more frequent than other instances of the construction, they are accessed as a single unit more often than other instances, leading to the loss of analysability as discussed above. The auxiliary within the prefab will become less connected to instances of locative *estar* in other constructions and will thus lose its locative meaning earlier than in other instances of the progressive construction. Bybee and Torres Cacoullos propose, then, that this bleaching of meaning in prefabs may have an effect on the meaning of the general construction, catalyzing its further grammaticalization.

This, then, is yet another way that reanalysis may be gradual – it occurs earlier in some instances of a construction than in others. Note that this is further evidence for an exemplar model, in which individual instances of constructions can develop their own properties. In this case it appears that the properties of the higher frequency exemplars of a construction may have an effect on the development of the general construction. See Chapter 10 for a discussion of the impact of the meaning of prefabs on grammaticalizing constructions.

8.9   Conclusions

In this chapter I have presented evidence that constituent structure arises through the application of the domain-general processes of chunking and categorization. As both of these processes produce gradient representations, based on how particular exemplars are processed in real-time language use, it follows that constituent structure is gradient on several dimensions. The basic point is that the degree to which a word in a sequence is analysable or associated with other exemplars of that word in other contexts can vary, depending upon how strongly that connection is activated during language use. The consequences of this variation are that (i) constructions of the same type (e.g. complex prepositions) can grammaticalize at different rates and (ii) the same grammaticalizing construction can be more advanced in its development with some lexical items than with others.

9 Conventionalization and the local vs. the general: Modern English *can*

9.1 Introduction

Given that chunking occurs with even low levels of repetition, there is much potential for word combinations to become conventionalized, accessed whole, and to accrue special uses or functions. In this chapter we study combinations of *can* and *can't* with verbs and their complements which have become conventionalized, some with special meaning or discourse function and some without. By using a large corpus of spoken American English (the *Switchboard* corpus) we discover certain regularities of usage that have escaped the notice of grammarians and which, indeed, defy many of the general principles of grammar. These 'subgrammatical' facts support the independence of conventionalization as one of the domain-general factors that is crucial to the emergence of grammar.

Of special interest also are cases where it appears that it is the meaning that has become conventionalized, not just the sequence of words. The role of meaning becomes apparent in cases where negation takes an alternate form, where *can* is replaced by *be able to* and where the requirement that a temporal phrase be present is met by that phrase in another clause. By conventionalization of meaning I mean that specific languages have specific concepts to which they call attention. Slobin (1996, 2003) refers to this phenomenon as 'thinking for speaking'. Its effect on language is evident in patterns of lexicalization, as Slobin 1997a points out, and also in layering in grammaticalization, where a language may develop multiple grammaticalized expressions in the same domain, for example obligation or degrees of remoteness in tense systems.

In Chapter 7 we discussed in detail the development of the English auxiliary via the emergence of the question and negative constructions. There we saw that over time, the use of the modal auxiliaries, including *can*, has increased considerably since Old English. Actually the use of *can* as an auxiliary begins in earnest in Middle English with a great expansion of the verbs with which it can be used (Bybee 2003b). Today, *can* is highly frequent and used with the meaning of ability or root possibility (see Coates 1983). This chapter examines the special uses of *can*, those found in high-frequency environments, for clues to the relation of the specific functions to the more general functions.

The study began as an inquiry into the present-day uses of the modal auxiliary *can*, following up on a diachronic study of the expansion of the co-occurring main verbs and the meanings of *can* into Early Modern English (Bybee 2003b). The previous study had already made it clear that by Early Modern English *can* could be used with passives, statives and dynamic verbs without apparent restriction. Interested in what further developments could ensue, especially with regard to *can* vs. *can't*, I chose to look at the most frequent verbs used with *can* in the *Switchboard Corpus* (Godfrey et al. 1992). Not surprisingly, when one studies frequent word combinations, one uncovers a lot of formulaic sequences.

9.2   General vs. local patterns: negation

The construction for forming sentence negation in English, as we saw in Chapter 7, follows the pattern shown in (1):

(1) General construction for the creation of a verb phrase:
     [... AUXILIARY + NEGATIVE + MAIN VERB...]

Many more specific constructions have developed from this general one so that there might be two ways to arrive at the same sequence of words. For instance, if *can't* is not always the direct negation of *can*, we would want to posit more specific constructions for *can't* with particular main verbs. The evidence from spoken American English strongly suggests that for some cognitive and communication verbs, there are very specific constructions that distinguish between *can* and *can't*. One indication of this is the relative frequency of the affirmative and negative forms. In general, we expect affirmative uses to be more common than negative ones, based on the cross-linguistic finding that all languages 'mark' negative with an overt marker, but no languages mark affirmative and leave the negative unmarked. As markedness relations correlate very highly with relative frequency (Greenberg 1963), we expect to find more affirmatives than negatives in any batch of data examined.

As predicted, overall *can* is three times more frequent than *can't*, but out of the top twenty-one verbs to follow *can* and the top twenty-one to follow *can't* in the Switchboard corpus, in six, the sequence with *can't* was more frequent. Table 9.1 lists these six and in addition a representative group of high-frequency verbs whose affirmative was more frequent than the negative as predicted.

All the cases in which the negative is more frequent than the affirmative are formulae or prefabs; in fact in some of the cases in which the affirmative is more frequent, the negative constructions are also prefabs. Most of the expressions with *can't* involve cognitive or epistemic verbs – verbs that give the speaker's subjective evaluation of a part of the discourse. Because these cases of 'local markedness' (Tiersma 1982) are owing to prefabs or local generalizations, the

Table 9.1 *Comparison of frequency of* can + VERB *to* can't + VERB

Negative more frequent than affirmative*			
	Can	*Can't*	Percentage affirmative
seem	2	19	11%
believe	20	73	22%
think	49	115	30%
remember	113	172	40%
say	56	83	40%
afford	73	93	43%
Affirmative more frequent than negative*			
go	125	20	86%
understand	36	11	80%
put	39	13	75%
get	98	51	66%
imagine	36	22	62%

*Raw numbers taken from different-sized portions of Switchboard

sequence of *can't* + certain verbs does not really constitute the negation of *can* but rather takes part in entirely different constructions.

9.3   Constructions with cognitive/epistemic verbs

9.3.1   Can't seem

Can't seem is much more frequent than *can seem*. The negative has a formulaic, non-transparent meaning of 'can't manage', perhaps due to an inference from a subjective meaning of 'not able to appear to' to 'appear not to be able to'.

(2) I *can't seem* to find the middle.
(3) They *can't seem* to read properly.

In the corpus, eighteen out of nineteen had such a meaning in this construction. One of the two instances of *can seem* listed in the table was actually negative also:

(4) A mess that nobody *can seem* to get out of.

Example (4) shows that the presence of *can't* is not required for the expression to have the formulaic meaning; any type of negation is possible. Thus it is not so much the expression *can't seem* that is conventionalized, but rather the meaning or the description of the situation in a particular way that is conventionalized.

Table 9.2 *Contexts for* can think *and* can't think

	Can	Can't
of	84% (41)	90% (90)
relative clause	78% (32/41)	0
of any, anything	0	22% (22)

Notice how the one example of the affirmative version (5) is quite compositional and not formulaic in its meaning.

(5) The violence *can seem* very realistic.

In this example, *can* takes its root possibility meaning ('general enabling conditions exist') and modifies *seem* to give the compositional sense of 'it is possible for the violence to appear very realistic'. Note that (2) does not have a parallel interpretation: 'it is not possible for me to appear to find the middle…' Thus *can't seem* cannot accurately be described as the negative counterpart of *can seem*; it is rather a separate construction.

9.3.2   Can't think, *can't believe, can't say:* skewed distribution
          in constructions

A quantitative look at the distribution of *can think/can't think, can believe/can't believe* and *can say/can't say* shows that the affirmative vs. negative expressions appear in different constructions. Consider first Table 9.2, which shows the number of occurrences in various contexts of all the instances of *can think* (N = 49) and 100 instances (out of a total of 115 in the corpus) of *can't think*. All of the *can't think* examples were first-person-singular (where the subject was elided, first singular was nonetheless apparent). The *can think* tokens were also primarily first singular, although first plural occurred once and second person *you* occurred six times. The two expressions share the strong tendency to occur with a following *of*: 84 per cent for *can think* and 90 per cent for *can't think*, see examples (6)–(9).

While both the affirmative and the negative occur with *of* + NP, the most common context for the affirmative with *of* is in a relative clause, as in (6) and (7). The heads of these relative clauses are indefinites, or phrases with *the only thing, the best thing,* and *the other thing.* Of course, indefinites such as *any* and *anything* only occur as the object of *of* when the modal is negative.

(6) That's about all I can think of to talk about right now.
(7) whatever ethnic background you can think of

Table 9.3 *Items following* can believe *and* can't believe

	Can (20)	*Can't* (73)
that-clause	**1**	**9**
clause	**0**	**26**
that (dem)	13	9
this (dem)	0	5
it	3	6
NP	1	5
how-clause	0	3
end of turn or S	0	8

(8) I can't think of the guy's name.

(9) I can't think of which one it was.

It is also semantically natural for the object of *I can't think of* to be a name, or a phrase such as *many alternatives.*

Since there are negative uses that occur in this construction that never (or rarely) occur with the affirmative construction, it would seem that they are not derived compositionally from negating *can*, but are themselves constructions that can be accessed without necessarily activating *can* (see the discussion in Chapter 8).

Can believe and *can't believe* are also skewed in their distributions. *Can't believe* was found eighty-three times in the corpus and *can believe* was found 20 times. It can be seen from Table 9.3 that *can't believe* occurs in a wider range of construction types than its affirmative counterpart.

Of course, it is well known that *I can't believe* is a common expression of astonishment on the part of the speaker. Of the seventy-three examples found, three had *you* as the subject and two had *they*; all the others were first person singular. Notice also that only one case of *I can believe* was followed by a finite clause (with *that*), while thirty-five cases of *I can't believe* were followed by a finite clause (nine with *that* and twenty-six without); examples (10) and (11) are typical.

(10) I can't believe the lady gave it to her.

(11) my husband said I can't believe that you made 500 dollars doing that

Interestingly, while both *it* and *that* occur as the object of *believe* in both affirmative and negative, it seems quite arbitrary that *this* occurs only with the negative version in the corpus.

Finally, consider the one instance of *I can believe* with a *that*-clause:

(12) that kind of a guy I can believe like that Bill Clinton would ...

Table 9.4 *Contexts for* can say *and* can't say

		Can	Can't
that-clause		3	23
clause		11	27
well-clause		4	3
okay			
you know			
all right	clause	**10**	**0**
yes			
in relative clause		10	0
miscellaneous		17	25

This might also represent a formulaic construction *I can believe that that kind of X would.* The absence of other examples suggests that *I can believe that* + CLAUSE is not a productive construction.

Can say occurred in the corpus fifty-three times and *can't say* occurred eighty-three times. *Can say* occurred with first person singular twenty times and it also occurred with *you* (fifteen times), *they* (eight times), *we* (six times), and other NPs (six times). *Can't say* also was predominantly used with *I* (sixty-one times), but also occurred with *you* (ten times), *we* (four times), *he* and a full NP once each and elided twice (presumably the subject was *I*).

The most frequent uses of both affirmative and negative could be regarded as epistemic: these uses reflect the older meaning of *can* which evolved from 'to know'. In Old English, when one said 'can say' it meant have the knowledge to say truthfully. This is still one use that is common today, more so in the negative than in the affirmative; examples (13) and (14) show the negative.

(13) I can't say that I would vote for him.
(14) I can't say I really enjoyed it.

Another use of *can say* that emerged in the corpus conversations is one for constructing an argument. Interestingly here there were several choices of emerging complementizers, such as *okay, you know, all right* and *yes*. This seems to be a shift from the use in 'can truthfully say' to something like 'can justifiably say'.

(15) her opponent can say well, look, they did it to us
(16) Then everybody can say okay nobody gets to do it.

In a construction similar to that found for *can think, can say* can be used in relative clauses with heads such as *the only thing, about all, what else* and *what more.* The negative is not used in such constructions.

Table 9.5 *Categories following* can afford
and can't afford

	Can	Can't
NP-object	60.3% (44)	54.8% (51)
Infinitive	34.2% (25)	39.8% (37)

The important point to note for these phrases with *can* is that their formulaic, subjective uses are different for the affirmative than for the negative. Despite the fact that they obey the general syntactic rules for modals and negatives, their interpretations have been shaped in discourse; they reflect common discourse maneuvers and subjective evaluations that speakers need.

9.4   A more equal distribution: *can* and *can't afford*

The other verb that is used more in the negative than in the affirmative does not have special meaning in the negative; both *can afford* and *can't afford* are prefabs in the sense that they are conventionalized. *Afford*, which formerly meant 'manage or achieve (something planned or desired)' is obsolete in that sense (where, by the way, it was often used with *may*) and is now used instead primarily with *can* to mean 'have the resources to do or have something'. The distribution with NP objects and infinitives is about the same for the negative and affirmative, again supporting their parallel meanings (see Table 9.5).

Further evidence for the conventionalization of the phrases is the fact that *afford* is not used in the sense described above with any other modal auxiliary. Instead, *afford* with other modals has the sense of 'provide', as in the following example:

(17) Said the President: "It is not a cure for business depression but *will afford* better organization for relief in future depressions." (*Time Magazine* 1931).

If a modal or other auxiliary is needed to express the meaning of *can afford*, *can* has to be paraphrased with *be able to,* as in the following examples:

(18) Ultimately no business house will be *able to afford* any mail but air mail. (*Time Magazine* 1923)
(19) I haven't been *able to afford* a TV ad since last Aug. 20, so help me God. (*Time Magazine* 1968)

The example of *can/can't afford* highlights the important issue mentioned earlier: it is not necessarily just the form of the expression that is conventionalized, but rather the meaning is also conventionalized, as shown by the fact that a paraphrase of the modal also will serve.

This point was not so evident in the epistemic examples we discussed earlier, because the expressions that are used to manage the discourse are more fixed in their form than the more propositional *can/can't afford*. Nevertheless, there are some examples that parallel those discussed above, where *be able to* has to be substituted for *can*. Example (20) has the same interpretation as *I can't think of any* (put in the Present Perfect), and example (21) means the same as *you can't believe it* with a future marker. However, (22) with its Present Perfect form and adverb *honestly* seems to have a more propositional meaning than the usual uses of *I can't believe it*.

(20)   There must be some worth mentioning. I just haven't been *able to think* of any. (*Time Magazine* 1966)
(21)   'Good God,' says Bush, 'it is so powerful, you won't be *able to believe it*.' (*Time Magazine* 1990)
(22)   'I just haven't honestly been *able to believe* that he is presidential timber.' (*Time Magazine* 1962)

It appears that some expressions, especially those that have taken on the discourse functions of expressing the subjective evaluations of the speaker, are likely to lose some of their pragmatic quality when put in different tenses or modalities if they have already become highly pragmaticized (Company Company 2006), while expressions which retain a more propositional function may be paraphrased, as it appears that the conceptual view of the situation described may be what is conventionalized, as in 'thinking for speaking' (Slobin 1996, 1997a, 2003).

9.5   Affirmatives more frequent than negatives

Of course, not all cognitive verbs are more frequent with *can't*, as their frequency depends upon what prefabs or discourse markers have evolved. For *imagine* and *understand*, the most frequent formulaic expression is in the affirmative, that is, *I can understand that* and *I can imagine*.

To put the cognitive/epistemic verbs in more perspective, consider the three high-frequency material verbs *go, get* and *put*. For these verbs *can* is more frequent than *can't* and it can be seen from Table 9.6 that all of the negative contexts correspond to an affirmative one. For these material verbs, the formulaic expressions found in the corpus are with particles and prepositions (P-words) rather than with *can*. For instance, we find *go to, go back, go out, get rid of, get enough, put in, put up* and *put on trial*.

Only a few formulaic expressions that require *can* or *can't* were found: one formulaic expression in the negative, *can't go wrong*, and one in the affirmative, *can go ahead and V*.

Table 9.6 *Material verbs with* can *and* can't

		Can	*Can't*
go	P-word	56% (70)	40% (8)
	verb	8% (10)	10% (2)
	intransitive	6% (8)	15% (3)
	NP place	13% (16)	15% (3)
	other	17% (21)	20% (4)
get	P-word	28% (27)	41% (21)
	NP	49% (48)	24% (12)
	adj./part.	8% (8)	8% (4)
	causative	8% (8)	4% (2)
	passive	1% (1)	6% (3)
	other	25% (25)	31% (16)
put	NP PP	51% (20)	54% (7)
	NP P	18% (17)	39% (5)
	P NP	13% (5)	8% (1)

9.6 Interim conclusions

Formulaic expressions drive up token or string frequency; this in turn makes these formulaic expressions easier to access, which then makes them more likely to be used again. Just as in grammaticalization, sufficient high frequency makes expressions more prone to meaning changes through inference; repetition of the same inferences builds their strength in the exemplar representation of meaning and context. Eventually the inferences become part of the meaning.

We have also seen that the function of the string determines what sorts of elements are conventionalized in it. Cognitive verbs with *can* and *can't* tend to move towards prefabs with discourse/pragmatic meaning. Material verbs combine with directionals or other types of adverbs, noun objects and prepositions to form their own set of prefabs.

9.7 *Can* and *can't remember*

Let us look now in more detail at the role of *can* and *can't* in expressions with cognitive verbs, by examining the distribution of *remember* without a modal compared to *remember* with *can* and *can't*.[1] In the corpus search we found the numbers shown in Table 9.7.

All four expressions occur commonly in the corpus. What is intriguing about these expressions is that there does not seem to be much semantic differentiation between *remember* and *can remember* or their negatives. If

Table 9.7 *Number of occurrences in Switchboard of four expressions*

I remember	396
I don't remember	120
I can remember	111
I can't remember	172

Table 9.8 *Distribution in Switchboard of items following four phrases (about 100 tokens each studied), pragmatically determined*

	I remember	*Don't remember*	*Can remember*	*Can't remember*
Time + clause	15	0	19	2*
When clause	14	0	17	0
Wh-word	0	37	0	46
Name	0	14	0	23

I remember something, then that implies that I can remember it; if I can remember it, then I remember it. This is true of the negatives as well. Despite these very similar meanings, the expressions have different syntactic distributions, a fact that is likely to go unnoticed without a corpus-based study. Tables 9.8 and 9.9 show the types of constructions each expression appears in. The tables are based on 100 tokens of each expression but each column does not add up to 100 because fragments, speaker changes, dysfluencies and miscellaneous uses are excluded. *Name* stands for a group of nouns such as *guy's name, his name, title, size, design,* and so on The skewing in distributions shown in Table 9.8 is due to pragmatic factors associated with affirmative and negative contexts.

Temporal phrases plus clause and *when* clauses do not occur in the negative for pragmatic reasons. If the speaker does not or cannot remember a situation, then that situation cannot be described in a temporal or *when* clause. The following examples illustrate the first two types.

(23) Time: I can remember once in high school I wanted some extra money.
           I remember as a kid my parents watching the Ed Sullivan show.
(24) *When*: I can remember when I bought my house I needed help.
           I remember when I was real little, I, we all went to some kind of scary movie.

The two exceptions marked with an asterisk in the table both instantiate a construction with an indefinite temporal followed by a negated clause.

Table 9.9 *Distribution in Switchboard of items following four phrases*

	I remember	Don't remember	Can remember	Can't remember
VERB + *ing*	21	14	21	0
Time + clause	15	0	19	2
Clause	23	0	2	0

(25) I can't remember a year when we didn't have one of some kind (a garden)

(26) I can't remember you know a day that I walked out and the wind wasn't blowing

Wh-objects and *name* objects do not occur in the affirmative in the corpus also for pragmatic reasons:

(27) Wh-word: I can't remember where I read that.
                I don't remember what it's called

(28) *Name:*   I can't remember that guy's name.
                I don't remember the name of it

Thus the distributions in Table 9.8 are due to general differences between affirmative and negative. Interestingly, the *remember/don't remember* and *can remember/can't remember* examples occur in the same constructions (except for the two examples shown in (25) and (26)). Any meaning differences between *remember* with and without *can* seem quite minimal. My intuition is that the use of *can't* implies that the speaker has tried to remember and failed, while the use of *remember* without the modal does not imply this.

In contrast, the distributions shown in Table 9.9 appear to be much more arbitrary. Table 9.9 includes one row – Time + clause – that also appears in Table 9.8. Here we will compare it to the simple clause following the expression. But first consider the distribution of the gerund clauses (VERB + *ing*).

The fact that VERB + *ing* doesn't occur with *can't remember* seems arbitrary as it occurs with both *don't remember* and *can remember,* as in (29).

(29) Verb -*ing:* I can remember being in those earthquakes
                   I don't remember doing all that stuff

The same construction with *can't remember* does not seem ungrammatical, but it simply did not occur in the corpus (# indicates that the utterance type did not occur in the corpus):

(30) #I can't remember doing all that stuff

Perhaps (30) has a slightly more compositional feel to it, as if someone had said *I can remember doing X* and someone else replied *I can't remember doing X.* If this is correct, it would suggest that *don't remember* VERB + *ing* is the prefab.

The other skewed distribution is with a clause that begins with a temporal phrase. While *I remember* takes a clause of any type and also clauses that begin with temporal phrases, overwhelmingly *I can remember* takes a clause beginning with a temporal phrase (time clause); see examples (31) and (32).

(31) Clause: I remember I saw him in a concert.
(32) Temporal phrase: I can remember in the late sixties early seventies you couldn't even hardly find a Japanese car around.

The complement clause with *can remember* always begins with a temporal phrase except in the following two examples. In (33) the complement to *I can remember* does not begin with a temporal phrase, but the phrase *many years ago* is in the previous discourse. It might be that a finite clause following *I can remember* requires a grounding in some specific time in the past.

(33) you know I- I my I remember my my grandmother many years ago when she was in a nursing home before she died ... I can- *I can remember she had several strokes* and the nursing home ...

On the other hand, (34) does not have such a ground. It does have a marker, *uh,* of a pause or disfluency. But even with this example, there is a strong skewing towards the clausal complement to *I can remember* beginning with a temporal phrase.

(34) I can remember uh the entire office got new electric typewriters because we hadn't spent all the budget money in December.

This would mean that the construction for a finite clause following *I can remember* would be as in (35):

(35) [*I can remember* + TEMPORAL PHRASE + CLAUSE]

This construction would predict that (36) would occur, but not (37):

(36) I can remember years ago I saw him in a concert.
(37) #I can remember I saw him in a concert.

There are three very odd properties of (35) as a construction. First, usually the main verb selects the complement type, but here the modal with the verb influences the complement type. This means the presence of the modal is not just the result of another construction, but the expression *can remember* itself must select the complement type. Second, the requirement that a complement begin with a temporal phrase is not usually part of the grammar. Temporal phrases are usually considered optional, especially at the clause level, and the set of factors that embedded clauses can have usually includes whether the verb is finite or not and how the arguments of the verb are marked. It is very unusual for a main verb to select otherwise optional properties of an embedded clause.

Third, while the temporal phrase introduces the complement clause 90 per cent of the time, in (33) it appears that the temporal phrase is in a previous clause. So the co-occurrence requirement may be semantic rather than structural. Even if it is semantic, I would argue that it is arbitrary since *I remember*, whose meaning is so similar to *I can remember,* does not have this requirement at all.

9.8   Why does English distinguish *remember* and *can remember*?

Among the top twenty-one verbs used with *can/can't* are the cognitive verbs, *remember, understand, imagine, think, believe,* and the communication verbs, *tell, say.* Interestingly, from the earliest documentation, *cunnan* OE 'to know' – the etymological source for *can* – was used with verbs of these semantic types, as well as those indicating skills (Goossens 1990).

Example (38) shows the main verb use of *cunnan*. Here it appears with a direct object and has the meaning of 'know'.

(38) Ge dweliað and ne cunnan halige gewritu (Ags. Gospel of Matthew xxii.29)
    'You are led into error and do not know the holy writing'

With cognitive verbs, as in (39), Bybee 2003b argues that it is not so much that *cunnan* is used with the cognitive verb with fuller lexical meaning as it is that the lexical verb is used to shore up and flesh out the cognitive meaning of *cunnan*. That is, the harmonic use of *cunnan* and other verbs of similar meaning may indicate the beginning of the bleaching of the meaning of *cunnan*.

(39) Nu cunne ge tocnawan heofenes hiw (Ags. Gospel of Matthew xvi.3)
    'Now you can distinguish heaven's hue'

With verbs of communication, *cunnan* adds the meaning of being able to say truthfully, that is, having the knowledge to say.

(40) Weras Þa me soðlice secgan cunnon. (c. 1000 Elena 317)
    'Then men can truly say to me'

While the main verb use of *cunnan* disappeared by the modern period, the use of *can* with cognitive and communication verbs is continuously documented (Bybee 2003b). As we mentioned in our discussion of *can say*, the meaning of this phrase still carries some of its earlier semantics of 'knowledge to say'. With cognitive verbs we continue the situation of the modal and the main verb being in a kind of harmony, such that the meaning of *can* + a cognitive verb is not that much different from the meaning of the cognitive verb alone. These examples make it clear that prefabricated sequences are highly conventional-ized and can remain in the language a long time. Furthermore, older meanings can be retained in prefabricated chunks (Hopper 1987, Bybee and Torres Cacoullos 2009).

9.9   Conclusions

This small study of the use of *can* and *can't* in high-frequency combinations has revealed a number of facts that seem out of sync with many assumptions about syntactic structures. First, as a marked category, we would expect negatives to be less frequent than affirmatives, but instead we found that with several high-frequency verbs, the negative *can't* was more frequent than the affirmative *can*. It turned out of course that the reason for this was that the negative modal combined with a cognitive or communicative verb to constitute a prefabricated sequence with special discourse functions. To underscore this conclusion we also saw that material verbs such as *go, get* and *put* had a much more usual distribution with regard to negation.

Then examining more carefully the differences between *(don't) remember* and *can/can't remember* we uncovered several interesting properties of the special *can remember* construction. First, counter to expectations based on more salient constructions across languages, the presence of the auxiliary makes a difference in determining what type of complement the main verb can take. Usually the main verb determines the complement type, for example, *that*-clause vs. *–ing* complement, so it is surprising that *remember* and *can remember* have different complement types. Second, the element that is conditioned by *can + remember* is an optional part of the embedded clause, an initial temporal phrase. What this example teaches us is that frequently repeated structures can become conventionalized, and therefore part of grammar, even if the elements that become conventionalized together are not elements that usually depend upon one another in the more familiar types of grammatical constructions.

Finally, a finding that emerges from this study is a contrast between discourse markers that have taken on pragmatic and subjective functions and tend not to be alterable by tense, person, or modifiers on the one hand (Scheibman 2000, Traugott and Dasher 2002, Company 2006) and formulae that constitute the usual way of describing a situation, which can have altered form, on the other. The former constitute prefabs in which the form is fixed while the latter constitute constructions in which some of the meaning may be expressed in other parts of the discourse.

10 Exemplars and grammatical meaning: the specific and the general

10.1 Introduction

It is important that meaning be specifically addressed in the context of usage-based theory, because as we have seen in many parts of our discussion, morphosyntactic form is very often influenced by meaning. The discussion so far has made reference to meaning a number of times, especially with regard to diachronic change, gradual reanalysis, meaning differences between prefabricated vs. compositional expressions and the meaning of members of categories that fill slots in constructions. Here I want to address directly the matter of grammatical meaning, as usage-based studies of grammaticalization and exemplar models make predictions about the nature of grammatical meaning which have not necessarily been heeded by those who approach meaning from a synchronic structural perspective.

Based on their success in dealing with phonetic and phonological problems, I have applied exemplar modelling to constructions in the previous chapters of this book. In this chapter we will see what the consequences are of analysing grammatical meaning in terms of experienced-based, rich memory representations. I will argue that the semantic categories for grammatical constructions and morphemes are not defined by necessary and sufficient conditions, but rather have the properties that have been discovered for other categories of grammar. Because of their rich category structure and pockets of high-frequency use, it is only natural that grammatical semantic categories (just as lexical ones) could split into two or more categories, creating polysemy in grammatical forms. Exemplar categorization both predicts and models such changes. Rich memory representations also entail that elements of context and inference from context would be included in exemplar representations. This would mean that repeated and conventionalized inferences do not need to be calculated each time, but could become part of a representation.

The basic tenets of a structural approach to meaning – the abstractness of grammatical meaning and the use of oppositions – come under examination with the result that these principles are shown not to be wrong, but to be only part of a fuller picture, which also includes concrete and polysemous categories and layering or overlapping meanings, rather than strict binary oppositions. Because what we talk about and how we talk about it provide a rich and varied landscape, the meanings we need to use cannot be apportioned into a one or two dimensional space, but must instead fit the curves and contours of human experience.

The organization of this chapter proceeds from an in-depth discussion of the mechanisms of semantic change in grammaticalization and what the processes of change indicate about the nature of grammatical meaning in comparison with the principles of abstraction and opposition in structural theories of grammatical meaning. The fact that grammatical meaning comes from lexical meaning is explored first in section 10.2, then the mechanisms of change and their effects are discussed: generalization of meaning in section 10.3, pragmatic strengthening in section 10.4, retention of lexical meaning in section 10.5 and absorption of meaning from context in section 10.6. The latter mechanism is operative in the development of zero morphemes, which is discussed in section 10.7. The remaining sections contrast this emerging view of grammatical meaning with the notions of abstract, invariant meaning in section 10.9, and of oppositions in section 10.10. Finally, the discussion addresses the interaction of human experiences with grammatical meaning.

10.2   Grammatical meaning comes from lexical meaning

The source of many of the ideas to be discussed here is not precisely exemplar theory, but rather the empirical examination of the way grammatical meaning arises and changes over time. The diachronic dimension is important, not because speakers know the source and history of the forms of their language, but because the diachrony determines a great deal about synchronic distributions and meanings of forms. It is also important as a source of evidence about cognitive categorization, since such categorizations make predictions about possible changes. Any synchronic characterization of meaning must be compatible with both prior and future changes in meaning. Finally, if we attempt to understand why grammatical meaning is the way it is, we must examine how and why it arises. To this end we examine the mechanisms by which meaning changes in grammaticalization in more detail than in Chapter 6.

Studies of grammaticalization make it abundantly clear that grammatical meaning arises out of lexical meaning in almost all cases (one important class of exceptions is zero morphemes, which will be discussed in section 10.7). That means that there is actual semantic substance that can be handed down across generations in grammatical morphemes just as in lexical morphemes. That semantic substance is discernible and acquirable through the contexts of use of grammatical morphemes within constructions. The semantic substance of grammatical morphemes is particularly evident in cases where we can compare two similar grammatical morphemes that have evolved from different source constructions, but we can also see it in contexts in which the grammatical morpheme has retained its older meaning and/or distribution.

In discussing meaning change from lexical to grammatical, we will mention the three mechanisms of semantic change that are most important in grammaticalization – bleaching or generalization of meaning, pragmatic strengthening through inference, and absorption of meaning from linguistic and extra-linguistic context.

10.3   Generalization of meaning: the case of English *can*

10.3.1   Overview

As we mentioned in Chapter 6, generalization of meaning occurs as a construction which gradually extends its distribution to occur with new lexical items and in new contexts. It is important to bear in mind that such changes are part of everyday language use; speakers need to be able to extend constructions to new uses in order to express new ideas. This section illustrates this process with the example of the development of the modal auxiliary *can* from Old English to the present. First, I present an overview of the generalization of the meaning of *can* and then I proceed to represent the changes in more detail via an exemplar representation of the meaning of this modal.

Generalizations of meaning entail the loss of some of the earlier specific meaning of the lexical item – in this case Old English *cunnan* which meant 'know'. When used with another verb, especially one indicating a skill, it meant 'know how to' and indicated mental ability. Later in Middle English it indicated both mental and physical ability of the agent. From there it generalized further to root possibility, which means 'general enabling conditions'. These are conditions outside the agent and include both physical and social conditions (Goossens 1990, Bybee 2003b), as the following two contemporary examples show:

(1) 'Why don't we just go for the biggest star we *can get*? Why don't we call Jack Nicholson?' (*Time Magazine* 2000)
(2) You *can read* all the profiles and other features at our two environmental websites. (*Time Magazine* 2000)

In these examples, it is not the particular abilities of the agents (*we* and *you*, which is generic in this example) but rather external circumstances that are indicated. This generalized meaning is also more abstract than ability or knowledge; in this case *can* is paraphrasable as 'it is possible for X to Y'.

At the same time, though, certain uses of *can* retain older meaning. It is still possible for *can* to indicate mental ability (3) or physical ability (4).

(3) But could any ritual prepare the six shamans – so removed from modernity that Don Nicolas *can read* the Incan code of knotted cords but speaks no Spanish – for the big city? (*Time* 2000)

(4) A sea lion *can swim* up to 25 m.p.h. for short bursts, enabling it to nab an underwater foe by snaring it in a clamp placed in its mouth. (*Time* 2003)

Also as we noted in Chapter 9, *can* is still used with cognitive and communication verbs in very much the same way it was in Old English. Thus it is important to note that despite the generalization of its meaning in some contexts, older, more specific meanings can still be invoked in particular contexts.

The complex interaction of senses of *can* is built up by speakers through their experience with particular tokens. Speakers store these tokens in exemplar representations, sorting them into clusters according to their interpretations in context. In the following I illustrate what such a set of exemplars would look like, using an older stage of English with comments about how the changes into Present Day English would be represented. In the process, we see more specifically how generalization (i.e. bleaching) is accomplished in use over time.

10.3.2   Can *in Middle English*

Consider the situation with *can* in Middle English, as based on the texts of *The Canterbury Tales* (Goossens 1990, Bybee 2003b). Continuing from Old English, the predecessor of *can, cunnan,* could be used as a main verb and with three classes of complement verbs. First, in the main verb use, *can* (spelled *kan*) in Chaucer's usage had a direct object and meant 'know'.

(5) In alle the ordres foure is noon that *kan*
    So muchel of daliaunce and fair langage. (Prologue, 210)
    'In all four orders there is none that knows so much of dalliance and fair language.'

Then there were uses with three classes of complement verbs. (1) With verbs denoting skills, the original 'know how to' meaning is basically equivalent to an ability sense (6):

(6) Ther seen men who *kan* juste, and who *kan* ryde,
    'Now see men who can joust and who can ride!' (The Knight's Tale, 1746)

(2) With communication verbs a different interpretation continues from Old English: as example (7) shows, the meaning with communication verbs indicated 'knowledge to say or tell truthfully'.

(7) As I cam nevere, I *kan* nat tellen wher (A. Kn. 2810)
    'As I was never there, I cannot say where'

However, a change occurred in Middle English such that certain prefabricated uses of *can say* and *can tell* developed as rhetorical devices for use in narrative (Bybee and Torres Cacoullos 2009). In these prefabs, as shown in (8)–(13), the meaning of *can* loses its knowledge interpretation and comes to indicate ability instead. For instance, in example (8), which appears to be a prefab since it occurred three times in only 300 tokens, and (9) through (11), which are variations on (8), the narrator is completing a description and moving on. He says no more, not because his knowledge is exhausted, but because he wants to continue with the tale. (Examples from Chaucer.)

(8) I kan sey yow namoore (B. ML. 175; B. NP. 4159; G. CY. 651)
     'I can tell you no more'
(9) I kan no more seye (TC. 1. 1051)
(10) I kan sey yow no ferre (A. Kn. 2060)
(11) I kan no moore expound in this manner (B. Pri. 1725)

The ability sense is especially apparent in (12) (which occurred four times) and (13) where *bettre* 'better' indicates that the quality being modified is not truthfulness, but ability.

(12) I kan no bettre sayn (B. ML. 42; B. ML. 874; E. Mch. 1874; I. Pars. 54)
     'I cannot say it better'
(13) I kan telle it no bettre (B. ML. 881)

(3) Finally, cognitive verbs were used in Old English with *cunnan* 'to know' in a kind of harmonic expression in which the particular lexical verb, such as 'discern, know, remember, distinguish, understand', made the 'knowing' indicated by *cunnan* more explicit. Such uses continue in Middle English, as example (14) shows and in Present Day English, where *can remember* means just about the same thing as *remember* as we saw in Chapter 9,

(14) To mannes wit, that for oure ignorance
     Ne *konne* noght knowe his prudent purveiance. (*The Man of Law's Tale*, 483)
     'For man's wit, which in its ignorance
     Cannot conceive His careful purveyance.'

The innovation apparent in Middle English is the use of *can* for ability with verbs other than those already mentioned, that is verbs indicating skills, communication or cognition. Here are some examples of *can* (*kan*) in uses where the interpretation could be either 'know how to' or 'is able'.

(15) He that me kepte fro the false blame,
     While I was on the lond amonges yow,
     He *kan* me kepe from harm and eek fro shame (*The Man of Law's Tale*, 29)
     'He that kept me from false blame while I lived among you, He can still keep me from harm and also from shame' (*He* = God)

(16) Thus *kan* oure Lady bryngen out of wo Woful Custance, and many another mo. (*The Man of Law's Tale*, 977)
'Thus can Our Lady bring from deepest woe Woeful Constance, and many another.'

(17) Now han ye lost myn herte and al my love! I *kan* nat love a coward, by my feith (B. NP. 4100–4101)
'Now have you lost my heart and all my love; I cannot love a coward, by my faith.'

(18) But I wol passe as lightly as I *kan*. (B. NP. 4129)
'But I'll pass on as lightly as I can.'

Since these combinations with *can* seem to be still analysable in the examples found in the texts, we have to think of the semantic characterization of *can* as an overlapping set of meanings conditioned in some cases by context – in particular, by the lexical verb. Figure 10.1 illustrates how the interpretations of *can* may have been organized by constructions especially in Middle English. The columns show a stage-like progression of meaning change.[1] Across the top of the figure are horizontal lines indicating which constructions were used in the period before Middle English (Old English) and subsequent to Middle English (Present Day English).

Because ability is the most general meaning and can be used with almost any verb to yield a coherent meaning, it is the interpretation that is most likely to become more frequent. While ability increases as the reading for *can* in Early Modern and Present Day English, the other uses become less frequent. The use of *can* as a main verb has, of course, completely disappeared.[2]

Figure 10.1 displays the complexity of the meaning of *can* in Middle English. Note that it includes both the more lexical senses and the more generalized ones, and that certain contexts favor certain of these meanings. Such a display for Present Day English would omit stage I [*can* + NP], it would show little if any extra meaning added to the *can* + Cognitive verbs construction and it would have very few exemplars of the 'knowledge to say' reading of *can* + Communication verbs. A huge [*can* + other verbs] cluster would have ability readings and in addition, the root possibility sense would occupy a large semantic space. We return in section 10.11 to some comments about how root possibility has evolved in Present Day English.

Once again, I would like to emphasize that the changes between Old English and Middle English are noticeable only because we are spanning several centuries and looking at 'before' and 'after' stages. The actual changes involved small choices made by speakers in individual speech events, based on their prior experience with these constructions. Thus in this section we have seen how a few very specific uses of OE *cunnan* expanded into a wide range of uses thereby generalizing the meaning of this modal.

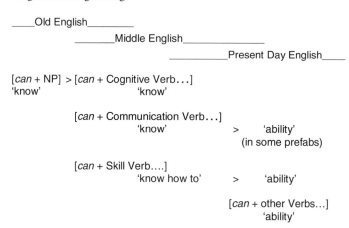

Figure 10.1 Exemplar representation of Middle English meanings of *can* and their persistence across time from Old English to Present Day English

10.4   Pragmatic strengthening

Pragmatic strengthening has been championed as a type of semantic change in grammaticalization by Elizabeth Traugott (Traugott 1989, Traugott and Dasher 2002, but see also Dahl 1985, Bybee 1988b, Bybee et al. 1994). This important mechanism of change allows inferences and meanings supplied by the context to become part of the meaning of a grammatical morpheme or construction. In contrast with generalization, pragmatic inference allows new meaning to become associated with a construction. Such new meanings derive from the context and do not form a direct line from the lexical meaning to the grammatical. However, it is interesting that inferential changes are cross-linguistically quite similar as predicted by the unidirectionality principle. This fact suggests that the inferences that are preferred in context are often very similar across cultures (see Chapter 11 for more discussion).

Inferential reasoning is an important, but quite routine, part of communication. As it would be much too cumbersome to express in overt form everything we need to convey with language, much is left to the hearer's knowledge of context and the powers of inference. Thus the interpretations that eventually lead to what we regard as a change in meaning are taking place all the time in ordinary language use. It is only when a construction is associated strongly with the same inference that speakers then might use it to express the inference in the absence of its earlier meaning. At this point we acknowledge that a change has occurred, but in fact many novel usage-events have set the stage and should themselves be regarded as 'changes'.

Change by inference (the conventionalization of implicature) does not produce the smooth semantic gradience that change by generalization does. Common inferences impute notions of intention or causation, for instance, where none was originally expressed. Thus the earlier meaning and the inferred meaning may produce ambiguity. Still the existence of many overlapping or ambiguous cases makes such change gradual in its implementation. In the following subsections I discuss two instances of semantic change involving pragmatic inference, both of which have been referred to earlier in the book – the case of grammaticalizing futures and the complex preposition *in spite of*.

10.4.1   Futures

Bybee et al. 1994 argue that the development of future tense markers usually involves a stage in which the markers express intention of the subject. This meaning of intention cannot come about by semantic generalization, but rather must be attributed to frequently made inferences. This hypothesis is supported by cross-linguistic reports of an intention use for futures that evolve from all sources – movement towards a goal, volition, obligation and even temporal adverbs. For instance, the English *be going to* phrase is used with its lexical meaning in Early Modern English, but often this lexical meaning implies intention, especially when the subject is first person singular. Thus in Shakespeare's English, in order to answer the question *Where are you going?*, it is appropriate to say *I am going to deliver some letters*, even though this answer does not give a place in answer to *where*. It can instead be taken to express the speaker's intention and apparently that is often satisfactory from the questioner's perspective. Thus from first person progressive movement towards a goal, the implication of intention can become conventionalized.

Future markers from volition sources (e.g. English *will*) and obligation sources (e.g. English *shall*) also have intention uses before they develop future uses. Consider this Middle English example from *Sir Gawain and the Green Knight*, where both *shall* and *will* are used with an intention sense, though at this point they both still express much of their earlier meaning of obligation and volition respectively, as I have tried to show in the translation.

(19) And I *schal* erly ryse, on hunting *wyl* I wende. (Gawain, 1101–2)
      'And I have to get up early, because I want to go hunting.'

Though futures much more rarely develop from temporal adverbs cross-linguistically, even in such a case, an intention use can be documented. Romaine 1995 shows for the creole language, Tok Pisin, that the future marker *bai,* which evolved from the phrase *by and by* or *bai m bai* is used to express intention, as in (20):

(20) Ating bai mi go long maket nau.
      'I think I will go to the market now.' (Romaine 1995: 413)

Thus from the expression of first-person volition (*I want to*), obligation (*I have to*), movement towards a goal (*I'm going to*) and time later (*I do it by and by*), the hearer can infer intention unless that inference is cancelled explicitly or in the context. Because both speakers and hearers are interested in one another's intentions, this particular inference is frequently made, and thus can become part of the meaning of the construction.

10.4.2   In spite of

Another typical case of meaning change by frequently made inferences is the shift to concessive meaning for the phrase *in spite of*, discussed in Chapter 8. There we saw that the phrase, whose meaning was earlier 'in defiance of', gradually generalized to the point that the object of *in spite of* could be any sort of opposing force or obstacle. The major inferential change, leading to a concessive meaning, was due to an inference that if a situation was attained in the face of obstacles, then given these obstacles, the situation was not expected to be attained. This meaning is more subjective, in the sense that it provides the speaker's evaluation of the unexpectedness of the situation described. Consider two examples from Chapter 8. The first (21) is an example of the opposing force or obstacle meaning, but it bears the implication that the main clause event is unexpected given these conditions. The second example has only the counter-expectation sense of *in spite of*, as the clause introduced by this phrase provides no obstacle to the main clause situation. The added subjectivity of both examples comes in the choice of the writer to juxtapose two clauses in such a way as to express his or her own surprise.

(21)   *In spite of* the rough conditions, travel advisories and the war on terror-ism, scores of older Americans are uprooting their lives to help needy nations improve their living conditions. (*Time Magazine* 2003)
(22)   Yet *in spite of* music's remarkable influence on the human psyche, scien-tists have spent little time attempting to understand why it possesses such potency. (*Time Magazine* 2000)

Like generalization of meaning, change by pragmatic inference produces a more abstract meaning. In the case of *in spite of* it expresses a concessive rela-tion, which can increase the frequency of use of the expression, as it can apply to more contexts than the obstacle meaning, as we see in (22), which has no obstacle interpretation.

We have already discussed the fact that the conventionalization of these prag-matic inferences as part of the meaning of an expression is nicely accounted for in a rich-memory representation in which the inferences drawn for each exemplar are registered in memory along with the construction used. Just as the representation in Figure 10.1 is complex, so must be the representations that include both an earlier, more concrete meaning and the inferences drawn from it, because once the inference becomes stable enough to be used without the concrete meaning, the concrete meaning does not instantly disappear.

10.5   Retention of lexical meaning

Because change in meaning takes place incrementally and because speakers are able to form many local generalizations (as predicted by an exemplar model), there are many examples of more specific meanings being retained as grammaticalization proceeds. Consider the English future as marked by *will*. In the previous section I commented on the diachronic development of *will*. It came from a verb meaning 'want', and acquired intention uses by inference, as described above. A further inference from some cases of intention is prediction. That is, what the subject intends to do, one can predict that he or she will do. A prediction is an assertion about future time; thus when the speaker asserts that someone has an intention, the hearer can infer (not always correctly, of course) that the speaker is also predicting what the subject will do. Consider the following Early Modern English example, where both intention and prediction can be taken to be conveyed:

(23) Madam, my lord *will* go away to-night; A very serious business calls on him. (*All's Well That Ends Well*, II.4)

Examples such as (24) with a dual intention/prediction interpretation still occur.

(24) The procedure is on the appeal and I *will* fight until the last drop of my blood to demonstrate my innocence. (COCA 1990)

In addition, example (25) has both interpretations because the main verb can be interpreted as either dynamic or stative.

(25) I *will* remember to my grave the response we got. The response was, "You have to do what you have to do." (COCA 1990)

As prediction may be thought of as the core meaning of future tense, it is fair to say that *will* marks future tense in Present Day English and examples where it functions this way are common. Consider the following:

(26) if she's not defeated in this current round, I suspect that she *will* be retiring within the next few months. (COCA 1990)
(27) Off of public lands in Nevada alone over the next five years, more than $10 billion worth of gold is going to be removed. And you and I *will* not get a penny for that. (COCA 1990)

However, this is not all that *will* does by any means. Corpora contain a good many examples of cases in which *will* reflects its lexical source meaning of volition by indicating willingness (Coates 1983, Bybee and Pagliuca 1987). One context is in *if*-clauses that are part of a conditional sentence.

(28) This hacker is offering me $1,000 if I *will* give him a declined credit card that has a mother's maiden name (COCA Spoken 2005)

(29) If they *will* just give me three weeks, this area will knock their eyes out. (The second *will* in (29) signals prediction.)

Another context is in a construction with the phrase *find/get someone who will ...* where the *will* signals willingness, as in (30):

(30) and now he got someone who *will* stand up and say, 'Well, this jury did a terrible job, because I know the case better, but gee, no one in law enforcement will listen to me.' (COCA 1990)

Perhaps the most common context in which we find the maintenance of the fuller lexical meaning is in the negative where *will not* or *won't* commonly indicates refusal or unwillingness, as in (31) (see also the second *will* in [30]):

(31) All right, Raymond, I guess the best question ... since she *will* not be specific, I'll follow up. (COCA 1990)

(32) she does not want to communicate. It's not that she can't, but she *will* not answer you. I tried – (COCA 1994)

Along with prediction, which is its most common use, *will* in Present Day English also expresses intention and willingness, and in a negative context, refusal or unwillingness. This situation of polysemy stemming from prior meanings of a future marker and more recent changes by inference is not at all unusual; the cross-linguistic survey in Bybee et al. 1994 turned up quite a number of cases in which an older modal meaning of a future, such as volition or obligation, were still available in certain contexts. The interesting point is that the lexical source of the future predicts which modal nuances will be available. Note that if one tries to substitute a different future marker, such as *be going to* or *shall* in examples (28)–(32), the result is a change in the meaning or even an anomalous interpretation.

The retention of some of the earlier meaning in specific contexts is a natural outcome of exemplar storage of constructions and their meaning. The particular constructions we have discussed here would not lend themselves to the prediction inference and thus a shift to prediction as their meaning. Hypothetical *if*-clauses do not contain assertions and thus do not contain predictions, though they might refer to future time. Future time reference for a hypothetical is expressed by the simple present in an *if*-clause.[3] Also, the *someone who will* relative clause construction can contain future time reference, but not the assertion of prediction.

However, as the examples show, special constructions are not necessary for the intention and willingness or unwillingness readings to show up. Examples

(24) and (25) are cases that can have both intention and prediction readings, but there are also examples where only intention is expressed:

(33)   And in a controversial compromise with the Sandinistas, Mrs. Chamorro announced she *will* keep Daniel Ortega's brother, Humberto, as commander of the 70,000 man Sandinista army. (COCA 1990)

Here only intention or willingness is a possible reading since Mrs. Chamorro would not make a prediction of this nature about herself. The existence of such cases as well as those where *will* occurs in a specific construction argues strongly for the recognition of polysemy in grammatical meaning. While a designation such as 'after the moment of speech' is common to all the examples we have seen, it in no way is sufficient for characterizing *will*. Despite the importance of context, the context alone cannot supply the intention and willingness meanings; they must be an inherent part of the semantic representation for *will*. Thus the meaning of *will* must include prediction, intention and willingness; what was formerly inferred is now part of the meaning.

10.6   Absorption of meaning from context

Grammatical morphemes are always part of a construction and their meaning can only be understood as deriving from the meaning of the whole construction. What might seem like a single grammatical morpheme could very well participate in a variety of constructions, each of which has a different meaning. The contribution of the grammatical morpheme to the construction can differ according to the stages of grammaticalization. In early stages the grammatical morpheme is meaningful in itself and supplies part of the meaning of the construction; later, however, as the grammatical morpheme becomes more and more bleached of its meaning, it may well be only conventionally a part of the construction and in fact may derive its meaning from the overall construction rather than making a contribution itself. This situation is described in Bybee et al. 1994 as 'absorption of meaning from the context'.

Consider the French sentence negator *ne ... pas*. The first part of this construction is the negator inherited from Latin, which occurs before the finite verb and the second part is from a noun meaning 'step'. The second part was presumably added as an emphatic, with the meaning 'to VERB not a step'. At first a number of other nouns occurred in the same position as *pas*, including Old French *mie* 'crumb', *gote* 'drop', *amende* 'almond', as well as *point* 'dot, point', which still occurs occasionally in this position (Hopper 1991). Thus *pas* did not originally have negative meaning, but today it is used independently to signal negation, as in the expression *pas beaucoup* 'not much' and when the negative particle *ne* is deleted in casual speech, as in *je sais pas* 'I don't know.' It seems evident that *pas* took on negative meaning from the construction it occurred in and is able to carry that negative meaning into other constructions.[4]

10.7   Zero morphemes

A zero morpheme expresses meaning but has no overt marker. An example is the singular of count nouns in English, where the lack of a suffix on, for example, *the horse*, signals that only one horse is referred to. A zero morpheme is always just one member of a grammatical category; the other members have to have an overt marker. Thus the English singular for nouns can be signalled by the absence of a suffix only because the plural is signalled by the presence of a suffix. Zeroes can only occur in grammatical categories that are obligatory. That is, zero can only indicate singular in count nouns because number is obligatorily expressed in English for count nouns. In a language without obligatory number marking on nouns, such as Japanese, the lack of a number marker does not necessarily express singular; thus it is not a zero morpheme.

The meaning of zero grammatical morphemes cannot develop in the same way as the meaning of overt morphemes, as there is no lexical source for their meanings. Instead it appears that zero morphemes develop because an opposing morpheme has grammaticalized, leaving zero to indicate its opposition (García and van Putte 1989, Bybee 1994). In this section we examine the development of 'zero' meaning.

It is well known that zero morphemes are not randomly distributed among the members of grammatical categories, but instead are cross-linguistically predictable (Greenberg 1966, Bybee 1985). For instance, zero markers are found cross-linguistically on singular nouns, but not duals or plurals; for present tense but not past or future; for inflectional perfective but not usually imperfective; for indicative but not usually subjunctive, and so on. Greenberg 1966 also shows that the zero morphemes or unmarked members of categories are also the most frequently occurring in discourse.

In Bybee 1994 I provide an explanation for these correspondences with reference to grammaticalization. Grammaticalization of overt markers occurs because of the use of extra words to divert the hearer from the most frequent interpretation. For example, referential nouns are most frequently individuated in discourse and referred to in the singular (Hopper and Thompson 1984). Thus if the singular is not intended, then some extra linguistic material is required to indicate plural. The continued use of this extra material can lead to its grammaticalization as a marker of plural. In such a case, no overt marker for singular develops because singular meaning is correctly inferred in most cases.[5]

Bybee 1994 considers the development of zeroes in tense/aspect systems. The distribution of zero morphemes in the sample of seventy-six languages used in Bybee et al. 1994 shows that the proportion of zeroes in tense and aspect systems is actually small: only seventeen markers coded were zeroes compared to over 200 overtly expressed markers. Among the commonly expressed inflectional tenses and aspects, present habitual and the general present can have zero expression, but present progressive does not; in the past, only perfective can have zero expression. In the following I propose an explanation of these facts with regard to the use of the English zero present in conversation.

As often noted, the structure of the present tense is quite different from that of the past (Binnick 1991, Bybee et al. 1994, Bybee 1994, Dahl 1995, Michaelis 2006). The past tense signals that the situation described by the clause occurred before the moment of speech. In terms of a timeline, the past encompasses a vast range. It follows that within the past a language can, but need not, also distinguish either a simple (narrative) past or a perfective form, contrasting with a past progressive and/or a past habitual. The present is more problematic, for while the parallel characterization of the present would be concurrent with the moment of speech, the moment of speech is a point rather than a range, so only statives and progressives can actually be concurrent with the speech event. Habitual and generic meaning describes situations that occur within a time period that includes the moment of speech, but may not be actually ongoing at speech time.[6]

In English, a zero verbal marker indicates present habitual, as in example (34). The present progressive is expressed by *be* + VERB + *ing,* which in (35) indicates a situation ongoing at the moment of speech.[7]

(34) He still *takes* the horses nobody else wants, older horses, horses with foals, with ears frozen off or otherwise less beautiful than those in cigarette ads. (COCA 1990)

(35) I'm *taking* a huge chance just talking to you now because it's not going to be liked. (COCA 1990)

Note that the lack of the Progressive as in (34) requires an habitual interpretation. A further use of the simple present is for narratives, sometimes called the 'historic present.' This use is very frequent in journalistic prose, such as that found the COCA database. Here is an example:

(36) The guy's standing there, this little photographer, and Tommy just comes running across the street, slams into him, knocks him down, breaks his pelvis. (COCA 1998)

The aspects available in the past differ from those of the present. In the past tense, we have narrative (perfective), habitual and progressive aspectual readings. Typical narrative sequences such as (37) use simple Past in English. But simple Past can also be used in habitual situations, such as (38). Other ways of expressing the past habitual are with *used to* and *would,* as in example (39) and (40) respectively.

(37) I *noticed* a woman who *came* up and she kind of *brushed* me aside and she *headed* right for one of the local photographers, one of the commercial photographers. (COCA 1990)

(38) The same local commercial photographers who *took* photos and then *sold* them back to the party goers night after night were also supplying the newspaper which, at the time, had only a small staff of its own. (COCA 1990)

(39) They *used to* stand in the back of the room and laugh for me. (COCA 1990)

(40) He kept asking me, "Well, could it have happened like this?" and I *would* say yeah and he *would* tell me to repeat it in my own words and the other officer *would* write it down. (COCA 1990)

Simple Past in English is not used, however, for progressive situations in the past – that is, situations taking place at the reference point in the past. Instead, the past progressive is used, as in (41).

(41) As he *was taking* me home, we were stopped by police and it turned out that he was wanted for about seven counts of rape in another state. (COCA 1990)

The difference between the aspectual marking in the present and in the past is that in the present the most usual interpretation of the zero-marked present is the habitual one, while a simple past (which has overt expression) is interpreted as narrative unless there are overt indications that it should be interpreted as habitual (see *night after night* as in example (38)). Why is there this difference between present and past and where does the meaning that is not overtly signalled come from?

The important point to note is that in the human experience, and in what humans want to communicate about, the present and past are not parallel. It is not just that the precise moment of speech does not serve as a very good reference time because it is a point rather than a range, but, in addition when people talk in the present tense they are talking more about how things are – in terms of states and habitual situations – than what happened (Thompson and Hopper 2001, Scheibman 2002). Thus I argued in Bybee 1994 that the default meaning of the present would more likely be habitual and the default interpretation of the past would be perfective.

This proposal can be fleshed out by considering again where the habitual meaning that is signalled by zero in English verbs comes from. In Old English there was a Past tense and a zero-marked Present, which was used for habitual, progressive and future meanings with dynamic verbs and of course for present with stative verbs. We have already mentioned the development of various future markers; in addition, the progressive construction of *be* + VERB + *ing* developed and became quite frequent in the last few centuries. These developments whittled away at the Present territory. The Present can still be used for future if the context makes it clear that future is intended, but it cannot be used for progressive. The result is that the usual interpretation of the present with dynamic verbs is habitual.

As I mentioned above, the more usual interpretation is often zero-marked and grammaticalization occurs to indicate the less usual or more specific meaning. In this case, the claim would be that in the present for dynamic verbs the default interpretation is present habitual. How can we show that this is the case? If the default interpretation is the most usual, then present habituals should be more frequent in language use than present progressives. In English we can count forms to determine the frequency relations since the progressive is overtly marked. We assume that in languages such as Middle English in which the distinction is not marked, the same proportion of progressives and habituals occurred as in Present Day English; the former were just not overtly marked.

Using the conversational data from the Corpus of Spoken American English which form the basis of Scheibman 2002, Table 10.1 shows that 78 per cent of dynamic verbs occur in the simple Present, while only 22 per cent are used in the Progressive. Simple Present has an habitual interpretation except in a small percentage of simple present uses which are narrative presents: only eleven instances were identified, fewer than 1 per cent of the total of simple Presents in these conversational interchanges. Given this preponderance of habitual uses in the present tense, it is reasonable to assume that the habitual reading would take precedence over the progressive even in languages where neither is marked, provided that conversational practice is similar to that of Present Day English.

The present habitual meaning did not arise from a lexical source, but rather from the most common interpretation of the present tense. In Bybee 1994 I argue that the context is very rich in meaning, and, as we have noted above, hearers and speakers are quite aware of the possible inferences one can make given the utterance and the rich context. As the Progressive becomes more frequent, hearers can infer that if it is not used, its meaning is not intended. Thus if the Progressive does not appear, habitual must be the meaning. García and van Putte 1989 argue that with repetition, the association of an inference such as 'the speaker did not say X, s/he must mean Y' can become automated; the brain constructs a shortcut by which the lack of a marker comes to have meaning and that meaning comes out of the rich context in which we communicate. We conclude, then, that while zero morphemes do not have meaning that is descended from lexical meaning as overt morphemes do, they are still ripe with meaning, which has been derived from their common contexts of use.

Table 10.1 *Simple present and progressive marking in non-modal predicates*[8]

	Progressive	Simple Present	*Total*
Dynamic verb types:			
material	67	140	**207**
perception	0	15	**15**
corporeal	13	24	**37**
feeling	1	27	**28**
verbal	14	134	**148**
Total dynamic types	**95 (22%)**	**340 (78%)**	**435**
Stative verb types:			
cognition	7	236	**243**
existential	5	53	**58**
relational	5	565	**570**
Total stative types	**17 (2%)**	**854 (98%)**	**871**
Total	**112**	**1194**	**1306**

10.8 Nature of semantic categories for grammatical forms

Thus the diachronic evidence suggests that grammatical forms and constructions are full of meaning, some of it originating in the lexical sources of the forms and some of it supplied by conventionalization of common discourse inferences. An exemplar model provides the means for describing this situation, where the meaning of grammatical forms and constructions can be varied in local contexts and supplied with the richness of the inferences hearers can make from the communicative situation. But even without the diachronic evidence, there is no reason to suppose that grammatical meaning is fully abstract and consists of necessary and sufficient conditions, because no other aspect of the linguistic meaning has these properties. The studies by Rosch and colleagues showed that semantic categories for the meanings of words show prototype effects rather than necessary and sufficient conditions (see the discussion in section 5.3). Lakoff 1987 develops the idea of radial categories that provide for the polysemy found in categories of various types. Thus there is every reason to suppose that grammatical meaning has a similar structure.

Surprisingly, however, there are many linguists, including those who subscribe to construction grammar, who hold the view that each grammatical morpheme or construction must have one and only one invariant meaning and that all deviations from this meaning are supplied by the lexical context. This view is particularly popular in studies of verbal aspect (Contini-Morava

1989, Smith 1997, Michaelis 2006), and arises from the fact that verbs of different lexical categories require different interpretations of aspectual markers (Vendler 1967). Thus the analyst hopes to simplify the aspectual system by showing that a single abstract meaning for a member of the system can be molded in context to give all the surface interpretations.

As we have seen, grammatical meaning is abstract and grammaticalization shows an increasing abstractness in such meaning. However, we have also seen that grammaticalization does not wipe the slate clean – often more specific meanings are retained over a long period of time, as we have seen in the discussion of English *shall*, *will* and *can*. Thus an error often made by linguists who see grammar as discrete structure is to elevate a tendency to an absolute constraint or principle. The evidence reviewed in this chapter suggests that the interesting feature of grammatical meaning is the way the abstract or general interacts with the more specific (Bybee and Torres Cacoullos 2009).

Thus the view presented here contrasts with a common view of grammatical meaning that can be traced back to the strong influence of Roman Jakobson. While many American structuralists and generativists shied away from the presumption of knowing what a morpheme or clause means, Jakobson articulated and applied a theory of grammatical meaning that was in keeping with the general principles of linguistic structure as he saw them. The most basic of these principles was that of semantic opposition, based on the binary oppositions that appeared in his work on phonology.

The concept of the opposition is a classical structuralist notion that is based on the assumption that the meaningful elements in a language are all defined in contrast to one another. Thus a grammatical morpheme is not thought to have inherent meaning, but rather to have meaning it has accrued by participation in a system of contrasts. Under this view of grammatical meaning, the present tense in a language that also has grammatical expression for past and a future tense will be different from a present tense in a language that expresses past tense but not future tense. Jakobson further proposed that these oppositions were decomposable into sets of binary features in which the minus value was the unmarked value (as unmarked was defined in Jakobson 1957, 1966). It also follows from this view that each member of the system has one abstract and invariant meaning that is present in all contexts of use. Variations in interpretation are attributed to co-occurring lexical items or other factors in the context.

Not all aspects of this theory have survived into current practice, but the goal of finding one abstract, invariant meaning for each grammatical form or construction still often provides the basis for analysis. In the next sections I argue that while grammatical meaning is often abstract, it is not feasible to reduce all the meaning and nuance found in specific contexts to one abstract feature.

10.9   Invariant, abstract meaning?

In this section I would like to examine the invariant meaning hypothesis and argue that it is incompatible with usage-based theory, exemplar modelling and the facts of grammaticalization, and further that many of the particular analyses proposed under this hypothesis are unworkable. Instead, I propose to recognize the interesting tension between generalized meanings and meanings associated with particular contexts. We have seen that grammaticalized markers have very general meanings; however, we have also seen that they can have specific meanings related to certain constructions or certain interactional situations. We will conclude, as does Dahl 1985, that the conceptual space to which grammatical morphemes refer is not one-dimensional nor are the things we talk about evenly distributed across conceptual space.

Let us consider as an example the analysis of English tense put forward in Michaelis 2006. Michaelis accepts the characterization of the English Past Tense as indicating that a situation obtained before the moment of speech.[9] However, as noted above, the present tense is more difficult to characterize since the moment of speech is a point in time and most situations unfold over time, making their relation with the moment of speech more complex. Michaelis observes that only states, which remain steady over time, can be truly simultaneous with the moment of speech.[10] She then moves from this observation to the proposal that the present tense is a 'state selector', meaning that it 'can impose stative readings on any dynamic verb with which it combines, thereby resolving semantic conflict between the verb and the inflection that is attached to it' (2006: 223). This one meaning, she argues, characterizes all the uses of the English present tense.

In section 10.7 above, we discussed the meanings of the zero-expressed English Present tense. I noted that the most commonly occurring meaning for dynamic verbs was present habitual or generic, but that journalistic prose in particular also uses the present for narrative quite often.[11] I did not mention the future uses of present tense, though these are important as well.[12] For instance, (42) shows the general property that some future time indication is necessary for the zero morpheme to be interpreted as future.

(42) And this meeting *takes* place next Thursday, so we'll keep you informed.
       (COCA 1990)

Michaelis proposes that all uses of the Present Tense can be characterized as imposing a stative interpretation on the situation and that that can give rise to both habitual and future readings. If the inflection (present zero) conflicts with the type of the verb, that is, if the verb is not stative, then the inflection coerces a stative interpretation on the verb.

It takes considerable manipulation of concepts to get this analysis to describe habitual and future sentences with the Present Tense. Consider the present habitual example provided above, shown here as (43):

(43) He still *takes* the horses nobody else wants, older horses, horses with foals, with ears frozen off or otherwise less beautiful than those in cigarette ads. (COCA 1990)

As with all habitual sentences this one is understood to describe a number of events of the same type that are repeated over time and that time includes the present moment. I find nothing at all stative about this sentence. Michaelis claims that all events have various phases and all include a 'rest', which is stative; the present tense selects that rest which includes reference time. If this is the case, then how do we get the information from this sentence that he has taken in horses on multiple occasions and continues to do so? The 'rest' for *takes* in the sense meant here – to take in, keep (at least for a while) and care for – must be the 'keep' part, yet that is not what the sentence means. If one wanted to express this more stative idea, one would say *he keeps horses no one else wants.*

A similar complex manipulation is necessary to get a future reading from a present tense sentence. Referring to the example *The flight arrives at noon,* Michaelis states:

Since arrival has an extended temporal profile that cannot fit inside the present moment, that event must be 'flipped' onto either one side or the other of the present partition in order for the semantic conflict between the tense inflection and the verb to be resolved. (2006: 234)

Given that such sentences always have an explicit temporal context, could we not suppose that rather than viewing futurate present sentences as statives whose interpretation must somehow be resolved, we could be content with an analysis that says that presents with future adverbs are interpreted as futures? Indeed, many authors have noted that the interpretation is of a 'scheduled future', not a general one (Comrie 1985: 47). Michaelis notes that this is a conventionalized interpretation in English and that other languages might have different interpretations. In an exemplar model, this conventionalized meaning would in fact be part of the semantic representation. In Michaelis' model, it is not clear how this interpretation is arrived at as speakers use language if the only meaning of the present is 'state selector'.

Further issues arise as Michaelis tries to justify the Present Tense as a state selector in the face of the use of the Present with Progressive and Perfect periphrases. She makes the assumption that '"Present-time adverbials", including *now* and *at this moment*, are compatible only with stative predications' because 'the present is conceived as a moment and only states are verifiable on the basis of a single momentaneous "sample" ' (2006: 239). She goes on to argue on that basis that future *will* makes a state predication, as in her example (39), shown here as (44):

(44) My daughter will now play the clarinet for you.

On a similar basis, Michaelis argues that Present Progressive and Present Perfect also indicate states, since they co-occur with *now*.

(45) She is playing the clarinet now.
(46) She has played the clarinet now.

However, (44) especially, indicates to me that *now* and indeed, the Present Tense, indicate not a point corresponding to the moment of speech, but rather a range of time that includes the moment of speech. When *now* is used, it appears that this range is rather short and projects more into the future than the past, but it is still a range, not a point.

Indeed, I would argue that the notion of stative predication has been stretched to the point of meaninglessness in the interest of finding only a single invariant meaning for the English Present Tense. Compare, for instance, the more specific definition of stativity proposed by Comrie 1976:

With a state, unless something happens to change that state, then the state will continue... With a dynamic situation, on the other hand, the situation will only continue if it is continually subject to a new input of energy (1976: 49).

Michaelis 2004 accepts this characterization, saying:

Unlike activities, however, state phases do not entail energy input. For example, one can try to sleep or lie on the floor, but one cannot try to be sick for three days or to be short as a child (2004: 11).

This characterization does not apply to all Present Tense predicates, as Michaelis would claim. In particular, Present Progressive predicates describe situations that require continued input of energy, as example (45) shows. Indeed, most analyses of the English Present Progressive focus on the greater activity and agent involvement of the Progressive over the simple Present (Hatcher 1951, Goldsmith and Woisetschlaeger 1982). In a detailed and highly nuanced study of the English Present Progressive, Hatcher 1951 indicates that the Progressive is used to describe overt activities (as in (47)) as well as non-overt ones (as in (48)), but in the latter cases the interpretation is that of development by degrees:

(47) She is washing dishes, sweeping the floor, tending the furnace … I'm slipping. I'm losing hold. It's falling to pieces. It's boiling over. It's spilling. Your teeth are chattering. Your nose is running.

(48) I'm getting hot. One of my headaches is coming on.   He is learning his lesson.   It is getting late.   This is driving me nuts. This is getting us nowhere.

Hatcher characterizes these examples as expressing or implying one of three following notions: (i) the subject is affected by his/her activity; (ii) the subject is busy or engrossed in the activity; or (iii) the subject is accomplishing something by his/her activity. Thus even though one can use *now* with most of these examples, they do not have the usual semantic properties of stative predications.

Finally, if the Present Progressive is stative, how can we explain the fact that the Present Progressive 'coerces' a stative predicate into a dynamic interpretation, as in these examples?

(49) He's being very obstinate.   I'm remembering it better now.

Thus Michaelis' attempt to reduce the English Present Tense meaning to a single invariant one of 'state selector' leads to a distortion of the meaning of 'state' or 'stative' to the point where it is no longer a coherent notion. While I have focused here on Michaelis' recent analysis it should only be considered one of many analyses in the Jakobsonian tradition that attempt to identify a single abstract meaning for each grammatical morpheme (others are Diver 1964, Waugh 1975, Reid 1991, for example). Besides the arguments given just above against the analysis of Present Tense as a state selector, the discussion in the first seven sections of this chapter, which outline the way grammatical meaning develops, provides many arguments against this theoretical position. The fact that the grammaticalization process leads to more and more abstract meanings provides some basis for arguing in favor of a single abstract meaning, but the evidence shows that older meanings related to the earlier lexical meaning of a form can be retained; these richer, less abstract meanings cannot be denied in the quest for the invariant meaning.

As argued in Chapters 6 and 8, changes that take place in grammaticalization demonstrate the importance of inference in meaning change. The theory discussed by Michaelis uses a similar notion, that of coercion, which describes how novel meanings can emerge when lexical and grammatical meanings are not compatible. The coercion theory seems to assume that instances of use that demand coercion have no effect on the meaning of a category. A usage-based approach, however, would propose that instances of language use have an effect on the more permanent representation of meaning. Thus to take the oft-cited example, if one uses an indefinite article with a mass noun, the resulting meaning that is coerced is that of a count noun: thus *a beer* indicates a unit (glass, bottle or can) of beer. This coercion does not have to happen anew with each instance of use, rather *a beer* can become registered in memory with its meanings. Similarly, the coerced meaning of a stative verb used with the Progressive, such as *being stubborn*, can be registered in memory. By such instances of use, the progressive itself can eventually change its meaning. If inference and coercion did not produce incremental changes in meaning representation, grammatical meaning would not change and there would be no grammaticalization process. It is in fact these local changes in meaning that contribute to the overall meaning change in grammaticalization.[13]

10.10   The importance of oppositions

Another legacy of Roman Jakobson's approach to meaning is the interest in contrasts or oppositions made within the system of grammar. The notion that grammatical morphemes get their meaning by opposing other grammatical morphemes is a classical example of a structural notion. We have already seen that it implies that grammatical morphemes do not themselves have inherent meaning, a proposition which studies of grammaticalization have laid to rest by showing how grammatical meaning is a direct result of processes acting upon lexical meaning, and that many features of lexical meaning are retained well into the grammaticalization process. However, we have also seen cases where other members of categories in the system do have an impact on meaning. Zero morphemes absorb their meaning from the context, but they are also limited by the meanings of the other obligatory markers in the system. Thus Present Day English Present Tense does not have a progressive reading (as older versions of English did) because of the development of the Progressive periphrasis.

As mentioned above, there is the interesting phenomenon of one member of an opposition being defined by the absence of the other. García and van Putte 1989 describe this development as the result of frequently made inferences creating a cognitive 'shortcut' from the form to the inference. In the case of the development of zeroes, the inference is 'the speaker did not say X, thus s/he must mean Y'. However, the range of application of such a process is quite limited. In fact, since overt markers have inherent meaning, it would only apply to cases where zeroes are developing, cases where the marker is highly bleached of its lexical meaning or other special cases.

Certainly broad distinctions such as perfective/imperfective, past/present, singular/plural are cross-linguistically well documented as major dividing lines in morphology, but my point here is to caution against the assumption that every grammatical distinction a language makes is of some broader cognitive importance. For example, an analysis of the distinction between the English Present and Progressive by Goldsmith and Woisetschlaeger 1982 argues that the semantic distinction being made is between the Progressive expressing 'what things happen in the world' vs. the Present, which expresses 'how the world is such that things happen in it' (1982: 80). I do not take issue with this description; in fact, I find it quite apt as it applies to the present habitual and stative uses of the Present Tense. However, it is interesting to read their further proposal:[14]

In fact, it is the fairly abstract nature of this particular semantic distinction that makes it of interest to us, for if the analysis proposed here is correct, then we have learned something directly about the conceptual distinctions a speaker of English uses in every sentence uttered. (1982: 79)

The assumption seems to be that a conceptual distinction expressed in the grammar must be of considerable importance. In fact, they go on to consider the possible cross-linguistic consequences of this distinction, noting that Spanish realizes a different distinction. They say that this distinction is so basic and important that it should be embedded within a more general theory of semantic contrasts which predicts which semantic domains a language may choose to incorporate under a single syntactic umbrella (1982: 89).

I would speculate that many linguists agree with this position – that semantic distinctions expressed grammatically are of basic cognitive importance. However, the facts of language change give us reasons to question this idea as generally applicable. Consider the fact that the English Progressive has developed rather recently, providing us with this distinction only in the last century or two; consider also the fact that the construction may continue to change its meaning, generalizing to express habitual meaning, and replacing the simple present, as has happened in a number of languages (Bybee et al. 1994). What then of the basic cognitive distinction? While the distinction between the English simple Present and Progressive is clearly a distinction that the human cognitive apparatus can deal with, its presence in a language is not necessarily evidence for its universal importance.

Consider the question from another perspective. As constructions grammaticalize they go through many stages which create semantic distinctions. At each stage one could consider the distinctions to be of great cognitive importance and yet these distinctions are not preserved; change continues and obliterates them. For example, as the French *passé composé* grammaticalized from a present perfect it went through a stage in the seventeenth century in which it expressed hodiernal past, 'past on the same day', while the older *passé simple* expressed past for situations on previous days (Lancelot and Arnauld 1660: 104). Such a distinction is made in many languages and could be considered quite important to human beings, yet in French this distinction disappeared as the *passé composé* replaced the *passé simple* in the spoken language. The Present Perfect in certain dialects of Spain, moreover, has now taken on the function of an hodiernal past, but one could certainly expect this to be a passing phase as well (Schwenter 1994).

Another phenomenon identified in the context of grammaticalization is layering (Hopper 1991), the build-up of multiple constructions in the same semantic domain through sequences of grammaticalizations. For instance, the expression of obligation in English can use the traditional modals *must, shall, should* and *ought to* (already four!) but in addition, *be to, have to* and *have got to* (> *got to*). In such a case are all seven expressions providing us with some important and very basic semantic distinction? How is it that some languages get along with only one perhaps fairly lexical expression for obligation? The cognitive process behind such excessive layerings obviously has little to do with important and overarching semantic distinctions, but rather with what Dan Slobin calls 'thinking for speaking' (Slobin 1996). Once English speakers become accustomed to expressing obligation (even in cases where other languages would leave it for inference) then multiple almost synonymous expressions can come into being and find occasions of use. Thus it is not always the case that grammatical distinctions are of great and universal cognitive importance.

My view is that languages are highly situated culturally and may allow many local generalizations to be conventionalized. Consider the pairs *remember/can remember, imagine/can imagine, believe/can believe,* discussed in Chapter 9. These express rather minor semantic distinctions, if they express any at all, and yet these conventionalized expressions (with *can*) are perpetuated in the language in their particular contexts of use. The hypotheses that repeated usage entrenches certain expressions and that exemplar storage allows minor generalization and specific usage patterns to be conventionalized explain why language is not entirely about major conceptual distinctions.

10.11   Meanings evolve to reflect experience

Under the invariant meaning hypothesis the conceptual space, for instance, time, which is expressed grammatically by tense and aspect, is divided up into abstract and supposedly uniform regions. The abstract meanings of tense and aspect interact with lexical meaning to provide varying interpretations. However, researchers who work with tense and aspect have to acknowledge that the grammaticalized concepts of past, present and future do not function in parallel ways in natural language. As we have seen it is more or less accurate to say that the English Past Tense designates situations occurring before the moment of speech, with the proviso that past states may persist into the present; as demonstrated above, the Present Tense is not so easily defined due to the fact that the relation between the reference point of the moment of speech and simultaneous situations may be quite complex. Also, the future tense as expressed in most languages, ranges across intention and prediction as well as other meanings, and therefore is not a simple tense in the sense that the past is. Thus it is clear that we as human beings do not experience time in a directly linear fashion, nor are we prone to talk about it that way. Rather, the mix of tenses and aspects that have evolved into grammatical expression in the languages of the world has come to reflect the human experience of situations and their temporal aspects and this experience is neither uniform nor symmetrical across the domain of time (Bybee et al. 1994).

When we consider what language is used for and that it must have the capacity to describe situations as humans see them, it does not seem so odd that grammatical markers and constructions might have very local meanings rather than abstract, global meanings. That would mean, for instance, that we do not have to find the feature that present states and present habitual situations have in common, nor need we be surprised that habitual in the past has different properties than in the present.

Examining the diachronic development of present tense in English is again instructive. In Old English and Middle English, the Present Tense could express present habitual, progressive, stative and even future meanings. Its meaning could be characterized in a very general way as describing a situation occurring within the range of the moment of speech (though without a thorough study, it is not clear how the future use of the present should be characterized). There is no special inflectional affix for present, so it can be regarded as unmarked or zero-expressed. With the development of the Progressive in the last few centuries – a development that has led to obligatory marking of the progressive/habitual distinction in dynamic verbs – the older present territory has been fragmented into present state for stative verbs and present habitual for dynamic verbs. This disjunctive characterization for present tense seems inelegant to supporters of the invariant meaning theory (see Michaelis 2006: 232). But again, the diachronic facts cannot be ignored. If there were a great pressure for grammatical meaning to be abstract and general and not disjunctive, then why would the more specific progressive develop and break apart the coherent simple present?

The fact is that grammaticalization does not occur in order to make meanings more general (although bleaching is often a byproduct); in fact it occurs because more specific meanings are very useful. It is the overuse of these specific meanings that contributes to their bleaching, not the goal of having more general meanings. The progressive apparently developed because it is very useful to express the notion that a dynamic situation is ongoing, counteracting the assumption that dynamic present situations are habitual.

Another interesting case concerns the use of *can* and *may* for permission. In section 10.3 we followed the semantic generalization of *can* from mental ability to general ability to root possibility. The latter asserts that general enabling conditions are in effect; these can include internal abilities of the agent, external physical enabling conditions and social enabling conditions. The social enabling conditions, which are included in root possibility, are equivalent to permission. The permission use of *may* develops as follows.

As is typical of grammaticalization paths, *may* underwent the same sequence of developments as *can* did, but somewhat earlier. It started with a meaning of physical ability (cf. *might* 'power') and generalized to all types of ability. In Middle English it could be used for both ability and root possibility. Here is an example of root possibility from *Sir Gawain and the Green Knight*:

(50) Make we mery quyl we *may* and mynne vpon joye (line 1681)
      'Let us make merry while we can and think of joyful things.'

This usage can be classified as root possibility because the conditions that allow us to 'make merry' are mostly external to the agents.

Among the external conditions included in root possibility are the social conditions that indicate permission. Bybee et al. 1994 argue that ability markers that come to signal permission do so through root possibility. In our cross-linguistic survey, we found that a majority of markers of permission also were used in the more general root possibility sense (Bybee et al. 1994: 193). Thus at the point at which *may* and *can* reach the generality of root possibility, their use for permission will also arise.

The granting, receiving and acknowledging of permission is a very well defined interactive niche in human societies. A grammatical element used in this social context will take on all the meaning afforded by that context, rather than maintaining the more general meaning of root possibility. That is why when *may* moved on to express epistemic possibility, the permission use remained even though other root possibility uses became less frequent. Thus Coates' 1983 examination of the use of *may* in current British usage turned up the following distribution of uses:[15]

(51) Uses of *may* (N = 200) (Coates 1983: 132)
      Epistemic possibility   147
      Root possibility   7
      Permission   32
      Indeterminate   13
      Benediction   1

Note that the root uses of *may* have grown rare, except where permission is signalled. As argued in Bybee 1988b, the epistemic uses of *may* evolved by inference from the root possibility uses. But now the data show a kind of gap or disjunction: epistemic possibility and permission are not a continuous category. Without root possibility to unite them, they are just two rather different uses of *may*. The fact that the permission use of *may* continues while other root possibility uses grow rarer indicates that *may* occupies this important social niche independently now of its other uses.

Can is following a similar path of development. Having reached the stage of root possibility in Early Modern English, it began specifically to be used for permission late in the nineteenth century, according to its *OED* entry. As many mid-twentieth-century school children found out, the use of *can* for permission was considered substandard for many decades. Presumably it is now replacing *may* as the auxiliary for permission.

Permission serves as an excellent example of a special communicative niche for a grammatical marker. Permission is an important and conventionalized social function that has a specific set of participants and conditions. An exemplar model would record these aspects of the context with the construction used in that context, providing a specific meaning for this construction that can grow autonomous from the root possibility meaning.

My proposal is that grammatical meaning in other domains is structured in the same way: it is associated with particular contexts of use and gravitates to certain niches which are socially and communicatively important (Dahl 1985, Bybee and Dahl 1989, Bybee et al. 1994). Some of these are fairly general and all of them have to be frequently used or else grammaticalization would never occur. Within the domain of tense and aspect we can name the narrative function, usually fulfilled by a past or perfective, but also sometimes by a present. We can also name the backgrounding function of describing how things are, which calls on the present or imperfective (used frequently with stative predicates) but also provides a habitual reading with dynamic predicates.[16] Rather than broad oppositions, such as [+ or − state] or [+ or − future] I suggest that grammatical meaning fills certain socio-cognitive niches which arise as language is used in context.

In this regard, it is worth noting the success of cross-linguistic study at the level of functional niches or focal categories. Drawing upon an analogy with the study of colour terms by Berlin and Kay 1969, Dahl 1985 bases his study of tense and aspect on specific categories that are characterized not by more abstract features but rather by their prototypical uses. Languages differ in which categories they utilize out of the cross-linguistic set and how these categories differ in their secondary or non-focal uses. Applying this type of analysis to a large sample of languages, Dahl was able to establish very clear, frequently expressed cross-linguistic categories for tense and aspect, a task which would not have been possible if each language had been analysed independently for the abstract invariant meanings. Given the range of secondary uses and meanings each language would have appeared very different from every other if analysed at this more abstract level.

The analogy with color terms is fitting. Berlin and Kay found that even though the color spectrum appears objectively continuous, as humans perceive it certain areas stand out and are therefore named by basic colour terms. Experiments show significant agreement about the meaning of such terms both within and across cultures. The human experience of temporal contours, modality or other domains that find grammatical expression can be similarly analysed as having a varied topology rather than being one or two dimensional and uniform in structure. Humans apparently perceive and care to talk about certain parts of the temporal domain more than others. Of course, for grammaticalization to proceed, there must be a certain frequency with which these temporal aspects are applicable and usable in communication. Thus the explanation for the particular tense/aspect/modality categories that find grammatical expression lies at the intersection of what is important to communication and what is general enough to become grammaticalized (Bybee 1985, Talmy 1985). Thus we conclude that human language has evolved to fit human experience and the way it is communicated; our experience is not linear, binary or abstract. This is not to say that there are no abstract categories – there certainly are. But not every instance of a category has to have the same underlying meaning.

10.12   Conclusions

In this chapter we have taken some lessons from grammaticalization studies in an attempt to identify the properties of grammatical meaning and its source in language history and usage. We took a closer look at the mechanisms of semantic change that are operating daily as language is used and the clues these give us for the cognitive representation of the meaning of grammatical forms. We find that context has a major impact on meaning and that aspects of the context and inferences made from the context can become a conventionalized part of grammatical meaning. While some inferences do arise at the moment of decoding utterances, we need to distinguish between those fleeting inferences and those that become part of the meaning through repetition. A rich memory representation allows the gradual increase in the importance of inferences over time, which leads to change in meaning.

Usage factors reveal language as a natural, organic social instrument, not an abstract logical one. The structures and meanings expressed grammatically in language are highly tied to our experience and the uses to which we put linguistic forms. As often noted, natural categorization is not accomplished in terms of necessary and sufficient features but rather proceeds with reference to similarity and frequency of exemplars. Our understanding of the grammatical forms of language are based rather concretely upon the range of contexts in which the forms have occurred, not on a predilection to reduce meaning to pure abstraction. Thus polysemy is to be expected in both lexical and grammatical meaning, as specific situations are coded in specific ways.

11 Language as a complex adaptive system: the interaction of cognition, culture and use

11.1 Typology and universals

A linguistic theory must strive to be applicable to all human languages and thus must recognize at some level what all languages have in common. Generative theory, for instance, has sought commonalities in the form of universals of grammar at the level of phrase structure rules and conditions and constraints on movement rules. While there are certainly many tendencies and repeated patterns cross-linguistically, stating universals at this level has largely been unsuccessful in accounting for the empirical data (see Newmeyer 2005). In this chapter we will consider tracing the tendencies and patterns observable across languages to the interaction of the cognitive processes that have been discussed in the previous chapters of this book. This approach allows us to integrate synchronic patterns with patterns of language change and provides the framework for forming a more comprehensive theory that explains the range of structures found in the languages of the world. But in addition to accounting for similarities among languages, it is also important to account for major typological differences. Towards this goal it is suggested here, following other research (Perkins 1992, Wray and Grace 2007) that cultural factors may come into play. Indeed social and cultural factors have remained in the background in the previous discussion, but clearly such factors cannot be ignored in a full account of the emergence of language.

Construction grammar as studied by Fillmore and colleagues emphasizes the idiomaticity of grammar. The burgeoning study of prefabs and formulaic language mentioned earlier (Wray 2002, and others) also emphasizes the extent to which linguistic knowledge is specific to particular words and phrases and therefore to particular languages. Radical Construction Grammar (Croft 2001) is typological in orientation but emphasizes the specifics of particular constructions within and across languages, arguing against static universals – for instance, on the level of 'the passive construction'. Following the Greenbergian tradition, this approach considers the universals to be evident in the way constructions develop over time. The new approaches to child language acquisition that were mentioned in earlier chapters also emphasize the child's use of specific instances of constructions at early stages, leading up gradually to more general constructions (Lieven et al. 1997, Tomasello 2003, Dbrowska and Lieven 2005). Despite the emphasis on the language-specific and local generalizations, none of these researchers would deny that all human languages are very similar; not only is this a firm intuition shared by researchers who work on language, but it is backed up by extensive demonstration of similarities across unrelated languages.

Usage-based theory developed directly out of, and is in a sense just a new name for, American functionalism, which has been practiced for many decades (Noonan 1998). The first usage-based linguist of the twentieth century was Joseph Greenberg. Although he is better known for his studies in typology and universals, he also showed an interest in frequency effects in helping to explain cross-linguistic patterns (Greenberg 1966). Other usage-based linguists who are also typologists include T. Givón (1975, 1979), Sandra Thompson (1988, 1998), Paul Hopper (Hopper and Thompson 1980, 1984), John Haiman (1985), and William Croft (2003). These researchers connect their dual interests in usage patterns and typology with the theoretical proposition that frequently occurring usage patterns will be reflected in cross-linguistically common grammatical patterns. Note that this approach, initiated by Greenberg in the 1960s, has the central properties of a complex adaptive systems approach: it postulates a small number of factors interacting locally from which emerge a dynamic, apparently global structure. Specifically, some concepts from complexity theory apply to the usage-based approach to language in the broadest sense – that is, to language as a world-wide phenomenon encompassing all known types. Thus the repeated grammaticalization paths alluded to in Chapter 6 can be thought of as 'strange attractors' in the sense that certain cycles seem to be repeated across languages and across time but without ever being precisely identical.

The goal of this chapter, then, is to present this view with several examples, showing that commonalities across languages can be explained with reference to language use as filtered through the processing mechanisms discussed in previous chapters. However, our first topic will be the general one of how cross-linguistic similarities can be incorporated into a theory of language.

11.2   Cross-linguistic similarities in a theory of language

A basic question for any linguistic theory to address is the nature of the human genetic endowment that makes language possible. Perhaps the most fundamental consideration is whether language similarities are to be attributed to domain-general or domain-specific processes and abilities. As we have noted in earlier chapters, 'domain-general' abilities are those that are also used outside of language – in general cognition – and include chunking, categorization, the use of symbols, the ability to make inferences and so on. 'Domain-specific' abilities would be those that are specific to language and not evidenced elsewhere. Aspects of the ability to process speech auditorily, for example, may turn out to be quite specific to language and not a process used elsewhere.

Among the domain-specific abilities that have been proposed one might distinguish between structural knowledge and processing tendencies. The innate parameters of generative grammar would be structural knowledge – specific knowledge about how languages are structured. An example of a processing constraint that might be innate would be the parsing constraint discussed in Hawkins 2009. The structural knowledge would become manifest during the acquisition of language by children, and the processing constraints would affect choices of structures and thus affect grammar through usage.

In earlier chapters I have argued against structural knowledge as innate. In Chapter 6 I also argued against the view that children play a more significant role than adults in changing language. The view that structural properties of language are innate requires that these properties appear in the acquisition process and that any changes in structure occur in this process. If we find that children in fact are not the major instigators of linguistic change, then the main link between innate universals and language structure cannot be established. In addition, I have demonstrated in several chapters of this book that the categories and constituents of grammar are gradient in their properties and change as language is used. The view that such properties are innate is not compatible with this demonstrated gradience. Finally, the fact that all categories and structures evolve gradually from other categories and structures also argues against the existence of static and innate universals of language (Bybee, 2009a and 2009b).

In fact it is more parsimonious to accept the challenge to derive language from non-language – that is, from domain-general principles – and to view language as a complex adaptive system. First, if we adhere to the assumption that the processes underlying language are specific to language, we will never discover if any of them applies outside of language. In contrast, if we start by examining the possibility of domain-general processes in operation, then we can eventually distinguish the domain-general from domain-specific. Second, in a complex-systems approach 'universals' or similarities across languages are emergent and dynamic, not static and given. Such a view is more in keeping with the facts: there are very few absolute universals; rather there are many possible typological patterns at every level and few pure types. These facts are consistent with the hypothesis that there are multiple factors involved in shaping a language.

11.3   Synchronic observations, diachronic paths and domain-general processes

American Structuralists, with their highly empirical orientation, emphasized the differences among languages and took great pains not to reduce all languages to the mold of what Benjamin Lee Whorf called Standard Average European (Whorf 1941; see also Sapir 1921). In contrast, in the middle of the twentieth century, both Noam Chomsky and Joseph Greenberg began to emphasize the many commonalities shared by distinct languages. Their approaches were, however, quite different: Chomsky postulated an innate 'Universal Grammar' as a starting point, so that 'universals' could be discovered by studying only a single language (Chomsky 1965). In contrast Joseph Greenberg studied hundreds of languages to establish their similarities and differences (Greenberg 1963, 1966, 1978a, 1978b). Based as it is on an understanding of the diversity as well as similarity among languages, Greenberg's theory is much more subtle and nuanced than Chomsky's in that it sees relations among the properties of languages that can be expressed in hierarchies and implicational statements, all of which are ultimately based on diachronic changes. In addition Greenberg tries to get closer to explanations for similarities while generativists seem satisfied with the a priori postulation that there are innate linguistic universals. In a Chomskian theory universals are properties that cannot be learned from experience; in Greenberg's theory or other usage-based theories patterns that turn out to be cross-linguistically similar are indeed learned from experience.

The generative idea of universals is carried to its logical conclusion in Optimality Theory where linguistic forms are derived by the application of universal constraints. Since the constraints can override one another, none of the 'universals' is absolute in its application. This fits with the facts – there are very few absolute universals – but it also makes the theory untestable. Practitioners of this theory play fast and loose with the empirical data, postulating 'universal constraints' on the basis of very little data, often on the basis of patterns that recur in a few related languages (see Bybee 2005).

The other common property of Universal Grammar found in work within generative theory and Optimality Theory is the view that structural properties of language are universal and innately given. That means that observational generalizations about grammar – distributions of consonants and vowels or ordering of subject, verb and object – are proposed to be a part of linguistic competence without any further search for the principles that underlie these observed generalizations. This is another reason why the Greenbergian approach is more sophisticated and satisfying. In the Greenbergian approach one does not stop at the observation stage, but rather one continues to piece together a sequence of diachronic developments that lead to both the similarities and the differences among languages (Greenberg 1969, 1978a and 1978b, Croft 2001,

Bybee 2006b). The ultimate goal is to identify the causal mechanisms that lead to the paths of development that underlie the observed regularities.

For instance, Greenberg 1978b discusses a diachronic continuum among languages (even some unrelated languages) from demonstratives to noun class markers. This continuum is a grammaticalization path, as demonstratives in some languages develop into noun class markers (e.g. Bantu languages). Many such paths have been discovered in the extensive literature on grammaticalization. They are paths of semantic development (paralleled by paths of development of form) that can be found approximated in different, related or unrelated languages across time (Givón 1979, Bybee and Dahl 1989, Bybee et al. 1994, Heine et al. 1991, Heine and Kuteva 2002). Just to take one example for which the empirical data are quite clear, there are many languages with a future form that is derived from a verb or construction meaning 'movement towards a goal'. In the seventy-six-language sample of Bybee et al. 1994, in which the languages studied were maximally unrelated genetically, the following languages were found to have a future marker built from a movement verb: Margi (Chadic), Tucano (Andean-Equatorial), Guaymí (Chibchan), Danish (Indo-European), Krongo (Kordofanian), Mwera (Benue-Congo), Tem (Gur), Mano (Mande), Tojolabal (Mayan), Cantonese (Sino-Tibetan), Cocamo (Tupi), Maung (Australian), Atchin (Oceanic), Abipon (Ge-Pano-Carib), Bari (Eastern Sudanic), Zuni (Native American isolate), and Nung (Tibeto-Burman).[1]

The next section contains a more detailed account of how diachrony in general and grammaticalization in particular provide a framework for tracking the similarities and differences among languages.

11.4   Grammaticalization paths as 'strange attractors'

In the literature on complex adaptive systems, 'attractor' is the name given to the path that a dynamic system takes. In a closed system, where there is no new input of energy, a fixed point can be the attractor, as in the case of a bob swinging on a string, which will come to rest at a fixed point or attractor. In a complex non-linear system, such as language, where there is new input of energy provided by language use, it can be observed that no cycle ever follows exactly the same path. Thus while cycles may seem very similar, yielding a global pattern, the details are always somewhat different (Larsen-Freeman 1997). Such a situation can be observed in language change, especially in grammaticalization, where paths of change can be identified that are cross-linguistically very similar, yielding a global pattern, even though the details show differences. In this section we will examine the paths of change for future markers across languages, demonstrating both similarities and differences. As mentioned earlier, viewing cross-linguistic patterns as patterns of change rather than as patterns of fixed states provides us with a more insightful basis of comparison.

In Chapter 10, the polysemy in the English future marker *will* was discussed and it was shown that *will* can indicate intention, prediction and willingness. That discussion made it clear that some of these meanings were expressed by *will* and not by the other English future markers. Also the occurrence of these meanings in specific constructions would suggest that they are particular to English. These facts would seem to make it very difficult to compare a grammatical category such as 'future' across languages. However, if we consider the way that grammatical morphemes develop diachronically, we find that the paths of development as well as the mechanisms behind them are very similar, providing us with a means for cross-linguistic comparison. The similarity among futures across languages can be summarized in the following set of grammaticalization paths proposed on the basis of documented changes as well as cross-linguistic synchronic patterns of polysemy (Bybee, Pagliuca and Perkins 1991, Bybee et al. 1994):

(1) Common paths of change resulting in future markers

'movement towards a goal'
'desire, volition'   > intention   > prediction   > epistemic or
'obligation'   subordinating
                                                                modality

Future markers are defined as any grammatical marker that indicates a prediction made by the speaker (Bybee and Pagliuca 1987, Bybee, Pagliuca and Perkins 1991). In the cross-linguistic survey cited here, all other uses of markers used for prediction were taken into account.

The list of meanings on the left side are meanings of lexical sources that appear in constructions that come to express the future. Surveys of many languages reveal that it is common to find a stage at which intention is expressed. The intention use comes about through an implication from the original lexical meanings used in first person contexts where expressions such as *I want to, I have to* and *I'm going to* can reasonably lead to the inference that the speaker intends to do something. It sets the stage for the move to future (prediction).

Since new meanings arise in specific contexts, they do not immediately replace old meanings; rather there can be long periods of overlap or polysemy where old and new meanings coexist. This fact is a major factor in accounting for the oft-cited modal meaning of future markers. That is, meanings of futures that indicate volition or willingness (as found for instance in Danish, Nimboran, Bongu, Dakota and Tok Pisin [Bybee, et al. 1994: 254]) probably are retentions from the original meaning of the lexical items and constructions that grammaticalized to form the future. The same can be said for futures that also have uses indicating obligation (such as found in Inuit, Basque, Danish and Slave [Bybee, et al. 1994: 258]). Futures derived from constructions indicating movement towards a goal usually do not have modal uses except for expressing intention. Thus a comparison based on grammaticalization paths affords a means to explain both similarities and differences among future markers.

Once the intention use is common in a language, the stage is set for the further inference of prediction, which can be taken to be the main diagnostic for a future marker. In the following examples from Chapter 10 *will* and *be going to* can be interpreted as expressing the intention of the subject of the sentence, a prediction by the speaker or just as likely, both.

(2) Madam, my lord *will* go away to-night; A very serious business calls on him. (*All's Well That Ends Well*, II. 4)

(3) She's *going to* take a poll in 1991 to find out what her chances are. (COCA 1990)

At each of the three stages mentioned so far – lexical source construction, intention and prediction – the new meaning is applicable in a wider range of contexts and thus the frequency of use increases at each stage. The generality of the meaning is also increasing and continues to increase. Later developments suggest that the meaning becomes applicable in a variety of contexts. In fact, the predictability of the path breaks down some in late stages and greater cross-linguistic diversity can be observed, as futures that have traversed this far on the path might be found to express imperative, the epistemic modalities of probability or possibility and to occur in some subordinate clauses (without their lexical meaning) such as protases of conditional sentences, temporal clauses and complements to certain kinds of verbs (Bybee et al. 1994).

In this way the grammaticalization paths in (1) act as 'strange attractors' in a complex adaptive system. We can observe this path being manifest in language after language and at different time periods, yet there are differences in detail from one manifestation of the path to another. One source of cross-linguistic differences are possibilities of differences in lexical source. Here it should also be mentioned that there are a few more attested lexical sources for futures that are less common, that is, temporal adverbs with meanings such as 'then', 'afterwards' and 'soon' and modals indicating ability and attempt. Interestingly, these very likely have gone through stages similar to the more common lines of development shown in (1), starting with 'intention'.

Another source of cross-linguistic differences in the manifestation of the future path is the existence of other constructions in the same functional domain in the same language. For instance, the existence of *shall* as a future marker earlier on limited the spread of *will*, which was not used with first person until recently (Coates 1983). In addition, as we saw Chapter 8, particular instances of constructions can be conventionalized, encouraging or inhibiting the spread of a construction and thus creating language-specific characteristics (Poplack, to appear).

The underlying mechanisms of change that occur in grammaticalization are the same in all languages, which leads to the similarity in the paths or the attractors, especially insofar as these mechanisms are nested in cross-culturally common discourse needs and communicative contexts. These mechanisms discussed in Chapter 6 include generalization of meaning, habituation and pragmatic inferencing. Interestingly, even the inferences that push the changes forward seem to be very similar across languages and cultures (see section 11.6). However, the context for grammaticalization in each language may be slightly different; the cultural context may differ as well (see section 11.7). Thus no two paths of development will be exactly the same, though very similar paths will occur over and over again in the languages of the world.

The knowledge of diachrony, then, provides us with a way of comparing the uses of futures across languages and making predictions about what kind of development will come next. Casting these developments in a complex adaptive systems framework helps us evaluate both the similarities and the differences in paths of development.

Note that these facts about similarity among languages cannot be listed in an innate Universal Grammar. They are rather facts that show that the paths of development for grammar are similar in the same way that dunes of sand or waves on the ocean are similar: because the forces that create them are the same and these forces interact dynamically over time to produce emergent structures that are similar but never identical.

Within cognitive and functional linguistics, there is mounting agreement that when we search for the 'universals of language' we need to focus our search on the processes that create and maintain language structures, not on the structures themselves (see Givón 2002 and Verhagen 2002). For this reason, the current book has been focused on the processes that create linguistic structure. To review, we have been concerned with the effects of the chunking which occurs in sequential processing, as this provides for groupings of morphemes and words that underlie constructions and constituents. Categorization, the most basic of cognitive processes, establishes the units of language, their meaning and form. The Law of Contiguity or cross-modal association (James 1950, Ellis 1996) allows for symbolization or meaning-form associations. These processes in combination with the effects of repetition on memory and access provide us with an explanation for many of the properties of linguistic form. When we consider that the content with which languages deal – what people choose to talk about and how they choose to talk about it – and the social interactive situation are often similar, we have a concrete basis for understanding how and why all languages are alike. In addition, as we will see in the next section, this view of grammar provides a framework for working out a very plausible view of language origins.

11.5   Origins of language from domain-general abilities

After a long hiatus it has again become acceptable and even popular to speculate on the origins of language. Given what we know about language change, particularly grammaticalization, which provides a well-documented account of how grammar emerges from repeated word sequences, there is every reason to suppose that the very first grammatical constructions emerged in the same way as those observed in more recent history (Bybee 1998a, Li 2002, Heine and Kuteva 2007). Moreover, the fact that we can relate the emergence of grammatical constructions to domain-general abilities that are present not only in humans, but also to varying degrees in other primates means that usage-based theory need not postulate an evolutionary event (whether of adaptation or mutation) by which the brain was rewired dramatically to contain the essence of Universal Grammar as necessitated in the theories of Pinker and Bloom 1990, Jackendoff 2002, Pinker 2003, and Chomsky 2006. Rather a theory based on domain-general cognitive abilities postulates the increasing capacity of such processes – increase in memory and access to memory, development of increasingly finer motor and perceptual skills, increased ability at imitation and at sequential processing, and greater abstraction in categorization, all of which could develop gradually while some form of language is being used (Bybee 1998a, Li 2002).

It is not my goal to pursue discussion of the biological foundations for language further in this section. Instead I will focus on theories of the evolution of grammar itself. The main thrust of this section will be to demonstrate that theories of the evolution of grammar must be based firmly on an understanding of language change and how it takes place.

In Chapter 6 I argued at length that the primary locus of language change is not in the first language acquisition process, but rather in the process of language use. Unfortunately, many researchers have embarked on a study of language evolution subscribing to the erroneous assumption that language change occurs primarily as language is transmitted across generations (for some examples, see Briscoe 2003, Kirby and Christiansen 2003). Applying a Darwinian model to this view, replication would occur with each individual's acquisition of a grammar. Faulty replication would create a grammar that is not identical to the adult model and would therefore introduce change. In contrast, the usage-based view, as presented in Croft 2000, takes the replicator to be the linguistic element and replication to occur in each utterance produced by speakers in a community. As pointed out in previous chapters, innovations in utterances often involve small articulatory adjustments due to neuromotor accommodations or extensions of constructions to new but related contexts. Such changes, if they are repeated over multiple speech events, add up to recognizable changes in phonological and grammatical structure.

Thus the evolution of grammar from the usage-based perspective requires that cross-modal association is already possible; that is, language users have begun to associate sound with meaning. Then if two sound–meaning symbols (or words) are produced in sequence, the stage is set for the elaboration of grammar, first through chunking, then through grammaticalization. The repetition of a two-word sequence can lead to the expansion of the lexicon through compounding, and compounds with repeated elements (*man-like, god-like, friend-like*) can lead to the development of derivational affixes (*manly, godly, friendly*). In addition, frequent word combinations can lead to the development of multi-word constructions and instances of such constructions can grammaticalize with repetition. It is important to note that innovations in the lexicon and the development of new grammatical elements and constructions through grammaticalization cannot occur in the first language acquisition process, but can only occur more gradually in language use.

Note that in this view, the first language or languages are thought not to be the same as present day languages. They would have had lexical items but not grammatical items or constructions. Grammar developed gradually as language was used and as the capacities of humans or our ancestors increased to accommodate a large vocabulary, more abstract categories and many automated sequences. Heine and Kuteva 2007 provide a set of explicit hypotheses, based on the now extensive literature on grammaticalization, which show how the modern categories of grammar could have been built up gradually in successive layers, as nouns and verbs followed their well-known grammaticalization paths. Thus rather than adopting a version of the uniformitarian hypothesis that says that the first languages had basically the same properties as documented languages, we should rather adopt the version that says that the processes of change were the same in the past as they are now (Heine and Kuteva 2007).

An alternate, but not mutually exclusive view, is taken by Wray and Kirby (Wray 2000, Kirby 2000, Wray and Grace 2007). These researchers do not take compositionality to be basic. Wray argues that complex structures could arise through the analysis of holistic structures rather than through the composition of simple structures. Wray 2000 notes the heavy use of holistic formulaic expressions in modern languages and Wray and Grace 2007 speculate further that unanalysed expressions may be even more common in social situations where one interacts primarily with people who share a similar background (see the next section for further discussion). Kirby 2000 demonstrates through a series of experiments that as the words of an artificial language are transmitted to new learners, the learners impose some order on the words, changing them to create recurrent parts that correspond to morphemes. Thus these researchers question the assumption made by many linguists, that compositionality – the regular and transparent combining of morphemes and words – is basic to grammar.

There is much to commend the view that holistic expressions are also natural. In Bybee 1985 I argued against the assumption that morphology is most natural when it is regular and compositional. By pointing to the fact that irregularity of form was most common in high-frequency items, I suggested that there is a natural place in the grammar for less analysable and more fused forms. The same theme has appeared in the current work as well. The previous chapters have demonstrated that loss of analysability and compositionality and the increase in autonomy are the natural consequence of the way language is processed and indeed provide us with a source for grammar. However, those who propose a role for analysis of holistic expressions should not lose sight of the nature of linguistic change as documented over many languages and many centuries. While this record does show some cases of folk etymologies and backformations that indicate that holistic units have been analysed, the vast majority of grammar-shaping changes start with two or more elements and fuse them into one. Thus for every case of folk etymology, as when *hamburger* is analysed as consisting of the noun for a type of meat or other ingredient plus an element that must mean 'sandwich on a bun', giving us by analogy new words such *fishburger* and *veggie-burger*, there are hundreds, if not thousands, of documented cases of changes going in the other direction – from analysable, complex formations to unanalysable formations. Thus I would ascribe a minor role to the analysis of holistic expressions in the evolution of grammar and a major role to grammaticalization. Note also that giving the analysis of holistic expressions a major role in language evolution is based on the assumption not accepted here that linguistic change occurs principally in language transmission.

11.6   Social factors that shape grammar

It follows from the premise of this book – that linguistic structure emerges through language use – that the social and cultural context in which language is used would have an impact on the structures that are created. We have already seen that frequency or repetition leads to loss of analysability and compositionality, reduction of form, generalization of meaning and conventionalization of inferences. To the extent that the conditions under which language is used are similar across cultures, the substance and form of grammar will also be similar; to the extent that these conditions differ, languages may has grammars of different types. Thus we might expect to find differences in typology relating to some extent to differences in cultural context. In contrast, a theory that relies on a set of innate givens, such as Universal Grammar, has very restricted means by which to account for typological differences among languages. In this section a few factors concerning the social interactional contexts in which language is used are discussed to show how these may impact grammar, providing in some cases for similarities across languages and in other cases for differences.

11.6.1   Similarities in pragmatic inferencing

Throughout the discussion in previous chapters we have seen the important role that pragmatic inference plays in semantic change, particularly in grammaticalization and the creation of new constructions. Clearly pragmatic inferencing is a universal mechanism that contributes to the creation of grammar. In section 11.4 we also noted that the similarity among semantic paths of grammaticalization across languages points to the fact that even across cultures that may be rather different, very similar inferences are made in similar situations. In the discussion of futures we saw that the inference of speaker intention is important in starting expressions of movement towards a goal, volition and obligation towards grammaticalization. A second inference of prediction also occurs to yield the future meaning. Since the same semantic sources and paths of change are documented across languages, it appears very likely that the same inferences are made in distinct cultures.

Another set of developments that point to inferences that are cross-linguistically similar are perfects and perfectives that can also be used to indicate present state. This occurs in Sango, Palaung, Tok Pisin, Engenni, Trukese, Island Carib, Kanuri, Mwera and in the Preterit-Present verbs of English (Bybee et al. 1994: 70–8). In these cases, when one expresses the concept of having entered a state, as in 'I learned' or 'it got dark' the inference is that the resulting state still holds: 'I learned' therefore 'I know'; 'it got dark' therefore 'it is dark'. Thus by the conventionalization of this implicature, polysemy results so that the perfect or perfective marker signals present with stative predicates. The impressive cross-linguistic similarity is a strong indication that people in different cultures can make very similar inferences.

A third example concerns the inference of causation from the expression of the temporal relation 'after'. Just as *since* in English has changed from having only a temporal meaning to expressing cause as well, this development has occurred in other languages. The English case, as discussed in Traugott and König 1991, shows a diachronic development from the temporal meaning in (4) to the cause meaning in (6) via examples such as (5) in which the context leads one to make a causal inference from the temporal meaning.

(4) I think you'll all be surprised to know that *since* we saw Barbara last, she made an amazing trip to China. (COCA 1990)
(5) After 50 years of sleepwalking, he hasn't walked once *since* he started taking the drug. (COCA 1990)
(6) *Since* the hunters all have CB radios, they can warn each other before he even gets close. (COCA 1990)

Heine and Kuteva 2002 cite such polysemy in English, French, Basque, and Aranda. The cross-linguistic pattern suggests that language users are particularly interested in finding causal relations even where they are not explicitly expressed. Thus we find cross-linguistic similarity in the actual inferences made: intention, prediction, resulting state and cause, and perhaps many others.

Of course, given different social and physical conditions, some inferences will undoubtedly vary across cultures.

11.6.2   Inferencing and morphological typology

Despite these similarities in the actual content of inferences, differences among languages also occur because of differences in the nature and extent of inferencing in discourse. In Bybee 1997 I examined the role of discourse inferencing in determining how far a language would carry the process of grammaticalization. The results of extensive cross-linguistic comparison of grammaticalization in Bybee et al. 1994 show that there are differences in the extent to which grammaticalization is carried out. We found in languages of the analytic or isolating type that not only were the grammaticalized forms longer and less fused with the verb (being less phonologically reduced in general), but also the meanings of grammatical categories were more specific and represented earlier stages of grammaticalization paths. For instance, a robust finding of Dahl 1985, Bybee and Dahl 1989 and Bybee et al. 1994 is that languages that lack inflections – that is, categories that are affixed and obligatory – also lacked perfective/imperfective and present/past distinctions. Such languages – the analytic types – tend rather to have perfects (or anteriors), which represent the earlier stages on the past and perfective path, or progressives, which represent the earlier stage of the present or imperfective paths.

This finding echoes the classification of morphological types proposed by Sapir 1921. While subsequent researchers tend to think of Sapir's proposed types as purely a matter of form, his actual discussion relates form to meaning and proposes that languages of different morphological types express different types of meaning. Thus Sapir distinguishes between Concrete Relational Concepts and Pure Relational Concepts, his names for types of grammatical meaning. He distinguishes these two types in terms of the degree of abstractness of their meanings. He does not place any grammatical categories permanently in one or the other category, but rather argues that a category such as number, gender or aspect may be more concrete in one language but more relational in another. For instance, where number is marked only on nouns it is more concrete, but where it also marks agreement on demonstratives, adjectives or verbs, it is more relational. In Bybee et al. 1994 and Bybee 1997 we proposed a rough equivalence of the more concrete relational concepts to meanings that occur earlier on grammaticalization paths and those that are more purely relational to more grammaticalized meanings. Given the parallelism of the development of form and meaning, then, languages which do not carry grammaticalization through to affixation would also not carry the semantic grammaticalization as far as inflectional languages do.

Thus the traditional morphological typology is underlyingly a typology of how far grammaticalization is carried in a language. The quantitative test of this hypothesis in Bybee et al. 1994 was based on the formal properties of morphemes associated with verbs in a seventy-six language sample on the basis of which each language could be classified by the phonological length of its grammatical morphemes, their dependence upon surrounding material and their fusion with the verb. Using these formal measures, we tested the correspondence of the overall morphological type of a language with the degree of semantic grammaticalization of its markers of completive, resultative, anterior (perfect) perfective and past, listed here in order from least grammaticalized to most grammaticalized. The correspondence with dependence on surrounding material and fusion with the verb were highly significant – the more fusion and dependence in the language in general, the more likely that the language had a highly grammaticalized morpheme for perfective and past. No correspondence was found for the length of the morphemes in the language. Of course, this is to be expected as no one has ever proposed a morphological typology of language based solely on the length of grammatical morphemes.

Thus the hypothesis that morphological typology depends upon how far a language carries the grammaticalization process is supported. On the inflectional end of the scale, grammaticalization proceeds to the development of the most abstract and general meanings. These are expressed by affixation and in some cases, because of further phonological changes, by stem changes. On the analytic end of the scale, grammaticalization proceeds less far – grammatical morphemes do not become affixes, nor do their meaning changes proceed so far as to establish the most abstract and obligatory categories of meaning. Rather, it appears that grammatical morphemes are replaced by other newly grammaticalizing morphemes before the older ones have had a chance to reach the end of a path of development (Lin 1991).

What prevents grammaticalization from proceeding as far in some languages as it does in others? In Bybee 1997 I suggested that an essential process in the later stages of grammaticalization is not available in languages of the analytic type. This process involves a particular type of inferencing which makes a category become obligatory, as obligatoriness of categories is the defining feature of inflection.

A characteristic of analytic or isolating languages is the lack of obligatory expression of items such as pronouns and the lack of obligatory categories, defined as categories for which some exponent must appear in the phrase or clause. Consider the Chinese sentence used by Bisang 2004 to illustrate this property of analytic languages:

(7) wǒ bú jiàn tā, yǐ   shǐ sān shǐ duō nián; jīntiān ø jiàn ø le.
    I   NEG see he already be 30   more year; today   see   PF
    'I haven't seen him for more than 30 years. Today [I] saw [him].'

Note that in the second clause there is no need for the expression of the pronominal forms as they can be inferred from context. Note also that there is no expression of tense in the first clause, but the lexical expression '30 years' makes the temporal reference clear. Typically, the form of expression in analytic languages contains very little in the way of redundancy or repetition. For instance, there are no explicit grammatical markers of the role of the arguments in the clause. Given a certain flexibility in word order, the listener is left to infer the relations among the NPs in a clause. In such cases, the semantics of the NPs, along with real world knowledge of agentivity, is the most important guide to semantic roles (Li, Bates and MacWhinney 1993). Rather than relying on explicit grammatical markers or word order, the listener must work actively to infer the relations among the NPs that the speaker intends. Similarly, in the domain of tense and aspect a lot can be left unexpressed; the listener again must apply the most reasonable inferences.

Bisang 2004 points out that there is a high degree of indeterminateness in both the morphosyntax and the lexicon of the analytic languages of East and Southeast Asia. Grammatical markers in these languages are polysemous and can express meanings from various functional domains, depending upon the context. Lexical items may be interpreted as either nouns or verbs, again, depending upon the context. As a result, grammatical markers lack two properties that Bisang considers would otherwise lead to the development of obligatory categories: frequency of use and a clear-cut semantic domain. Because markers are not used redundantly, they do not undergo the kind of frequency increase that usually characterizes grammaticalization. Because they operate in various semantic domains, no paradigms emerge. These two properties, which both reference the use of markers in discourse context, are features of these languages which inhibit grammaticalization.

Let us now consider the role of redundancy in promoting grammaticalization. Redundant expression can be of at least two types. One sort of redundancy comes about when a speaker expresses an idea as part of an utterance, where that particular idea would be assumed even without expression. For instance, English uses modal elements expressing obligation much more often than the cognate or similar items would be used in other European languages. For instance, an American English speaker would say *I have to go now* in the same context in which a Dutch speaker would simply say *Ik ga nu* or a Spanish speaker would say *me voy ahora*. If the context is one of, say, going to a doctor's appointment, the notion of obligation is implicit; however, English expresses it and the other languages do not. The increase in frequency in early stages of grammaticalization are probably due to this sort of redundancy – where a notion might have gone unexpressed in the past (because it was easily inferable), it is now expressed wherever it is intended.

A second type of redundancy is supplied by the actual linguistic elements: within a discourse in most cases one expression of tense may be enough if several clauses have the same temporal reference. However, in languages in which tense is obligatory, it is expressed in every clause. Similarly, in languages with subject-verb agreement it appears whether it is necessary for comprehension or not. The same type of redundancy occurs where determiners and adjectives agree with the noun in number and gender. This second type of redundancy indicates an even more advanced stage of grammaticalization, the stage at which categories have become obligatory. Both types of redundancy are characteristic of synthetic languages but not analytic languages.

What leads to the development of redundancy and obligatoriness? These are of course very difficult questions. In the extreme frequency increases during grammaticalization one senses an inexorable movement by which each frequency increase leads to another. One possible factor is that the constructions that are grammaticalizing become all the more accessible because of their frequency; not only is their articulation automated, but their cognitive access is as well. One might say they reach a high level of resting activation and as a result are more likely to be selected for production.

Redundant activation might be inhibited, however, by discourse conventions that favour non-redundant utterances. In such cases, repeated constructions must be interpreted as new contributions to information. Given such interpretational conventions, speakers are not likely to use constructions redundantly. One source of increased frequency is thus constrained.

As mentioned in Chapter 10, high frequency of use, including redundant use, is a prerequisite to obligatoriness. As suggested by García and van Putte 1989, obligatoriness arises by pragmatic inference. If the expression of a category becomes common enough, the listener is entitled to infer that if the category is NOT expressed, then its opposite was intended. Thus the absence of expression comes to be considered the zero expression of the complementary category. In section 10.7 this development was illustrated with the English Simple Present, which developed an habitual interpretation when the Progressive grammaticalized.

Consider now conventions for making inferences. In a culture in which utterances contain fewer redundancies, each element is taken as meaningful, so the absence of elements can mean either that the absent meanings are intended to be inferred, or that they are not intended. Thus the listener is required to fill in information that goes unexpressed. The listener is not accustomed to make the kind of inference that assigns meaning to the absence of mention. Compared to synthetic languages with many obligatory categories, the listener in an analytic language does not have linguistic cues that eliminate certain possible meanings, as when a case marker or verb agreement confirms which NP is the subject. Rather the listener is making probabilistic judgements based on semantics and prior context to determine the role of NPs, as well as other factors, such as temporal reference. With this type of inference, obligatory categories will not become established; thus an analytic language will remain analytic as long as the inferencing strategy remains the same.

It is important to note that inferencing strategies are conventional and must be learned. Children learn through experience with utterances in context what can be inferred and what must be explicitly expressed, and as we have seen this differs from language to language. Once such conventions are established, I would argue, they have an effect on how far grammaticalization can proceed in a language. Are such cultural conventions related to other properties of the culture? I see no reason to assume such relations as far as inferencing strategies are concerned. However, as we see in the next section, certain types of morphological categories may be highly related to the nature of the culture within which the language is spoken.

11.7   Deictic morphology and cultural type

It has been noted that speech used in an intimate environment – where participants know each other well and share many experiences – is different from that spoken in more public contexts, among participants who are not intimate and who cannot be presumed to share many past experiences or current conditions (Bernstein 1972, Kay 1977, Givón 1979, Perkins 1992). In situations where speakers share backgrounds, utterances can, for instance, have more pronominal use or omission of NPs, fewer subordinate clauses and the markers of those clauses. A number of researchers have noticed similar differences between spoken and written language (Chafe 1982, Biber 1986). Givón 1979: 207–33 writes of a 'pragmatic' mode characteristic of unplanned and informal discourse compared to a 'syntactic' mode used in more planned and formal discourse. He argues that evolutionarily the pragmatic mode precedes the syntactic one, which develops as a response to the speech situation in a more complex culture where we often talk to strangers.

Perkins 1992 has devised a rigorous means of testing the hypothesis that the social and cultural context in which language is used affects grammatical structure. In particular, working from the observations referred to above from Bernstein, Givón and others, Perkins hypothesizes that languages spoken in cultures where small groups share a limited physical and social background will have more inflectional or affixal markers of deixis than languages spoken in cultures where large numbers of people of diverse background communicate with one another. The hypothesis relies on the fact that inflectional affixes arise by grammaticalization and that in order for forms to grammaticalize they must be used with high frequency. Thus Perkins proposes that in cultures where communication commonly occurs among familiars, deictic expressions, such as *here, there, now, then, she, he* will occur often enough to become grammaticalized. In contrast, in cultures in which communication has to be more explicit, such markers will not grammaticalize as readily. Because there is always the cyclic loss and replacement of grammaticalized forms, as cultures grow more complex and the speech situation changes, deictic inflections will be lost and not replaced.

The test of this hypothesis relies on resolving three important issues.

First and foremost, the hypothesis must be tested on a large sample of cultures and languages, but it is very important that genetic and areal bias in such a sample be controlled. Perkins solved this problem by using a sampling technique by which he chose languages randomly from a matrix that separated languages by genetic affiliations and the potential for areal contact. It was important that the languages be chosen randomly rather than 'by convenience' so that additional bias did not creep into the sample, as only well-studied languages came to the fore. Perkins' selection by this method yielded a sample of forty-nine languages on which to base his study.

Second, a method of measuring cultural complexity must be selected. Perkins used a scale derived from the report in Murdock's *Ethnographic Atlas* (1967 and 1967–71) based on nine cultural features which referenced the type and intensity of agriculture in a culture, rules for inheritance, regional organization, craft specialization, class stratification and size of settlements. Such measures are appropriate for the hypothesis as they indicate the extent to which members of the society share background assumptions and current presuppositions.

Third, for the linguistic test of the hypothesis, Perkins selected inflectional markers of deixis, which include person markers bound to nouns or verbs, dual marking (usually in second person), the inclusive/exclusive distinction in first person, bound demonstratives, and inflectional tense. In addition, Perkins coded gender distinctions in person markers as a frequently occurring, but non-deictic category in order to test whether the absence of deixis is merely due to an absence of inflection.

The results of the survey of the forty-nine languages/cultures supported the hypothesis. A significant correspondence was found between person affixes on nouns and verbs and cultural complexity such that languages spoken in the less complex cultures had more person affixes. A significant correspondence in the same direction was found for the dual distinction and the inclusive/exclusive distinction. The presence of tense affixes on verbs showed a trend in the predicted direction and came close but did not reach significance. The few cases of demonstrative elements in nouns and verbs also showed a non-significant trend in the predicted direction. Thus most of the categories tested aligned with cultural complexity in the predicted way. In contrast, the non-deictic category tested, gender agreement on verbs, showed a non-significant association with cultural complexity (in the same direction as the deictic affixes), indicating that it is not just the presence of inflection that is predicted by cultural measures, but deictic inflection in particular, as predicted by the hypothesis.

Other attempts at similar hypotheses have been less successful. It is not known how they would fare if tested empirically because the proponents of these theories have not submitted them to empirical testing. The prospect for empirical success, however, is diminished by certain flaws in the reasoning behind them. These hypotheses are based on the observation that second-language learners simplify aspects of grammar, particularly the inflection (Trudgill 2001, Wray and Grace 2007). Extreme examples of simplification occur in pidgin and creole languages. Such languages have fewer inflectional categories than languages with more normal development and they have fewer inflectional categories than their lexifier languages (the languages from which the majority of the vocabulary is derived) (as noted by many researchers, e.g. Bickerton 1981, McWhorter 2001). It is also known that adult second-language learners often do not fully master the inflectional system of the target language and on this basis, Wray and Grace 2007 advance the opinion that languages used 'exoterically' – that is, when talking to strangers – would tend to lose morphological distinctions. Wray and Grace 2007: 551 state the hypothesis as follows:

Thus, languages that are customarily used exoterically will tend to develop and maintain features that are logical, transparent, phonologically simple and, significantly, learnable by adults. (Thurston 1989; Trudgill, 1989, 2002)

These researchers assume that the mechanism for the loss of inflection is the process of second language learning. Thus they claim that languages which are often the target of second language learning will develop properties that simplify them and make them more learnable by adults.

Several problems come to light when this hypothesis and its associated mechanisms are examined carefully. We will examine some of these problems here.

First, it is not necessarily valid to assume a continuum from what happens in the pidginization process to what happens in language contact situations in languages undergoing normal development (McWhorter 2001, Dahl 2001 contra Trudgill 2001). As is well known, pidgin languages arise in restricted social situations (plantations, trade situations) where multiple languages are spoken natively. A particular language is chosen for communication in this setting, but access to native speakers of the language, and thus the language itself is very limited. Failure of adult learners to master the language is at least in part due to this limited access. In contrast, in more ordinary cases of language contact or bilingualism (as in the case of immigrant populations, such as guest workers in Europe), second-language learners are embedded in the target language and culture. While in such cases adults still show a lesser ability to acquire a language than children, their failures do not affect the language as a whole. Rather, the effect of second-language learners is fleeting in the sense that their children have full access to the language and acquire it, becoming native speakers. The presence of adult second language learners does not change the language; rather the immigrant population gradually shifts to the language of the majority.

Second, it is important to note that not all inflection is lost in pidgin and creole languages. Roberts and Bresnan 2008 survey the categories lost and retained in twenty-seven pidgin languages from all around the world and report that fifteen of these languages retain some inflection. Certain tendencies for which type of inflection is retained also emerged:

> We have encountered evidence that the reduction of inflection is asymmetric and not always total. Inflections that contribute semantic and grammatical information pertaining to the stem are retained slightly but significantly more often than inflections that pertain more to building the syntax of the sentence outside the word. (Roberts and Bresnan 2008: 293)

Nor do second-language learners eliminate all morphology from their version of the target language (Dietrich, Klein and Noyau 1995, Prévost and White 2000). Studies of adult second language learners in natural settings (outside the classroom) are inconclusive on the issue of the use of inflections. Dietrich, Klein and Noyau 1995 and Klein and Perdue 1997 argue that the Basic Variety of the first 30 months shows very little morphological marking of tense or aspect; however, after this period some learners go on to use some inflections for tense (especially if the target language is French or English). As for agreement, Prévost and White note many correct agreement uses in the first three years for learners of French and German. Thus it is certainly incorrect to conclude that adult language learners eliminate all inflection. It is also incorrect to assert, as Wray and Grace do, that adults learn rules, while children learn the specifics and generalize less. Dietrich, Klein and Noyau observe that for all the target languages represented in their study (English, German, Dutch, Swedish and French) adult learners started with the irregular past tense formations, apparently overlooking the simpler rules of the regulars.

Finally, theories based on the notion that language change occurs in transmission to new speakers and in particular that second language adult learners simplify inflection provide no means for explaining why languages have inflection in the first place. In contrast, the theory of Perkins, which is based on the well-supported premise that language change occurs in language use, explains through grammaticalization why languages have inflections in the first place, as well as why deictic categories are not replaced in certain cultural contexts. With respect to grammaticalization, it is important to note that when inflectional categories are created anew in pidgin and creole languages, the process by which this happens is the same as in languages with normal development – that is, new categories are created by grammaticalization. This fact provides further evidence that the usage-based process of grammaticalization is responsible for the origins of grammar wherever grammar is created – in language origins, in pidgin and creole languages as well as in mature languages.

11.8   Grammaticality, frequency and universals

In this final section we treat another way in which usage patterns determine cross-linguistic patterns by considering the factors that make particular constructions frequent or infrequent within a culture. An important component of this discussion rests on the usage-based notion that high frequency of usage leads to conventionalization and further elaboration, while very low frequency of use leads to unacceptability and eventual loss. Thus we find that some construction types are robustly represented across and within languages (transitive clauses, possessive constructions) while others vary considerably across languages in their frequency of use (serial verbs [Hopper 2008]), and some that are rare in the languages in which they occur are ungrammatical in others (oblique relative clauses [Keenan 1975]; see discussion below).

In usage-based theory, grammaticality or acceptability judgements are considered to be gradient; both grammatical and ungrammatical combinations of words, morphemes or sounds can be rated for degrees of acceptability. As mentioned in Chapter 5, acceptability judgements within a language are postulated to be based on familiarity, where familiarity rests on two factors: the frequency of a word, construction or specific phrase, and similarity to existing words, constructions or phrases. Items will be judged as acceptable to the extent that they are frequent in the subject's experience or similar to frequent items. In the experiment reported in Bybee and Eddington 2006, the stimuli were taken from corpora and thus were presumably grammatical, but subjects were still able to rate them for degrees of acceptability. The highly significant results showed that high-frequency verb + adjective combinations were judged most acceptable followed closely by lower frequency combinations which were semantically similar to high-frequency combinations. Low-frequency combinations lacking semantic similarity to high-frequency ones were rated the least acceptable.[2] Thus we view the line between extremely low frequency and ungrammaticality as a gradient one.

The same factors that make a construction frequent or infrequent in one language can make it completely acceptable or unacceptable in another. High-frequency patterns are highly conventionalized and may be highly productive, while rare patterns may be retained only in fixed phrases or fall into unacceptability. Hawkins (1994, 2004, 2009) proposes the Performance-Grammar Correspondence Hypothesis, which he states as follows:

Grammars have conventionalized syntactic structures in proportion to their degree of preference in performance, as evidenced by patterns of selection in corpora and by ease of processing in psycholinguistic experiments. (Hawkins 2004: 3)

Hawkins envisions the primary factor determining frequency in corpora to be ease of processing, but it should be noted that a wide variety of factors influences frequency in corpora. In the following I would like to mention some of these and demonstrate how they influence both frequency or infrequency in language use and the patterns of occurrence in the languages of the world.

11.8.1   What people want to talk about

We have already seen that the most usual inferences or assumptions can determine factors such as the distribution of zero expression, as zeroes take on the meaning that is the most usual in the context. Highly generalized grammatical categories also gravitate towards what people talk about most – perfectives for narration, present for habitual states and situations. In addition, one might mention the high frequency of first-person-singular pronouns and verb forms, as conversation is highly subjective. First-person-singular verb forms are often highly autonomous, resisting change. Thus many cross-linguistic generalizations about both form and meaning are partially determined by what people tend to talk about.

11.8.2   What constructions speakers choose to use

There are also strong tendencies in the particular ways that information is presented and interaction is managed that determine some cross-linguistic properties of grammar. The tendency to put topics first and to choose (human) agents as topics leads to the development of the category of 'subject' and its tendency to occur before the object (Tomlin 1986, Siewierska 2002). Hawkins 1994, 2009 reports that in languages which allow both the order subject-object and object-subject, the former is much more frequent in discourse; this is paralleled, of course, by the cross-linguistic finding that subject-object order is much more common than the opposite.

Strategies for organizing discourse can also lead to the establishment of grammatical properties such as the inflectional marking of argument roles on verbs. Du Bois 1985, 1987 shows that a persistent discourse strategy in Sacapultec Maya introduces full NPs into a narrative in the absolutive role, usually as the subject of an intransitive. Further narrative mention of the referent then occurs in the ergative, but this reference is signalled only by agreement marking on the verb. Du Bois takes this pattern to be the source of the zero expression of the third singular of the absolutive – it co-occurs more often with a lexical NP, while the ergative inflection derived presumably from a pronoun and thus has overt marking.

The NP Accessibility Hierarchy was one of the first widely discussed cases in which it could be shown that what was rare in one language was non-occurring (or unacceptable) in another (Keenan 1975). This hierarchy is based on the role of the NP within the relative clause that is co-referential with the head noun. Keenan and Comrie 1977 demonstrated on a large cross-linguistic sample that if a language could form a relative clause on a case role in the following list, it could also form a relative clause using all the case roles to the left of that one.

Accessibility Hierarchy:
Subject > Direct Obj. > Indirect Obj. > Oblique > Genitive > Obj. of Comp.

That is, some languages allow relative clauses to be formed only with Subjects (Malagasy), others only on Subjects and Direct Objects (Welsh), and so on.[3] Keenan 1975 also demonstrates that in English written prose, the frequency of occurrence of each type of relative also follows this scale: subject relatives are the most common (constituting 46 per cent of the set of 2,200 relative clauses examined), direct object relatives the next most common (24 per cent), oblique and indirect object relatives next (15 per cent) and genitive relatives last (5 per cent). This correlation between acceptability in the languages of the world and frequency within one language is open to various interpretations. Keenan 1975 suggests that "there may be some sense in which it is 'easier' or more 'natural' to form RCs on the Subjects (or higher) end of the [hierarchy] than on the lower end" (1975: 138). Keenan and Comrie 1977 argue that relative clause formation with NPs in certain grammatical roles is psychologically easier because the meanings are easier to encode. They also cite studies in which it is shown that children comprehend relative clauses formed on the left end of the scale more easily than those on the right. Diessel and Tomasello 2005 offer a competing explanation of the ease with which English-speaking children use subject relatives: a subject relative retains the same word order structure as in main clauses.

Hawkins 1994 refers to 'complexity' in his suggested explanation. He proposes a formal grammatical account in which the structural description of each grammatical role is compared, and it is found that one cannot supply a structural description for a Direct Object without making reference to the Subject; further Indirect Objects require reference to Subject and Direct Object and so on. From these characterizations, one would have to further say that the 'easier', 'more natural' or less complex structures occur more frequently in the discourse of a single language and are more likely to be acceptable across languages; see Hawkins' Performance-Grammar Correspondence Hypothesis, given in the previous section. The causal link between the intra-language and the cross-language hierarchies must be that what is rarely used may come to be considered unacceptable.

The explanations provided by Keenan and Comrie and Hawkins leave much to be desired. Keenan does not specify what he means by 'easier' or more 'natural' nor does he say why certain meanings are 'easier' than others. Hawkins' formal proposal is strictly internal to the grammar in that it takes as givens the notions of Subject, Direct Object, and so on, notions that themselves need explanations.

Another possible explanation comes from what is known about how speakers tend to organize their discourse. Fox 1987 and Thompson and Fox 1990 take this approach to the examination of relative clauses in English conversation. Of course, relative clauses may not be used in exactly the same way across languages, but their studies of the use of relative clauses in English conversation is strongly suggestive of a discourse-based explanation for the Accessibility Hierarchy. Fox 1987 notes in the data she examined that subject and object relatives were equally frequent, but that most of the subject relatives were actually not agents but rather the subject of an intransitive verb. Thus by far the preponderance of examples shows the noun phrase playing the role of absolutive – subject of the intransitive or object of the transitive in the relative clause. In Fox's study and a more detailed one by Thompson and Fox 1990, it is determined that the discourse or conversational role of relative clauses is to establish the referent as relevant or related to referents that are already given in the discourse. This is done by presenting relevant characteristics of the referent (the subject function, as in 10) or by presenting the referent as the object of a transitive predication in which the agent is a pronoun (one of the discourse participants or referents already introduced, as in 11). Not that other functions are not possible; indeed they are, but these functions performed by relative clauses are the most common, making the grammar of subject and object (or absolutive) relatives the most accessible and conventionalized.

(10) She's married to this guy who's really very quiet.
(11) This man who I have for linguistics is really too much.

If other languages also use absolutive relatives for these functions, they will be frequent in discourse, and other types will be infrequent and may even be ungrammatical. Thus there are languages such as Dyirbal (Dixon 1972) in which only absolutives can be relativized and agents (ergatives) cannot.

For the Accessibility Hierarchy, then, we see various explanations being offered: processing preferences, semantic ease/difficulty, grammatical complexity, and discourse functions. In each case, the link between these factors and the relative grammaticality or acceptability of the structure is frequency in usage. One could even argue that none of these proposed explanations is necessary since the higher frequency of absolutives (subjects and objects) over other argument types would in itself render them more likely to be relativized and thus more acceptable.

The question of why more relativization positions are acceptable in some languages than in others can be addressed in the context of Perkins' theory of communication in more or less intimate communities. As outlined above, reference can be established through the use of deictic markers in smaller, more intimate cultures because of shared knowledge. In larger, more complex cultures, however, more explicit means for establishing reference, such as relative clauses, provide a necessary strategy for making reference explicit. Thus Perkins hypothesized a relation between a scale of cultural complexity and the extent to which a language allows relative clauses on the right end of the Accessibility Hierarchy. Using the languages whose relativization possibilities were discussed in Keenan and Comrie 1977, Perkins established that this cultural to grammatical association was significant, further supporting the hypothesis that contexts of language use determine what structures are grammatical.

11.8.3   Specificity or generality of meaning

Both the specificity and the generality of meaning have an effect on what is frequent in a language. Specific members of grammatical categories, such a dual number, occur less frequently within a language (Greenberg 1966) and are also more prone to loss than singular and plural. In contrast, as grammaticalizing elements, such as verbs, become more frequent and more generalized in meaning in the grammaticalizing construction, they may lose the ability to occur as main verbs. Thus the English modal verbs, such as the ancestors of *can, may, shall, will* and *must*, occurred in Old English primarily in their finite forms, with infinitive and gerund forms being very rare or non-existent. Many dialects of English now find the use of these auxiliaries as main verbs to be unacceptable, as seen in the double modal examples such as *shall can*, which formerly occurred but which are no longer acceptable. Thus the fact that many auxiliaries in the languages of the world lack nonfinite forms is due to the extreme bleaching of their meaning.

11.8.4   Processing ease/difficulty

As mentioned above, Hawkins 2004 attributes high or low frequency in discourse to processing ease or difficulty. One example that illustrates this point concerns the tendency for members of the same constituent to be adjacent syntactically. Example (12) shows the complement of *waited* to be adjacent to that verb, while in example (13) it is not.

(12) The man waited for his son in the cold but not unpleasant wind.
(13) The main waited in the cold but not unpleasant wind for his son.

Hawkins shows that tokens such as (12), which are much easier to process, are also more common in corpora of English, and that examples such as (13) would be unacceptable in some languages (Tomlin 1986).

11.8.5   Conventionalization of thinking for speaking

Another determinant of what is frequent in languages is conventionalized ways of packaging concepts for speaking, or 'thinking for speaking', as Slobin (1996) puts it. Slobin (1997a, 2003) deals primarily with the lexical features of verbs and what features they incorporate. He finds that languages fall into different types, depending upon whether they tend to incorporate directional information into motion verbs, as in Spanish, where verbs such as *entrar* 'go in', *salir* 'go out', *bajar* 'go down' and *subir* 'go up' are good examples, or whether they tend to include manner of motion information as in English *amble, saunter, run* or *swim*.

Another more grammatical example of thinking for speaking might be the extent to which a language uses serial verb constructions, that is, constructions in which two or more finite verbs are used inside the same clause to form part of the same predication (Hopper 2008: 254). Languages in which such constructions are quite commonly used are located in West Africa, Papua New Guinea and in other places throughout Africa and Asia. Serial verb constructions are not common in European languages, but they are not unknown. For instance, Hopper 2008 presents an in-depth analysis of the *take + NP and* construction of English, as in the following sentence:

(14) And unfortunately we are going to have to *take all these people and* squish them into a church that seats four hundred...

This example represents a serial verb usage in the sense that *take* and *squish* do not represent distinct events, but rather together provide the predication. Other examples in English are *go get,* as in *Let's go get some coffee,* and the *try and* construction.

Hopper's (2008) point is that what may be a minor construction-type in one language may be a dominant one in another language. That is, it seems all languages are capable of arriving at serial verb constructions through grammaticalization, but only some languages carry the tendency to an extreme. Surely this is not because one set of speakers needs serial verbs more than others. Rather, it seems that a convention of thinking for speaking – packaging information in a certain way – may become established, and then extend to more and more verbal sequences in a language.

11.9   Conclusion: explanation for linguistic structures

Following the Greenbergian approach, which we have seen presages the complex adaptive systems approach, we can consider similarities and differences among languages at various levels. At the level of specific constructions, inventories, or lexical items we tend to find some core similarities of both form and function, but with many differences. Croft 2001 argues that constructions are necessarily language-specific, yet in particular domains such as voice one can categorize constructions and find similarities among them on several dimensions, including both grammatical and distributional properties. These similarities are related to the diachronic sources from which the constructions arise and how advanced they are on their particular grammaticalization paths.

To take an example we have discussed previously, one can give a semantic definition to a construction that expresses future tense by saying that one of its uses should be for a prediction by the speaker. This definition would specify a core set of constructions cross-linguistically but they would differ in many ways: some might also express other meanings, such as intention, obligation, willingness or probability. Some might be more frequent in discourse than others; some might be inflectional and others periphrastic. Some might be prohibited from *if* clauses while others are allowed there. As we have said before, to understand the differences we can trace their diachronic development: the particular lexical source for the construction will determine which modality meanings – obligation, volition or willingness – occur; the extent of the development along the path will determine the relative frequency of modality, intention and prediction readings as well as the formal properties of the marker.

Thus the paths of change for constructions – such as voice, tense and aspect constructions – project stronger universals than the simple cross-linguistic comparisons of synchronic states. However, these cross-linguistic paths can also be further decomposed into the mechanisms and factors that create them as language is used. As mentioned in Chapters 6 and 10, chunking and phonological reduction, along with meaning changes traceable to habituation, generalization and inferencing, give rise to these changes. Thus an even stronger level for the statement of universals resides in the mechanisms of change that produce the paths as these do not vary across languages or across time (Bybee et al. 1994, Bybee 2001a, 2006b).

Yet another dimension in which language universals can be identified is constituted by the continua we have identified in the properties of constructions: analysability, compositionality, autonomy, schematicity, productivity and prototype effects in categories. All constructions in all languages have these properties to some degree or other. Thus while grammar itself is emergent and language-specific, the properties of the units of grammar on these dimensions are quite comparable across languages.

As we have seen, however, even these properties derive from the more basic cognitive processes of categorization by similarity, chunking of repeated sequences and association by contiguity. Categorization by similarity produces the categories of meaning of words and constructions, the grouping of bits of experience into the formal units of language, the categories for slots in constructions and degrees of analysability. Chunking of repeated sequences of units cements the parts of constructions together, and gives us degrees of constituency or coherence among morphemes and words. Association by contiguity allows forms to take on meaning and allows meaning to change from association with context and with frequently made inferences.

These domain-general processes operate through repetition on a massive scale, within individuals and certainly within communities; this repetition within the context of what humans like to talk about and how they structure their discourse gives shape to the grammar and lexicon of particular languages. To the extent that context, meaning, and discourse patterns are shared across languages, similarities in structure arise. Thus taking language to be an embodied activity that occurs in real time, in real situations and passes through real cognitive systems has great potential for leading to the explanation of what we perceive as linguistic structure.

Notes

CHAPTER I A USAGE-BASED PERSPECTIVE ON LANGUAGE

1 This example is from the Corpus of Contemporary American English (COCA) (Davies 2008), spoken section, and the date is 1990. In future references to this and other corpora, the citation will give the name of the corpus and the year the example occurred, e.g. COCA 1990.

CHAPTER 2 RICH MEMORY FOR LANGUAGE

1 Despite the effect of frequency on the lexical diffusion of sound changes, many turn out to be completely regular in the end.
2 Whether this is mediated by the frequency with which each word is used in other contexts as proposed by Gregory et al. 1999, Jurafsky et al. 2001 and other works by Jurafsky and colleagues is still to be determined.

CHAPTER 3 CHUNKING AND DEGREES OF AUTONOMY

1 Here and elsewhere, language-specific names of forms, such as Preterit, will be given with an initial uppercase letter. Terms for cross-linguistically defined meaning categories, such as perfective, will appear with a lowercase initial.
2 Elsewhere I have described autonomy as the extreme version of the Conserving Effect. I hope that putting the relation the other way does not create confusion.
3 Studies seeking an invariant meaning for grammatical morphemes are too numerous to cite exhaustively. Some early examples are Jakobson 1957, Diver 1964, Steele 1975, Waugh 1975, Langacker 1978; more recently, Reid 1991, Goldsmith and Woisetschlaeger 1982 and in the construction-grammar tradition, Michaelis 2006.

CHAPTER 4 ANALOGY AND SIMILARITY

1 Tomasello 2003 uses the term 'analogy' to refer to the process by which higher-order grammatical abstractions such as the categories 'noun' and 'verb' are formed by young children. He would refer to the creation of a category in a construction as schematization.
2 Reactions to potential 'garden-path' sentences are also subject to influence from prior experiences of word sequences (Jurafsky 1996).
3 Of course there are various ways such a segment of discourse could be divided into prefabs.

4 There might be inter-speaker variation on the assignment of words to prefabs or prefabs might overlap in ways not shown here. For instance, *when I was younger* may be
a prefab overlapping *I can remember when*. For evidence of the prefabricated nature
of the latter, see Chapter 9.

CHAPTER 5 CATEGORIZATION AND THE DISTRIBUTION
OF CONSTRUCTIONS IN CORPORA

1 Jackendoff 2002 and Culicover 1999 also view idiomaticity as the main reason for
adopting constructions; however, they do not consider the more general patterns of
syntax to also be accounted for by constructions.
2 The 'total number of types' will be fewer than the total of types in each corpus because some of the same types occurred in both the written and spoken corpora.
3 I am grateful to Clay Beckner for calculating the Collostructional Strength for the
Spanish constructions. He used the software in Gries 2004.
4 In the Collostructional Analysis all items were 'attracted' to the construction, except
convencido and *redondo*, which were repelled.

CHAPTER 6 WHERE DO CONSTRUCTIONS COME FROM?

1 Presumably this claim does not count the infinitives in the frequently occurring
emerging auxiliaries such as *wanna, hafta* and *gonna,* and so on.

CHAPTER 7 REANALYSIS OR THE GRADUAL CREATION
OF NEW CATEGORIES?

1 Treatments of the semantic changes in the modals can be found for *will* and *shall* in
Bybee and Pagliuca 1987, for *may* in Bybee 1988b, for *would* and *should* in Bybee
1995, and for *can* in Bybee 2003b (also see Traugott 1989 on *must*).
2 Approximately 100 clauses of the following texts were counted;
1460–80:
Ludus Conventriae 1460–77
'Mankind', *The Macro Plays* 1465–70
1550–70:
Udall, Nicholas *Roister Doister* 1566
Stevenson, William *Gammer Gurton's Needle* 1550
1594–1602:
Shakespeare, William *Love's Labour's Lost* 1594, *A MidsummerNight's Dream*
1595, *As You Like It* 1599–1600, *The Merry Wives of Windsor* 1599–1600, *All's Well
That Ends Well* 1602, *Measure for Measure* 1604.
1630–1707:
Middleton, Thomas *A Chaste Maid in Cheapside* 1630
Vanbrugh, John *The Relapse* 1697. Act II, Scene 1
Farquhar, George *The Beaux Stratagem* 1707. Act I, Scene 1
3 Modern Spoken data is taken from the Switchboard corpus. Note that spoken data is
not quite comparable to the written plays. In the Switchboard data 15 per cent of the
finite verbs were *think* and *know*, which are used as discourse markers.
4 Questions were sampled in the following way: they were extracted from the Shake-
spearean comedy *All's Well That Ends Well*. Then the last twenty of each 100 in the

first 1000 were examined and extracted if they were questions containing a verb or auxiliary. This yielded 118 examples of questions.

5 These negative examples were sampled in the following way: all instances of *not* were extracted from the comedy *All's Well That Ends Well*. Then 160 examples of *not* were selected by taking the last twenty examples from each 100, up to 800. Examples of *not* used without a verb were excluded.

6 The plays used for these counts were as follows:
1566–1588:
Udall, Nicholas *Roister Doister* 1566
Stevenson, William *Gammer Gurton's Needle* 1550
Lyly, John, *Endymion The Man in the Moon* 1585–8
1599–1602:
Shakespeare, William *All's Well That Ends Well* 1660, *Measure for Measure* 1604
1621–49:
Massinger, Phillip *A New Way to Pay Old Debts* 1621–5
Shirley, James *The Lady of Pleasure* 1635
D'Avenant, William *Love and Honour* 1649
1663–97:
Villiers, George *The Rehearsal* 1663
Etherege, George *The Man of Mode (Sir Fopling Flutter)* 1676
Vanbrugh, John *The Relapse* 1697. Act II, Scene 1

CHAPTER 8 GRADIENT CONSTITUENCY AND GRADUAL REANALYSIS

1 Lichtenberk 1991 mentions a fourth way in which reanalysis may be gradual: it can gradually diffuse through the speech community.

CHAPTER 9 CONVENTIONALIZATION AND THE LOCAL VS. THE GENERAL

1 Tao 2003 also studies the uses of *remember* in discourse.

CHAPTER 10 EXEMPLARS AND GRAMMATICAL MEANING

1 Figure 10.1 is very similar to Goossens' 1992 radial category analysis of *can* in Middle English.

2 This fact indicates that the main verb use remained connected to the auxiliary use but as the ability use became the more common interpretation, using *can* as a main verb to mean 'know' became less common and less acceptable.

3 In large corpora, however, one does find some examples of *will* in an *if*-clause that expresses future rather than willingness. Consider this example:
   (i) If I would really get tired from this, and if I *will* start to sing worse, I will just change it. (COCA 2004)

4 Another set of examples concerns indicatives that become subjunctives, as discussed in Bybee et al. 1994: 230–6.

5 In some languages both singular and plural have affixes (e.g. the noun class prefixes in Bantu languages). In such cases, Greenberg 1978b has argued that the singular and plural markers derive from demonstratives.

6 As argued in Bybee 1994, Dahl 1995 and Michaelis 2006, the aspectual meaning in present habitual and generic sentences is the same; thus when I use the term 'present habitual' I intend to include generic.

7 Note that many Progressive instances are not actually happening at the moment of speech either, as in this example:
   we get to the people who *are taking* drugs and we try to treat them

8 I am very grateful to Joanne Scheibman for preparing this table to use in this chapter.

9 To be thorough, Michaelis notes, as have many others, that the interpretation of past for states does not indicate whether the state has or has not continued into the present.

10 This point is subject to some differences of interpretation. A present habitual situation which describes repeated situations within a time range including the present could be seen as simultaneous with the moment of speech. (Cf. Comrie's 1976 definition of habitual as 'a situation which is characteristic of an extended period of time…' (27–8).)

11 Michaelis misinterprets the following statement in Bybee et al. 1994 as claiming that the English present has no meaning. Diachronically it has no lexical meaning, as we have argued above, but it takes on meaning from the context:
   "The present tense, according to Bybee et al. (1994: 152), 'carries no explicit meaning at all; it refers to the default situation from which other tenses represent deviations'. Because of its neutral semantics, they argue, the present tense can 'absorb the meaning inherent to normal social and physical phenomena, and this meaning if described and broken down explicitly, consists of habitual occurrence and behavior as well as ongoing states' (ibid.)" (Michaelis 2006: 231–2)

12 No future uses of the simple Present occurred in the samples analysed for Table 10.1.

13 For another example of an attempt at a highly abstract meaning that fails to provide a realistic description both language-internally and cross-linguistically, see Bybee 1998b, which discusses the putative category 'irrealis'.

14 I also make this point in Bybee 1988b.

15 The data reported are from the more informal corpus which Coates takes to be more representative of spoken English.

16 See Bybee et al. 1994, Chapter 8, for further specifications of these functions.

CHAPTER 11 LANGUAGE AS A COMPLEX ADAPTIVE SYSTEM

1 A further illustration of the cross-linguistic similarity in grammaticalization paths is the book-length reference work by Heine and Kuteva 2002, which lists well-documented changes from lexical to grammatical that have occurred in two or more unrelated languages.

2 Similar results have been found in acceptability studies of phonotactics (Vitevitch et al. 1997, Bailey and Hahn 2001).

3 Because it is not directly relevant to the current discussion, I omit a discussion of the difference between primary and other strategies.

Bibliography

Andersen, Henning. 1973. Abductive and deductive change. *Language* **49**: 765–93.

Anderson, John R. 1982. Acquisition of cognitive skill. *Psychological Review* **89**: 369–406.

1993. *Rules of the mind.* Hillsdale, NJ: Lawrence Erlbaum.

Anderson, John R. and Gordon H. Bower. 1973. A propositional theory of recognition memory. *Memory and Cognition* **2**(3): 406–12.

Arbib, Michael A. 2003. The evolving mirror system: a neural basis for language readiness. In Morten H. Christiansen and S. Kirby (eds.), *Language evolution*, 182–200. Oxford: Oxford University Press.

Aske, Jon. 1990. Disembodied rules vs. patterns in the lexicon: testing the psychological reality of Spanish stress rules. *Berkeley Linguistics Society* **16**: 30–45.

Baayen, Harald. 1993. On frequency, transparency, and productivity. In G. E. Booij and J. van Marle (eds.), *Yearbook of morphology*, 181–208. Dordrecht: Kluwer Academic.

2003. Probabilistic approaches to morphology. In R. Bod, J. Hay and S. Jannedy (eds.), *Probability theory in linguistics*, 229–87. Cambridge, MA: MIT Press.

Bailey, Todd M., and Ulrike Hahn. 2001. Determinants of wordlikeness: phonotactics or lexical neighborhoods? *Journal of Memory and Language* **44**: 568–91.

Baron, Naomi. 1977. *Language acquisition and historical change.* Amsterdam: North Holland.

Bates, Elizabeth. 1994. Modularity, domain specificity and the development of language. In D.C. Gajdusek, G.M. McKhann, and C.L. Bolis (eds.), *Evolution and the neurology of language. Discussions in neuroscience* **10**(1–2): 136–49.

Bates, E., I. Bertherton and L. Snyder. 1988. *From first words to grammar: individual differences and dissociable mechanisms.* New York: Cambridge University Press.

Bates, Elizabeth, Donna Thal and Virginia Marchman. 1991. Symbols and syntax: a Darwinian approach to language development. In N. Krasnegor, D. M. Rumbaugh, R. L. Schiefelbusch and M. Studdert-Kennedy (eds.), *Biological and behavioral determinants of language development*, 29–65. Hillsdale, NJ: Lawrence Erlbaum.

Beckner, Clay, and Joan Bybee. 2009. A usage-based account of constituency and reanalysis. *Language Learning* **59**: Suppl. 1, December, 27–46.

Bell, Alan, Daniel Jurafsky, Eric Fosler-Lussier, Cynthia Girand, Michelle Gregory and Daniel Gildea. 2003. Effects of disfluencies, predictability, and utterance position on word form variation in English conversation. *Journal of the Acoustical Society of America* **113**(2): 1001–24.

Berlin, Brent and Paul Kay. 1969. *Basic color terms: their universality and evolution.* Berkeley, CA: University of California Press.

Bernstein, Basel. 1972. Social class, language and socialization. In P. Giglioli (ed.), *Language and social context*. Baltimore, MD: Penguin.

Beths, Frank. 1999. The history of DARE and the status of unidirectionality. *Linguistics* **37**: 1069–10.

Biber, Douglas. 1986. Spoken and written textual dimensions in English. *Language* **62**: 384–414.

Bickerton, Derek. 1981. *Roots of language*. Ann Arbor, MI: Karoma.

Binnick, Robert I. 1991. *Time and the verb*. Oxford: Oxford University Press.

Bisang, Walter. 2004. Grammaticalization without coevolution of form and meaning: the case of tense-aspect-modality in East and mainland Southeast Asia. In W. Bisang, N. Himmelmann, and B. Wiemer (eds.), *What makes grammaticalization? A look from its fringes and its components*, 109–38. Berlin: Mouton de Gruyter.

Boas, Hans. 2003. *A constructional approach to resultatives. (Stanford Monographs in Linguistics)*. Stanford, CA: CSLI Publications.

Bowdle, Brian F. and Dedre Gentner. 2005. The career of metaphor. *Psychological Review* **112**: 193–216.

Boyland, Joyce T. 1996. *Morphosyntactic change in progress: a psycholinguistic approach*. Dissertation. University of California, Berkeley, CA.

Bradley, H. 1904. *The making of English*. New York: Macmillan.

Bransford, J. D., and J. J. Franks. 1971. The abstraction of linguistic ideas. *Cognitive Psychology* **2**: 331–50.

Brinton, Laurel and Traugott, Elizabeth C. 2005. *Lexicalization and language change*. Cambridge: Cambridge University Press.

Briscoe, Ted. 2003. Grammatical assimilation. In M. Christiansen and S. Kirby (eds.), *Language evolution*, 295–316. Oxford: Oxford University Press.

Browman, Catherine P., and Louis M. Goldstein. 1992. Articulatory phonology: an overview. *Phonetica* **49**: 155–80.

Brown, Esther. 2004. *Reduction of syllable initial /s/ in the Spanish of New Mexico and southern Colorado: a usage based approach*. Dissertation. University of New Mexico, Albuquerque, NM.

Bybee, Joan L. 1985. *Morphology: a study of the relation between meaning and form*. Amsterdam/Philadelphia: John Benjamins.

  1986. On the nature of grammatical categories: a diachronic perspective. In S. Choi (ed.), *Proceedings of the Second Eastern States Conference on Linguistics*, 17–34.

  1988a. Morphology as lexical organization. In M. Hammond and M. Noonan (eds.), *Theoretical morphology*, 119–41. San Diego, CA: Academic Press.

  1988b. Semantic substance vs. contrast in the development of grammatical meaning. *Berkeley Linguistics Society* **14**: 247–64.

  1988c. The diachronic dimension in explanation. In J. Hawkins (ed.), *Explaining language universals,* 350–79. Oxford: Basil Blackwell.

  1994. The grammaticization of zero: asymmetries in tense and aspect systems. In W. Pagliuca (ed.), *Perspectives on grammaticalization*, 235–54. Amsterdam/ Philadelphia: John Benjamins.

  1995. The semantic development of past tense modals in English. In J. Bybee and S. Fleischman (eds.) *Modality in grammar and discourse*, 503–7. Amsterdam: John Benjamins.

1997. Semantic aspects of morphological typology. In J. Bybee, J. Haiman and S. Thompson (eds.), *Essays on language function and language type*, 25–37. Amsterdam/Philadelphia: John Benjamins.

1998a. A functionalist approach to grammar and its evolution. *Evolution of Communication* **2**: 249–78.

1998b. 'Irrealis' as a grammatical category. *Anthropological linguistics* **40**: 257–71.

1998c. The emergent lexicon. *CLS 34: the panels*, 421–35. Chicago: Chicago Linguistic Society. Reprinted in Bybee 2007: 279–93.

2000a. Lexicalization of sound change and alternating environments. In M. Broe and J. Pierrehumbert (eds.), *Laboratory Phonology 5: Language acquisition and the lexicon*, 250–68. Cambridge: Cambridge University Press. Reprinted in Bybee 2007: 216–34.

2000b. The phonology of the lexicon: evidence from lexical diffusion. In M. Barlow and S. Kemmer (eds.), *Usage-based models of language*, 65–85. Stanford, CA: CSLI Publications. Reprinted in Bybee 2007: 199–215.

2001a. *Phonology and language use*. Cambridge: Cambridge University Press.

2001b. Main clauses are innovative, subordinate clauses are conservative: consequences for the nature of constructions. In J. Bybee and M. Noonan (eds.), *Complex sentences in grammar and discourse: essays in honor of Sandra A. Thompson*, 1–17. Amsterdam/Philadelphia: John Benjamins.

2002a. Sequentiality as the basis of constituent structure. In T. Givón and B. Malle (eds.), *The evolution of language from pre-language, 109–32*. Amsterdam/ Philadelphia: John Benjamins. Reprinted in Bybee 2007: 313–35.

2002b. Word frequency and context use in the lexical diffusion of phonetically conditioned sound change. *Language Variation and Change* **14**: 261–90. Reprinted in Bybee 2007: 235–64.

2003a. Cognitive processes in grammaticalization. In M. Tomasello (ed.), *The new psychology of language*, Vol. II, 145–67. Mahwah, NJ: Lawrence Erlbaum.

2003b. Mechanisms of change in grammaticization: the role of frequency. In B. D. Joseph and R. D. Janda (eds.), *The handbook of historical linguistics*, 602–23. Oxford: Blackwell. Reprinted in Bybee 2007: 336–57.

2005. Restrictions on phonemes in affixes: a crosslinguistic test of a popular hypothesis. *Linguistic Typology* **9**: 165–222.

2006a. From usage to grammar: the mind's response to repetition. *Language* **82**: 711–733.

2006b. Language change and universals. In R. Mairal and J. Gil (eds.), *Linguistic universals*, 179–94. Cambridge: Cambridge University Press.

2007. *Frequency of use and the organization of language*. Oxford: Oxford University Press.

2008. Formal universals as emergent phenomena: the origins of Structure Preservation. In J. Good (ed.), *Language universals and language change*, 108–21. Oxford: Oxford University Press.

2009a. Grammaticization: implications for a theory of language. In J. Guo, E. Lieven, S. Ervin-Tripp, N. Budwig, S. Özçalişkan, and K. Nakamura (eds.), *Crosslinguistic approaches to the psychology of language: research in the tradition of Dan Isaac Slobin*, 345–56. New York: Psychology Press.

2009b. Language universals and usage-based theory. In M. H. Christiansen, C. Collins, and S. Edelman (eds.), *Language universals*, 17–39. Oxford: Oxford University Press.

Bybee, Joan L., and Mary A. Brewer. 1980. Explanation in morphophonemics: changes in Provençal and Spanish preterite forms. *Lingua* **52**: 201–42. Reprinted in Bybee 2007: 41–73.

Bybee, Joan L., and Elly Pardo. 1981. On lexical and morphological conditioning of alternations: a nonce-probe experiment with Spanish verbs. *Linguistics* **19**: 937–68. Reprinted in Bybee 2007: 74–100.

Bybee, Joan L., and Dan I. Slobin. 1982. Why small children cannot change language on their own: evidence from the English past tense. In A. Alqvist (ed.), *Papers from the 5th International Conference on Historical Linguistics*, 29–37. Amsterdam/Philadelphia: John Benjamins.

Bybee, Joan L., and Carol L. Moder. 1983. Morphological classes as natural categories. *Language* **59**: 251–70. Reprinted in Bybee 2007: 127–47.

Bybee, Joan L., and William Pagliuca. 1987. The evolution of future meaning. In A. Giacalone Ramat, O. Carruba and G. Bernini (eds.), *Papers from the 7th International Conference on Historical Linguistics*, 109–22. Amsterdam/Philadelphia: John Benjamins.

Bybee, Joan L., and Östen Dahl. 1989. The creation of tense and aspect systems in the languages of the world. *Studies in language* **13**(1): 51–103.

Bybee, Joan L., William Pagliuca, and Revere Perkins. 1991. Back to the future. In E. Traugott and B. Heine (eds.), *Approaches to grammaticalization*, Vol.II, 17–58. Amsterdam/Philadelphia: John Benjamins.

Bybee, Joan, Revere Perkins, and William Pagliuca. 1994. *The evolution of grammar: tense, aspect and modality in the languages of the world*. Chicago: University of Chicago Press.

Bybee, Joan, and Joanne Scheibman. 1999. The effect of usage on degrees of constituency: the reduction of *don't* in English. *Linguistics* **37**(4): 575–96. Reprinted in Bybee 2007: 294–312.

Bybee, Joan, and Sandra A. Thompson. 2000. Three frequency effects in syntax. *Berkeley Linguistics Society* **23**: 65–85. Reprinted in Bybee 2007: 269–78.

Bybee, Joan, and James L. McClelland. 2005. Alternatives to the combinatorial paradigm of linguistic theory based on domain general principles of human cognition. In N. A. Ritter (ed.), *The role of linguistics in cognitive science*. Special issue of *The Linguistic Review*, **22**(2–4): 381–410.

Bybee, Joan, and David Eddington. 2006. A usage-based approach to Spanish verbs of 'becoming'. *Language* **82**: 323–55.

Bybee, Joan, and Rena Torres Cacoullos. 2009. The role of prefabs in grammaticization: How the particular and the general interact in language change. In R. Corrigan, E. Moravcsik, H. Ouali, and K. Wheatley (eds.), *Formulaic language,* Vol. I, 187–217. Typological Studies in Language. Amsterdam: John Benjamins.

Campbell, Alistair. 1959. *Old English grammar*. Oxford: Oxford University Press.

Campbell, Lyle. 2001. What's wrong with grammaticalization? In L. Campbell (ed.), *Grammaticalization: a critical assessment*. Special issue of *Language Sciences* **23** (2–3), 113–61.

Carey, Kathleen. 1994. The grammaticalization of the Perfect in Old English: an account based on pragmatics and metaphor. In W. Pagliuca (ed.), *Perspectives on grammaticalization*, 103–17. Amsterdam/Philadelphia: John Benjamins.

Casenheiser, Devin, and Adele E. Goldberg. 2005. Fast mapping of a phrasal form and meaning. *Developmental Science* **8**: 500–08.

Chafe, Wallace. 1982. Integration and involvement in speaking, writing and oral literature. In D. Tanner (ed.), *Spoken and written language: exploring orality and literacy*, 35–53. Norwood, NJ: Ablex.

Chevrot, Jean-Pierre, Laurence Beaud and Renata Varga. 2000. Developmental data on a French sociolinguistic variable: post-consonantal word-final /R/. *Language Variation and Change* **12**: 295–319.

Chomsky, Noam. 1957. *Syntactic structures*. The Hague: Mouton.

  1965. *Aspects of the theory of syntax*. Cambridge, MA: MIT Press.

  2006. On phases. In R. Freidin, C. Otero and M. Zubizaretta (eds.), *Foundational issues in linguistic theory*, 133–66. Cambridge, MA: MIT Press.

Clausner, Tim, and William Croft. 1997. The productivity and schematicity of metaphor. *Cognitive Science* **21**: 247–82.

Coates, Jennifer. 1983. *The semantics of the modal auxiliary*. London: Croom Helm.

Coleman, John, and Janet Pierrehumbert. 1997. Stochastic phonological grammars and acceptability. *Computational phonology: proceedings of the 3rd meeting of the ACL Special Interest Group in Computational Phonology*, 49–56. Somerset: Association for Computational Linguistics.

Company Company, Concepción . 2006. Subjectification of verbs into discourse markers: semantic-pragmatic change only? In B. Cornillie and N. Delbecque (eds.), *Topics in subjectification and modalization*, 97–121. Amsterdam/Philadelphia: John Benjamins.

Comrie, Bernard. 1976. *Aspect*. Cambridge: Cambridge University Press.

  1985. *Tense*. Cambridge: Cambridge University Press.

Contini-Morava, Ellen. 1989. *Discourse pragmatics and semantic categorization: the case of negation and tense-aspect with special reference to Swahili*. Berlin: Mouton de Gruyter.

Coste, Jean, and Augustin Redondo. 1965. *Syntaxe de l'espagnol moderne*. Paris: Société d'Edition d'Enseignement Superieur.

Croft, William. 2000. *Explaining language change*. Harlow: Longman Linguistic Library.

  2001. *Radical construction grammar: syntactic theory in typological perspective*. Oxford: Oxford University Press.

  2003. *Typology and universals* (2nd edn). Cambridge: Cambridge University Press.

Croft, William, and Alan Cruse. 2004. *Cognitive linguistics*. Cambridge: Cambridge University Press.

Culicover, Peter W. 1999. *Syntactic nuts: hard cases, syntactic theory, and language acquisition*. Oxford: Oxford University Press.

Culicover, Peter W., and Ray Jackendoff. 2005. *Simpler syntax*. Oxford: Oxford University Press.

Curme, George O. 1931. *A grammar of the English language*. Essex: Verbatim.

Dąbrowska, Eva, and Elena Lieven. 2005. Towards a lexically specific grammar of children's question constructions. *Cognitive Linguistics* **16**: 437–74.

Dahl, Östen. 1985. *Tense and aspect systems*. Oxford: Basil Blackwell.

1995. The marking of the episodic/generic distinction in tense-aspect systems. In G. Carlson and F. Pelletier (eds.), *The generic book*, 412–25. Chicago: University of Chicago Press.

2001. Inflationary effects in language and elsewhere. In J. Bybee and P. Hopper (eds.), *Frequency and the emergence of linguistic structure, 471–80*. Amsterdam/ Philadelphia: John Benjamins.

Davies, Mark. 2004. BYU-BNC: The British National Corpus. 100 million words, 1980s–1993. Available online at http://corpus.byu.edu/bnc.

2006. Corpus del español. (100 million words, 1200s–1900s). Available online at www.corpusdelespanol.org. Accessed Autumn 2006.

2007. Time Magazine Corpus. 100 million words, 1920s-2000s. Available online at http://corpus.byu.edu.time.

2008. The Corpus of Contemporary American English (COCA): 400+ million words, 1900–present. Available online at www.americancorpus.org.

Denison, David. 1985. The origins of periphrastic 'do': Ellegård and Visser reconsidered. In R. Eaton, O. Fischer, F. van der Leek, and W. F. Koopman (eds.), In *Papers from the 4th International Conference on English Historical Linguistics*, 45–60. Amsterdam/Philadelphia: John Benjamins.

1993. *English historical syntax: verbal constructions*. London: Longmans.

Díaz-Campos, Manuel. 2004. Acquisition of sociolinguistic variables in Spanish: do children acquire individual lexical forms or variable rules? In T. Face (ed.), *Laboratory approaches to Spanish phonology*, 221–36. Berlin: DeGruyter.

D' Introno, Franco, and Juan Manuel. Sosa. 1986. Elisión de la /d/ en el español de Caracas: aspectos sociolingüísticos e implicaciones teóricas. In R. A. Núñez Cedeño, I. Páez Urdaneta, and J. Guitart (eds.), *Estudios sobre la fonología del español del Caribe*, 135–63. Caracas: Ediciones La Casa de Bello.

Diessel, Holger, and Michael Tomasello. 2005. A new look at the acquisition of relative clauses. *Language* **81**: 1–25.

Dietrich, R., Wolfgang Klein and C. Noyau. 1995. *The acquisition of temporality in a second language*. Amsterdam/Philadelphia: John Benjamins.

Diver, William. 1964. The system of agency in the Latin noun. *Word* **20**: 178–96.

Dixon, R. M. W. 1972. *The Dyirbal language of North Queensland*. Cambridge: Cambridge University Press.

Dobzhansky, Theodosius. 1964. Biology, molecular and organismic. *American Zoologist* **4**: 443–52.

Donald, Merlin. 1991. *Origins of the modern mind: three stages in the evolution of culture and cognition*. Cambridge, MA: Harvard University Press.

1998. Mimesis and the executive suite: missing links in language evolution. In J. R. Hurford, M. Studdert-Kennedy and C. Knight (eds.), *Approaches to the evolution of language*, 44–67. Cambridge: Cambridge University Press.

Downing, Pamela. 1977. On the creation and use of English compound nouns. *Language* **53**: 810–42.

Drachman, Gaberell. 1978. Child language and language change: a conjecture and some refutations. In J. Fisiak (ed.), *Recent developments in historical phonology*, 123–44. Berlin: Walter De Gruyter.

Dryer, Matthew S. 1988. Object-verb order and adjective-noun order: dispelling a myth. *Lingua* **74**: 185–217.

Du Bois, John W. 1985. Competing motivations. In J. Haiman (ed.), *Iconicity in syntax*, 343–65. Amsterdam/Philadelphia: John Benjamins.

1987. The discourse basis of ergativity. *Language* **63**: 805–55.

Eddington, David. 1999. On 'becoming' in Spanish: a corpus analysis of verbs of expressing change of state. *Southwest Journal of Linguistics* **18**: 23–46.

2000. Stress assignment in Spanish within the analogical modeling of language. *Language* **76**: 92–109.

Ellegård, Alvar. 1953. *The auxiliary DO: the establishment and regulation of its use in English.* Stockholm: Almqvist and Wiksell.

Ellis, Nick C. 1996. Sequencing in SLA: phonological memory, chunking and points of order. *Studies in Second Language Acquisition* **18**: 91–126.

Ellis, Nick C., and Diane Larsen-Freeman. 2006. Language emergence: implications for applied linguistics – introduction to the special issue. *Applied linguistics* **27**(4): 558–89.

Erman, Britt, and Beatrice Warren. 2000. The Idiom Principle and the Open Choice Principle. *Text* **20**: 29–62.

Fente, R. 1970. Sobre los verbos de cambio o devenir. *Filología Moderna* **38**: 157–72.

Fidelholtz, James. 1975. Word frequency and vowel reduction in English. *Chicago Linguistic Society* **11**: 200–13.

Fillmore, Charles J., and Paul Kay. 1999. Grammatical constructions and linguistic generalizations: the What's X doing Y? construction. *Language* **75**(1): 1–33.

Fillmore, Charles J., Paul Kay and Mary C. O' Connor. 1988. Regularity and idiomaticity in grammatical constructions. *Language* **64**: 501–38.

Fischer, Olga. 2007. *Morphosyntactic change.* Oxford: Oxford University Press.

Foulkes, Gerald, and Paul Docherty. 2006. The social life of phonetics and phonology. *Journal of Phonetics* **34**: 409–38.

Fowler, Carol A., and Jonathan Housum. 1987. Talkers' signaling of "new" and "old" words in speech and listeners' perception and use of the distinction. *Journal of Memory and Language* **26**: 489–504.

Fox, Barbara A. 1987. The Noun Phrase Accessibility Hierarchy reinterpreted: subject primacy or the absolutive hypothesis. *Language* **63**: 856–70.

Frisch, Stefan A., Nathan R. Large, Bushra Zawaydeh and David B. Pisoni. 2001. Emergent phonotactic generalizations in English and Arabic. In J. Bybee and P. Hopper (eds.), *Frequency and the emergence of linguistic structure*, 159–80. Amsterdam/Philadelphia: John Benjamins.

García, Erica., and Florimon van Putte. 1989. Forms are silver, nothing is gold. *Folia Linguistica Historica* **8**(1–2): 365–84.

Gentner, Dedre. 1983. Structure-mapping: a theoretical framework for analogy. *Cognitive science* **7**: 155–70.

Gentner, Dedre, and Arthur B. Markman. 1997. Structure mapping in analogy and similarity. *American Psychologist* **52**: 45–56.

Gibbs, Raymond W., and Jennifer E. O' Brien. 1990. Idioms and mental imagery: the metaphorical motivation for idiomatic meaning. *Cognition* **36**(11): 35–68.

Givón, Talmy. 1971. Historical syntax and synchronic morphology: an archeologist's field trip. *CLS* **7**: 384–415. Chicago: Chicago Linguistic Society.

1973. The time-axis phenomenon. *Language* **49**: 890–925.

1975. Serial verbs and syntactic change: Niger-Congo. In Charles N. Li (ed.), *Word order and word order change*, 47–112. Austin, TX: University of Texas Press.

1979. *On understanding grammar*. New York/San Francisco: Academic Press.

1984. *Syntax: a functional-typological introduction*, Vol. I. Amsterdam/Philadelphia: John Benjamins.

2002. *Biolinguistics: the Santa Barbara lectures*. Amsterdam/Philadelphia: John Benjamins.

Godfrey, John, Edward Holliman and Jane McDaniel. 1992. SWITCHBOARD: Telephone speech corpus for research and development. In *Proceedings of the IEEE ICASSP-92*, 517–20. San Francisco: IEEE.

Goldberg, Adele E. 1995. *Constructions: a construction grammar approach to argument structure*. Chicago: University of Chicago Press.

2003. Constructions: a new theoretical approach to language. *Trends in Cognitive Science* **7**: 219–24.

2006. *Constructions at work: the nature of generalization in language*. Oxford: Oxford University Press.

Goldberg, Adele E., Devin Casenheiser and N. Sethuraman. 2004. Learning argument structure generalizations. *Cognitive Linguistics* **14**: 289–316.

Goldinger, Stephen. 1996. Word and voices: episodic traces in spoken word identification and recognition memory. *Journal of Experimental Psychology* **22**: 1166–83.

Goldinger, Stephen, Paul Luce and David Pisoni. 1989. Priming lexical neighbors of spoken words: effects of competition and inhibition. *Journal of Memory and Language* **28**: 501–18.

Goldsmith, John, and E. Woisetschlaeger. 1982. The logic of the English progressive. *Linguistic Inquiry* **13**: 79–89.

Goossens, Louis. 1987. The auxiliarization of the English modals: a functional grammar view. In M. Harris and P. Ramat (eds.), *Historical development of auxiliaries* (*Trends in linguistics*, 35), 111–43. Berlin: Mouton de Gruyter.

1990. *Cunnan, conne(n), can*: the development of a radial category. In G. Kellermann and M. D. Morrissey (eds.), *Diachrony within synchrony: language history and cognition*, 377–94. Frankfurt am Main: Peter Lang.

Greenberg, Joseph H. 1963. Some universals of grammar with particular reference to the order of meaningful elements. In J. Greenberg (ed.), *Universals of language*, 73–113. Cambridge, MA: MIT Press.

1966. *Language universals: with special reference to feature hierarchies*. The Hague: Mouton.

1969. Some methods of dynamic comparison in linguistics. In J. Puhvel (ed.), *Substance and structure of language*, 147–203. Berkeley/Los Angeles: University of California Press.

1978a. Diachrony, synchrony and language universals. In J. Greenberg, C. Ferguson and E. Moravcsik (eds.), *Universals of human language: method and theory*, Vol.I, 61–92. Stanford, CA: Stanford University Press.

1978b. How do languages acquire gender markers? In J. Greenberg, C. Ferguson and E. Moravcsik (eds.), *Universals of human language*, Vol.III, 47–82. Stanford, CA: Stanford University Press.

Greenberg, Joseph H., Charles Ferguson and Edith Moravcsik (eds.). 1978. *Universals of human language: method and theory*. Stanford, CA: Stanford University Press.

Gregory, Michelle, William Raymond, Alan Bell, Eric Fosler-Lussier and Daniel Jurafsky. 1999. The effects of collocational strength and contextual predictability in lexical production. *CLS* **35**: 151–66. Chicago: Chicago Linguistic Society.

Gries, Stefan Th. 2004. Coll. analysis 3. A program for R for Windows.

Gries, Stefan, Beate Hampe and Doris Schönefeld. 2005. Converging evidence: bringing together experimental and corpus data on the association of verbs and constructions. *Cognitive Linguistics* **16**(4): 635–76.

Gurevich, Olga, Matt Johnson, and Adele E. Goldberg. To appear. Incidental verbatim memory for language. *Language and Cognition*.

Haiman, John. 1985. *Natural syntax*. Cambridge: Cambridge University Press.

1994. Ritualization and the development of language. In W. Pagliuca (ed.), *Perspectives on grammaticalization*, 3–28. Amsterdam/Philadelphia: John Benjamins.

2002. Systematization and the origin of rules: the case of subject-verb inversion in questions. *Studies in Language* **26**(3): 573–93.

Halle, Morris. 1962. Phonology in generative grammar. *Word* **18**: 54–72.

Harrington, Jonathan. 2006. An acoustic analysis of 'happy-tensing' in the Queen's Christmas broadcasts. *Journal of Phonetics* **34**: 439–457.

Harris, Alice C., and Lyle Campbell. 1995. *Historical syntax in cross-linguistic perspective*. Cambridge: Cambridge University Press.

Haspelmath, Martin. 1989. From purposive to infinitive – a universal path of grammaticization, *Folia Linguistica Historica* **10**: 287–310.

1998. Does grammaticalization need reanalysis? *Studies in Language* **22**(2): 315–51.

Hatcher, Anna G. 1951. The use of the Progressive form in English. *Language* **27**: 254–80.

Hawkins, John A. 1983. *Word order universals*. New York: Academic Press.

1994. *A performance theory of order and constituency*. Cambridge: Cambridge University Press.

2004. *Efficiency and complexity in grammars*. Oxford: Oxford University Press.

2009. Language universals and the Performance-Grammar Correspondence Hypothesis. In M. Christiansen, C. Collins and S. Edelman (eds.), *Language universals*, 54–78. Oxford: Oxford University Press.

Hay, Jennifer. 2001. Lexical frequency in morphology: is everything relative? *Linguistics* **39**: 1041–70.

2002. From speech perception to morphology: affix-ordering revisited. *Language* **78**: 527–55.

Hay, Jennifer, and Harald Baayen. 2002. Parsing and productivity. *Yearbook of Morphology 2001*, 203–35.

Hay, Jennifer, and Joan Bresnan. 2006. Spoken syntax: the phonetics of giving a hand in New Zealand English. *The Linguistic Review* **23**(3): 321–49.

Heine, Bernd. 1993. *Auxiliaries: cognitive forces and grammaticalization*. Oxford: Oxford University Press.

Heine, Bernd, and Tania Kuteva. 2002. *World lexicon of grammaticalization*. Cambridge: Cambridge University Press.

2007. *The genesis of grammar: a reconstruction*. Oxford: Oxford University Press.

Heine, Bernd, and Mechthild Reh. 1984. *Grammaticalization and reanalysis in African languages*. Hamburg: H Buske.

Heine, Bernd, Ulrike Claudi and Friederike Hünnemeyer. 1991. *Grammaticalization: a conceptual framework*. Chicago: University of Chicago Press.

Hoffman, Sebastian. 2005. *Grammaticalization and English complex prepositions: a corpus-based study*. London/New York: Routledge.

Hook, Peter Edwin. 1991. The emergence of perfective aspect in Indo-Aryan languages. In E. Closs T. and B. Heine (eds.) *Approaches to grammaticalization,* Vol. II, 5989. Amsterdam: John Benjamins.

Hooper, Joan B. 1976. Word frequency in lexical diffusion and the source of morphophonological change. In W. Christie (ed.), *Current progress in historical linguistics,* 96–105. Amsterdam: North Holland. Reprinted in Bybee 2007: 23–34.

1979. Child morphology and morphophonemic change. *Linguistics* **17**: 21–50. Reprinted in J. Fisiak (ed.) 1980. *Historical morphology,* 157–87. The Hague: Mouton.

Hooper, Joan B. and Sandra A. Thompson. 1973. On the applicability of root transformations. *Linguistic Inquiry* **4**: 465–97.

Hopper, Paul J. 1987. Emergent grammar. *Berkeley Linguistic Society* **13**: 139–57.

1991. On some principles of grammaticization. In E. C. Traugott and B. Heine (eds.), *Approaches to grammaticalization,* Vol.I, 17–35. Amsterdam/Philadelphia: John Benjamins.

1994. Phonogenesis. In W. Pagliuca (ed.), *Perspectives on grammaticalization,* 29–45. Amsterdam/Philadelphia: John Benjamins.

2008. Emergent serialization in English: pragmatics and typology. In J. Good (ed.) *Language universals and language change,* 253–84. Oxford: Oxford University Press.

Hopper, Paul J., and Sandra A. Thompson. 1980. Transitivity in grammar and discourse. *Language* **56**: 251–99.

1984. The discourse basis for lexical categories in universal grammar. *Language* **60**(4): 703–52.

Hopper, Paul J., and Elizabeth Traugott. 2003. *Grammaticalization* (2nd edition). Cambridge: Cambridge University Press.

Huddleston, Rodney D., and Geoffrey K. Pullum. 2002. *The Cambridge grammar of the English language.* Cambridge: Cambridge University Press.

Israel, Michael. 1996. The way constructions grow. In A. E. Goldberg (ed.), *Conceptual structure, discourse, and language,* 217–30. Stanford, CA: CSLI.

Jackendoff, Ray. 1975. Morphological and semantic regularities in the lexicon. *Language* **51**: 639–71.

2002. *Foundations of language.* Oxford: Oxford University Press.

Jakobson, Roman. 1957 [1971]. Shifters, verbal categories and the Russian verb. Reprinted in *Roman Jakobson, Selected Writings II,* 130–47. The Hague: Mouton.

1966 [1971]. Quest for the essence of language. *Diogenes,* 51. Reprinted in *Roman Jakobson, Selected Writings II,* 345–59. The Hague: Mouton.

1990. Some questions of meaning. In L. R. Waugh (ed.), *On language: Roman Jakobson,* 315–23. Cambridge, MA: Harvard University Press.

James, William. 1950 [1890]. *Principles of psychology.* New York: Dover.

Janda, Richard D. 2001. Beyond 'pathways' and 'unidirectionality': on the discontinuity of language transmission and the counterability of grammaticalization. In L. Campbell (ed.), *Grammaticalization: a critical assessment.* Special issue of *Language Sciences,* **23**(2–3): 265–340.

Jespersen, Otto. 1942. *A modern English grammar on historical principles, Part VI: Morphology.* London: George Allen & Unwin; Copenhagen: Ejnar Munksgaard.

Johnson, Keith. 1997. Speech perception without speaker normalization. In K. Johnson and J. W. Mullennix (eds.), *Talker variability in speech processing*, 145–65. San Diego, CA: Academic Press.

Johnson-Laird, P., and R. Stevenson. 1970. Memory for syntax. *Nature* **227**: 412.

Johnson-Laird, P., C. Robins and L. Velicogna. 1974. Memory for words. *Nature* **251**: 704–705.

Jurafsky, Daniel. 1996. A probabilistic model of lexical and syntactic access and disambiguation. *Cognitive Science* **20**: 137–94.

Jurafsky, Daniel, Alan Bell and Cynthia Girand. 2002. The role of the lemma in form variation. In C. Gussenhoven and N. Warner (eds.), *Papers in laboratory phonology VII*, 1–34. Berlin/New York: Mouton de Gruyter.

Jurafsky, Daniel, Alan Bell, Michelle Gregory and William Raymond. 2001. Probabilistic relations between words: evidence from reduction in lexical production. In J. Bybee and P. Hopper (eds.), *Frequency and the emergence of linguistic structure*, 229–54. Amsterdam/Philadelphia: John Benjamins.

Kay, Paul. 1977. Language evolution and speech style. In B. Blount and M. Sanchez (eds.), *Sociocultural dimensions of language change*, 21–33. New York: Academic Press.

Keenan, Edward L. 1975. Variation in universal grammar. In E. Keenan, R. Fasold and R. Shuy (eds.), *Analyzing variation in language*, 136–48. Washington, DC: Georgetown University Press.

Keenan, Edward L., and Bernard Comrie. 1977. Noun phrase accessibility and Universal Grammar. *Linguistic Inquiry* **8**(1): 63–99.

Kiparsky, Paul. 1968. Linguistic universals and linguistic change. In E. Bach and R.T. Harms (eds.), *Universals in linguistic theory*, 171–204. New York: Holt Rinehart and Winston.

  1985. Some consequences of lexical phonology. *Phonology yearbook* **2**: 85–138.

  1995. The phonological basis of sound change. In J. Goldsmith (ed.), *The handbook of phonological theory*, 640–70. Oxford: Blackwell.

Kirby, Simon. 2000. Syntax without natural selection: how compositionality emerges from vocabulary in a population of learners. In C. Knight, J. Hurford & M. Studdert-Kennedy (eds.), *The evolutionary emergence of language: social function and the origins of linguistic form*, 303–23. Cambridge: Cambridge University Press.

  2001. Spontaneous evolution of linguistic structure: an iterated learning model of the emergence of regularity and irregularity. *IEEE Journal of Evolutionary Computation* **5**(2):102–10.

Kirby, Simon, and Morten Christiansen. 2003. From language learning to language evolution. In M. Christiansen and S. Kirby (eds.), *Language evolution*, 279–94. Oxford: Oxford University Press.

Klein, Wolfgang, and Clive Perdue. 1997. The basic variety (or: couldn't natural languages be much simpler?). *Second Language Research* **13**(4): 301–47.

Köpcke, Klaus-Michael. 1988. Schemas in German plural formation. *Lingua* **74**: 303–35.

Kotovsky, Laura, and Dedre Gentner. 1996. Comparison and categorization in the development of relational similarity. *Child Development* **67**: 2797–822.

Kroch, Anthony. 1989a. Function and grammar in the history of English: periphrastic *do*. In R. W. Fasold and D. Schiffren (eds.), *Language change and variation*, 134–69. Amsterdam/Philadelphia: John Benjamins.

  1989b. Reflexes of grammar in patterns of language change. *Language Variation and Change* **1**: 199–244.

Kroch, Anthony, John Myhill and Susan Pintzuk. 1982. Understanding *do*. *CLS* **18**: 282–94. Chicago: Chicago Linguistics Society.

Krott, Andrea, Harald Baayen and R. Schreuder. 2001. Analogy in morphology: modeling the choice of linking morphemes in Dutch. *Linguistics* **39**(1): 51–93.

Krug, Manfred. 1998. String frequency: a cognitive motivating factor in coalescence, language processing and linguistic change. *Journal of English Linguistics* **26**: 286–320.

Labov, William. 1966. *The social stratification of English in New York City*. Arlington, VA: Center for Applied Linguistics.

1972. *Sociolinguistic patterns*. Philadelphia, PA: University of Pennsylvania Press.

1982. Building on empirical foundations. In Winfred P. Lehmann and Yakov Malkiel (eds.), *Perspectives on historical linguistics*, 17–92. Amsterdam: John Benjamins.

1994. *Principles of linguistic change: internal factors*. Oxford: Blackwell.

Lakoff, George. 1987. *Women, fire, and dangerous things: what categories reveal about the mind*. Chicago: University of Chicago Press.

Lancelot, C. and A. Arnauld. 1660. *Grammaire générale et raisonnée*. Paris: Pierre le Petit.

Langacker, Ronald. 1978. The form and meaning of the English auxiliary. *Language* **54**: 853–82.

1987. *Foundations of cognitive grammar: theoretical prerequisites*, Vol.I. Stanford, CA: Stanford University Press.

2000. A dynamic usage-based model. In M. Barlow and S. Kemmer (eds.), *Usage-based models of language*, 1–63. Stanford, CA: CSLI.

Larsen-Freeman, Diane. 1997. Chaos/complexity science and second language acquisition. *Applied Linguistics* **18**: 141–65.

Lehmann, Christian. 1982. *Thoughts on grammaticalization: a programmatic sketch*, Vol. I. (Arbeiten des Kölner Universalien-Projekts 48). Köln: Universität zu Köln. Institut für Sprachwissenschaft.

Li, Charles N. 1975. *Word order and word order change*. Austin, TX: University of Texas Press.

1976. *Subject and topic*. New York: Academic Press.

(ed.) 1977. *Mechanisms of syntactic change*. Austin, TX: University of Texas Press.

2002. Some issues concerning the origin of language. In J. Bybee and M. Noonan (eds.), *Complex sentences in grammar and discourse: essays in honor of Sandra A. Thompson*, 203–21. Amsterdam/Philadelphia: John Benjamins.

Li, P., Elizabeth Bates and Brian MacWhinney. 1993. Processing a language without inflections: a reaction time study of sentence interpretation in Chinese. *Journal of Memory and Language* **32**: 169–92.

Liberman, A. M., K. Safford Harris, H. Hoffman and B. C. Griffith. 1957. The discrimination of speech sounds within and across phoneme boundaries. *Journal of Experimental Psychology* **54**: 358–68.

Lichtenberk, Frantiek. 1991. On the gradualness of grammaticalization. In E.C. Traugott and B. Heine (eds.), *Approaches to grammaticalization*, 37–80. Amsterdam/ Philadelphia: John Benjamins.

Lieven, Elena, Julian M. Pine and Gillian Baldwin. 1997. Lexically-based learning and early grammatical development. *Journal of Child Language* **24**: 187–219.

Lightfoot, David. 1979. *Principles of diachronic syntax*. Cambridge: Cambridge University Press.

1991. *How to set parameters: arguments from language change*. Cambridge, MA: MIT Press.

Lin, Zi-Yu. 1991. *The development of grammatical markers in Archaic Chinese and Han Chinese.* Dissertation. SUNY, Buffalo, NY.

Lindblom, Björn. 1990. Explaining phonetic variation: a sketch of the H&H theory. In W. J. Hardcastle and A. Marchal (eds.), *Speech production and speech modelling,* 403–39. Dordrecht: Kluwer.

Lindblom, Björn, Peter MacNeilage and Michael Studdert-Kennedy. 1984. Self-organizing processes and the explanation of language universals. In B. Butterworth, B. Comrie and Ö. Dahl (eds.), *Explanations for language universals,* 181–203. Berlin/New York: Walter de Gruyter.

Lord, Carol. 1976. Evidence for syntactic reanalysis: from verb to complementizer in Kwa. In S. B. Steever, C. A. Walker and S. Mufwene (eds.), *Papers from the parasession on diachronic syntax,* 179–91. Chicago: Chicago Linguistic Society.

Los, Bettelou. 2005. *The rise of the* to-*infinitive.* Oxford: Oxford University Press.

Losiewicz, Beth L. 1992. *The effect of frequency on linguistic morphology.* Dissertation. University of Texas, Austin, TX.

Luce, Paul, David Pisoni, and Stephen Goldinger. 1990. Similarity neighborhoods of spoken words. In G. Altmann (ed.), *Cognitive models of speech processing: psycholinguistic and computational perspectives,* 122–47. Cambridge, MA: MIT Press.

MacFarland, T., and Janet Pierrehumbert. 1991. On ich-Laut, ach-Laut and structure preservation. *Phonology* **8**: 171–80.

MacWhinney, Brian. 1978. The acquisition of morphophonology. *Monographs of the Society for Research in Child Development* **174**(43).

Malt, B. C., and E. E. Smith. 1984. Correlated properties in natural categories. *Journal of Verbal Learning and Verbal Behavior* **23**: 250–69.

Mańczak, Witold. 1980. Laws of analogy. In J. Fisiak (ed.), *Historical morphology, 28388.* The Hague: Mouton.

Marchese, Lynell. 1986. *Tense/aspect and the development of auxiliaries in Kru languages.* Arlington, VA: Summer Institute of Linguistics.

Marcos Marín, Francisco. 1992. *Corpus oral de referencia del español contemporáneo.* Textual corpus, Universidad Autónoma de Madrid.

Marcus, Gary F., Steven Pinker, M. Ullman, M. Hollander, T. J. Rosen and F. Xu. 1992. Overregularization in language acquisition. *Monographs of the society for research in child development* **57**(4): 1–182.

McClelland, James L., and Joan Bybee. 2007. Gradience of gradience: a reply to Jackendoff. *The Linguistic Review* **24**: 437–55.

McWhorter, John. 2001. Defining 'creole' as a synchronic term. In I. Neumann-Holzschuh and E. Schneider (eds.), *Degrees of restructuring in creole languages,* 85–124. Amsterdam/Philadelphia: John Benjamins.

Medin, Douglas. L., and Marguerite M. Schaffer. 1978. Context theory of classification learning. *Psychological Review* **85**: 207–38.

Meillet, Antoine. 1912. L'évolution des formes grammaticales. *Scientia (Rivista di scienza)* **6**(12): 384–400.

Michaelis, Laura A. 2004. Type shifting in Construction Grammar: an integrated approach to aspectual coercion. *Cognitive Linguistics* **15**(1): 1–67.

   2006. Tense in English. In B. Aarts and A. MacMahon (eds.), *The handbook of English linguistics,* 220–34. Oxford: Blackwell.

Miller, George A. 1956. The magical number seven, plus or minus two: some limits on our capacity for processing information. *Psychological Review* **63**: 81–97.

Miller, Joanne. 1994. On the internal structure of phonetic categories: a progress report. *Cognition* **50**: 271–85.

Moonwomon, Birch. 1992. The mechanism of lexical diffusion. Paper presented at the Annual Meeting of the Linguistic Society of America, January, Philadelphia.

Morton, J. 1967. A singular lack of incidental learning. *Nature* **215**: 203–04.

Mossé, Fernand. 1952. *A handbook of Middle English.* Translated by James A. Walker. Baltimore, MD: Johns Hopkins University Press.

    1968. *Manual of Middle English.* Baltimore, MD: Johns Hopkins University Press.

Mowrey, Richard, and William Pagliuca. 1995. The reductive character of articulatory evolution. *Rivista di Linguistica* **7**(1): 37–124.

Munson, Benjamin, and Nancy P. Solomon. 2004. The effect of phonological neighborhood density on vowel articulation. *Journal of Speech, Language, and Hearing Research* **47**: 1048–58.

Murphy, G. L., and A. M. Shapiro. 1994. Forgetting of verbatim information in discourse. *Memory and Cognition* **22**: 85–94.

Nader, K., G.E. Schafe, and J.E. le Doux. 2000. Fear memories require protein synthesis in the amygdale for reconsolidation after retrieval. *Nature* **406**: 722–6.

Nagle, Stephen J. 1989. *Inferential change and syntactic modality in English.* Frankfurt am Main: Lang.

Newell, Allen. 1990. *Unified theories of cognition.* Cambridge, MA: MIT Press.

Newmeyer, Frederick J. 1998. *Language form and language function.* Cambridge, MA: MIT Press.

    2005. *Possible and probable languages: a generative perspective on linguistic typology.* Oxford: Oxford University Press.

Noonan, Michael. 1998. Non-structuralist syntax. In M. Darnell, E. Moravcsik, F. Newmeyer, M. Noonan and K. Wheatley (eds.), *Functionalism and formalism in linguistics*, Vol. I, 11–31. Amsterdam/Philadelphia: John Benjamins.

Norde, Muriel. 2001. Deflexion as a counterdirectional factor in grammatical change. In L. Campbell (ed.), *Grammaticalization: a critical assessment.* Special issue of *Language Sciences* **23**(2–3): 231–64.

Nosofsky, Robert M. 1988. Similarity, frequency, and category representations. *Journal of Experimental Psychology: learning, memory, and cognition* **14**: 54–65.

Nunberg, Geoffrey, Ivan A. Sag and Thomas Wasow. 1994. Idioms. *Language* **70**: 491–538.

Ogura, M. 1993. The development of periphrastic *do* in English: a case of lexical diffusion in syntax. *Diachronica* **10**(1): 51–85.

O'Neill, John. 1999. *Electronic Texts and Concordances of the Madison Corpus of Early Spanish Manuscripts and Printings,* CD-ROM. Madison and New York; Hispanic Seminary of Medieval Studies.

Patterson, Janet L. 1992. *The development of sociolinguistic phonological variation patterns for (ing) in young children.* Dissertation. University of New Mexico, Albuquerque, NM.

Pawley, Andrew, and Frances Hodgetts Syder. 1983. Two puzzles for linguistic theory: nativelike selection and nativelike fluency. In J. C. Richards and R. W. Schmidt, *Language and communication*, 191–226. London: Longman.

Perkins, Revere. 1992. *Deixis, grammar, and culture*. Amsterdam/Philadelphia: John Benjamins.

Peters, Ann M. 1983. *The units of language acquisition*. Cambridge: Cambridge University Press.

Pierrehumbert, Janet. 1994. Syllable structure and word structure: a study of triconsonantal clusters in English. In Patricia Keating, ed., *Phonological structure and phonetic form: papers in laboratory phonology III*, 168–90. Cambridge: Cambridge University Press.

—— 2001. Exemplar dynamics: word frequency, lenition and contrast. In J. Bybee and P. Hopper (eds.), *Frequency and the emergence of linguistic structure*, 137–57. Amsterdam/Philadelphia: John Benjamins.

—— 2002. Word-specific phonetics. In C. Gussenhoven and N. Warner (eds.), *Laboratory phonology 7*, 101–39. Berlin: Mouton de Gruyter.

—— 2003. Phonetic diversity, statistical learning, and acquisition of phonology. *Language and speech* **46**(2–3): 115–54.

Pine, Julian M., and Elena Lieven. 1993. Reanalysing rote-learned phrases: individual differences in the transition to multiword speech. *Journal of Child Language* **20**: 551–71.

Pinker, Steven. 1991. Rules of language. *Science* **253**: 530–35.

—— 1999. *Words and rules*. New York: Basic Books.

—— 2003. *The blank slate: the modern denial of human nature*. New York: Viking.

Pinker, Steven, and Paul Bloom. 1990. Natural language and natural selection. *Behavioral and Brain Sciences* **13**: 707–26.

Phillips, Betty S. 1984. Word frequency and the actuation of sound change. *Language* **60**: 320–42.

—— 2001. Lexical diffusion, lexical frequency, and lexical analysis. In J. Bybee and P. Hopper (eds.), *Frequency and the emergence of linguistic structure*, 123–36. Amsterdam/Philadelphia: John Benjamins.

Plank, Frans. 1984. The modals story retold. *Studies in Language* **8**(3): 305–64.

Poplack, Shana. To appear. A variationist perspective on grammaticalization. In B. Heine and H. Narrog (eds.) *Handbook of grammaticalization*. Oxford University Press.

Poplack, Shana, and Sali Tagliamonte. 1996. Nothing in context: variation, grammaticization and past time marking in Nigerian Pidgin English. In P. Baker and A. Syea (eds.), *Changing meanings, changing functions: papers relating to grammaticalization in contact languages*, 71–94. London: University of Westminster.

Pountain, Christopher J. 1984. How 'become' became in Castilian. In *Essays in honour of Robert Brian Tate from his colleagues and pupils*, 101–11. University of Nottingham Monographs in the Humanities.

Prévost, P., and L. White. 2000. Missing surface inflection or impairment in second language acquisition? Evidence from tense and agreement. *Second language research* **16**(2): 103–33.

Quirk, Randolf, Sydney Greenbaum, Geoffrey Leech, and Jan Svartvik. 1985. *A comprehensive grammar of the English language*. New York: Harcourt Brace Jovanovich.

Reid, Wallis. 1991. *Verb and noun number in English: a functional explanation*. New York: Longman.

Reyna, V. F., and B. Kiernan. 1994. The development of gist versus verbatim memory in sentence recognition: effects of lexical familiarity, semantic content, encoding instruction, and retention interval. *Developmental Psychology* **30**: 178–91.

Roberts, Ian. 1985. Agreement parameters and the development of the English modal auxiliaries. *Natural Language and Linguistic Theory* **3**: 21–58.

Roberts, Ian, and Anna Roussou. 2003. *Syntactic change: a minimalist approach to grammaticalization.* Cambridge: Cambridge University Press.

Roberts, Julie. 1994. *Acquisition of variable rules: (-t, d) deletion and* (ing) *production in preschool children.* Dissertation, University of Pennsylvania, Philadelphia.

1997. Acquisition of variable rules: a study of (-t, d) deletion in preschool children. *Journal of Child Language* **24**: 351–72.

Roberts, Sarah J., and Joan Bresnan. 2008. Retained inflectional morphology in pidgins: a typological study. *Linguistic Typology* **12**: 269–302.

Romaine, Suzanne. 1995. The grammaticalization of irrealis in Tok Pisin. In J. Bybee and S. Fleischmann (eds.), *Modality in grammar and discourse*, 389–427. Amsterdam/Philadelphia: John Benjamins.

Rosch, Eleanor H. 1973. Natural categories. *Cognitive Psychology* **4**: 328–50.

1975. Cognitive representation of semantic categories. *Journal of Experimental Psychology* **104**: 573–605.

1978. Principles of categorization. In E. H. Rosch and B. B. Lloyd (eds.), *Cognition and categorization*, 27–48. Hillsdale, NJ: Lawrence Erlbaum.

Rumelhart, David E., James L. McClelland, and the PDP research group. 1986. *Parallel distributed processing: explorations in the microstructure of cognition*, vols. 1–2. Cambridge, MA: MIT Press.

Sachs, Jacqueline S. 1967. Recognition memory for syntactic and semantic aspects of connected discourse. *Perception and Psychophysics* **2**(9): 437–43.

Sankoff, Gillian, and Hélène Blondeau. 2007. Language change across the lifespan: /r/ in Montreal French. *Language* **83**: 560–614.

Sapir, Edward. 1921. *Language: an introduction to the study of speech.* New York: Harcourt Brace.

Savage, Ceri, Elena Lieven, Anna Theakston and Michael Tomasello. 2003. Testing the abstractness of children's linguistic representations: lexical and structural priming of syntactic constructions in young children. *Developmental Science* **6**(5): 557–567.

Scheibman, Joanne. 2000. *I dunno but* … a usage-based account of the phonological reduction of *don't. Journal of Pragmatics* **32**: 105–24.

Scheibman, Joanne. 2002. *Point of view and grammar: structural patterns of subjectivity in American English conversation.* Amsterdam: John Benjamins.

Schwenter, Scott A. 1994. The grammaticalization of an anterior in progress: evidence from a Peninsular Spanish dialect. *Studies in Language* **18**: 71–111.

Seppänen, Aimo, Rhonwen Bowen, and Joe Trotta. 1994. On the so-called complex prepositions. *Studia Anglia Posnaniensia* **29**: 3–29.

Sienicki, Ben. 2008. The *dare* and *need* constructions in English: a case of degrammaticization? Unpublished manuscript. University of New Mexico, Albuquerque, NM.

Siewierska, Anna. 2002. Word order. In N. Smelser and P. Baltes (eds.), *International encyclopedia of the social and behavioral sciences* (16552–5). Amsterdam: Elsevier.

Sinclair, John. 1991. *Corpus, concordance, collocation.* Oxford: Oxford University Press.

Skousen, Royal. 1989. *Analogical modeling of language.* Dordrecht: Kluwer.

Slobin, Dan I. 1977. Language change in childhood and in history. In J. Macnamara (ed.), *Language learning and thought,* 185–214. New York: Academic Press.

    1985. Cross-linguistic evidence for the language-making capacity. In D. Slobin (ed.), *The cross-linguistic study of language acquisition: theoretical perspectives,* Vol.II, 1157–256. Hillsdale, NJ: Lawrence Erlbaum.

    1994. Talking perfectly: discourse origins of the Present Perfect. In W. Pagliuca (ed.), *Perspectives on grammaticalization,* 119–33. Amsterdam/Philadelphia: John Benjamins.

    1996. From "thought" and "language" to "thinking for speaking." In J.J. Gumperz and S.C. Levinson (eds.), *Rethinking linguistic relativity,* 70–96. Cambridge: Cambridge University Press.

    1997a. Mind, code, and text. In J. Bybee, J. Haiman and S. Thompson (eds.), *Essays on language function and language type,* 437–67. Amsterdam/Philadelphia: John Benjamins.

    1997b. The origins of grammaticizable notions: beyond the individual mind. In D. Slobin (ed.), *The cross-linguistic study of language acquisition: expanding the contexts,* Vol.V, 1–39. Mahwah, NJ: Lawrence Erlbaum.

    2003. Language and thought online: cognitive consequences of linguistic relativity. In D. Gentner and S. Goldin-Meadow (eds.), *Language in mind: advances in the investigation of language and thought,* 157–91. Cambridge, MA: MIT Press.

Smith, Geoff P. 2002. *Growing up with Tok Pisin: contact, creolization, and change in Papua New Guinea's national language.* London: Battlebridge.

Smith, K. Aaron. 2001. The role of frequency in the specialization of the English anterior. In J. Bybee and P. Hopper (eds.), *Frequency and the emergence of linguistic structure,* 361–82. Amsterdam/Philadelphia: John Benjamins.

Smith, Carlota S. 1997. *The parameter of aspect.* Dordrecht: Kluwer.

Steele, Susan. 1975. Past and irrealis: just what does it all mean? *International Journal of American Linguistics* 41: 200–17.

Stefanowitsch, Anatol, and Stefan Gries. 2003. Collostructions: investigating the interaction of words and constructions. *International Journal of Corpus Linguistics* **8**(2): 209–43.

Studdert-Kennedy, Michael, Alvin Liberman, Katherine Harris and Franklin Cooper. 1970. Motor theory of speech perception: a reply to Lane's critical review. *Psychological Review* **77**: 234–49.

Taeymans, Martine. 2004. What the Helsinki Corpus tells us about DARE in late Middle English to Early Modern English. Paper presented at 13 ICEHL, University of Vienna, August.

    2006. *An investigation into the emergence and development of the verb* need *from Old to Present-Day English: a corpus-based approach.* Dissertation. University of Antwerp, Belgium.

Talmy, Leonard. 1985. Lexicalization patterns: semantic structure in lexical forms. In Timothy Shopen (ed.), *Language typology and syntactic description,*

Vol. III: Grammatical categories and the lexicon, 57–149. Cambridge: Cambridge University Press.

Tao, Hongyin. 2003. A usage-based approach to argument structure: 'remember' and 'forget' in spoken English. *International Journal of Corpus Linguistics* **8**(1): 75–95.

Taylor, John. 1995. *Linguistic categorization* (2nd edn), Oxford: Oxford University Press.

Thompson, Sandra A. 1988. A discourse approach to the cross-linguistic category "adjective". In J. A. Hawkins (ed.), *Explaining language universals*, 167–85. Oxford: Basil Blackwell.

1998. A discourse explanation for the cross-linguistic differences in the grammar of interrogation and negation. In A. Siewierska and J. J. Song (eds.), *Case, typology and grammar*, 309–41. Amsterdam/Philadelphia: John Benjamins.

Thompson, Sandra, and Barbara Fox. 1990. A discourse explanation of the grammar of relative clauses in English conversation. *Language* **66**(2): 297–316.

Thompson, Sandra A., and Paul J. Hopper. 2001. Transitivity, clause structure, and argument structure: evidence from conversation. In J. Bybee and P. Hopper (eds.), *Frequency and the emergence of linguistic structure*, 27–60. Amsterdam/ Philadelphia: John Benjamins.

Thurston, William R. 1989. How exoteric languages build a lexicon: esoterogeny in West New Britain. In R. Harlow and R. Hooper (eds.), *VICAL 1: Oceanic languages, Papers from the Fifth International Conference on Austronesian Linguistics*, 555–79. Auckland: Linguistic Society of New Zealand.

Tiersma, Peter. 1982. Local and general markedness. *Language* **58**: 832–49.

Tomasello, Michael. 1992. *First verbs: a case study of early grammatical development.* Cambridge: Cambridge University Press.

2003. *Constructing a language: a usage-based theory of language acquisition.* Cambridge, MA: Harvard University Press.

Tomasello, Michael, A. Kruger, and H. Ratner. 1993. Cultural learning. *Behavioral and Brain Sciences* **16**: 495–552.

Tomlin, Russell S. 1986. *Basic word order: functional principles.* London: Croom Helm.

Torres Cacoullos, Rena. 1999. Variation and grammaticization in progressives: Spanish *-ndo* constructions. *Studies in Language* **23**(1): 25–59.

2000. *Grammaticization, synchronic variation, and language contact: a study of Spanish progressive* -ndo *constructions.* Amsterdam/Philadelphia: John Benjamins.

2001. From lexical to grammatical to social meaning. *Language in Society* **30**: 443–78.

2006. Relative frequency in the grammaticization of collocations: nominal to concessive *a pesar de*. In T. Face and C. Klee (eds.), *Selected proceedings of the 8th Hispanic Linguistics Symposium*, 37–49. Somerville: Cascadilla Proceedings Project.

Torres Cacoullos, Rena, and Scott Schwenter. 2005. Towards an operational notion of subjectification. *Berkeley Linguistics Society* **31**: 347–58.

Torres Cacoullos, Rena and James A. Walker. 2009. The present of the English future: grammatical variation and collocations in discourse. *Language* **85**(2) 321–54.

Tottie, Gunnel. 1991. Lexical diffusion in syntactic change: frequency as a determinant of linguistic conservatism in the development of negation in English. In D. Kastovsky (ed.), *Historical English syntax*, 439–67. Berlin: Mouton de Gruyter.

Trask, Robert. L. 2007. *Historical linguistics* (2nd edn.). Revised by Robert McColl Millar. London: Arnold.

Traugott, Elizabeth C. 1972. *A history of English syntax*. New York: Holt, Rinehart, & Winston.

1989. On the rise of epistemic meanings in English: an example of subjectification in semantic change. *Language* **65**: 31–55.

2001. Legitimate counterexamples to unidirectionality. Paper presented at Freiberg University, October.

2003. Constructions in grammaticalization. In B. Joseph and R. Janda (eds.), *A handbook of historical linguistics*, 624–47. Oxford: Blackwell.

Traugott, Elizabeth C., and Richard B. Dasher. 2002. *Regularity in semantic change*. Cambridge: Cambridge University Press.

Traugott, Elizabeth C., and Ekkehard König. 1991. The semantics-pragmatics of grammaticalization revisited. In E.C. Traugott and B. Heine (eds.), *Approaches to grammaticalization*, Vol.I, 189–218. Amsterdam/Philadelphia: John Benjamins.

Trudgill, Peter. 2001. Contact and simplification. *Linguistic Typology* **5**: 371–74.

1989. Contact and isolation in linguistic change. In L. Breivik and E. Jahr (eds.), *Language change: contributions to the study of its causes*, 227–37. Berlin: Mouton de Gruyter.

2002. Linguistic and social typology. In J. Chambers, P. Trudgill and N. Schilling-Estes (eds.), *Handbook of language variation and change*, 707–28. Oxford: Blackwell.

Van Bergem, Dick. 1995. *Acoustic and lexical vowel reduction, Studies in language and language use*, 16. Amsterdam: IFOTT.

Van Gelderen, Elly. 2004. *Grammaticalization as economy*. Amsterdam/Philadelphia: John Benjamins.

Vendler, Zeno. 1967. Verbs and times. In Z. Vendler (ed.), *Linguistics in philosophy*, 97–121. Ithaca, NY: Cornell University Press.

Verhagen, Arie. 2002. From parts to wholes and back again. *Cognitive Linguistics* **13**: 403–39.

2006. English constructions from a Dutch perspective: where are the differences? In M. Hannay and G. J. Steen (eds.), *Structural-functional studies in English grammar*, 257–74. Amsterdam/Philadelphia: John Benjamins.

Vihman, Marilyn. 1980. Sound change and child language. In *Papers from the 4th International Conference on Historical Linguistics*. Amsterdam/Philadelphia: John Benjamins.

Vitevitch, Michael S., Paul A. Luce, Jan Charles-Luce and David Kemmerer. 1997. Phonotactics and syllable stress: implications for the processing of spoken nonsense words. *Language and Speech*, **40**: 47–62.

Warner, Anthony. 1983. Review article of Lightfoot 1979 (*Principles of diachronic syntax*). *Journal of Linguistics* **19**: 187–209.

2004. What drove 'do'? In C. Kay, S. Horobin, and J. J. Smith (eds.), *New perspectives on English historical linguistics: syntax and morphology*, Vol.I, 229–42. Amsterdam/Philadelphia: John Benjamins.

Watkins, Calvin. 1962. *Indo-European origins of the Celtic verb I: the sigmatic aorist*. Dublin: Dublin Institute for Advanced Studies.

Waugh, Linda. 1975. A semantic analysis of the French tense system. *Orbis* **24**: 436–85.

Wedel, Andrew B. 2006. Exemplar models, evolution and language change. *The Linguistic Review* **23**(3): 247–74.

2007. Feedback and regularity in the lexicon. *Phonology* **24**: 147–85.

Whorf, Benjamin Lee. 1941 [1956]. Language, mind, and reality. In J. B. Carroll (ed.), *Language, thought, and reality: selected writings of Benjamin Lee Whorf*, 134–59. Cambridge, MA: MIT Press.

Wilson, Damián Vergara. 2009. From 'remaining' to 'becoming' in Spanish: the role of prefabs in the development of the construction *quedar(se)* + ADJECTIVE. In R. Corrigan, E. Moravcsik, H. Ouali and K. Wheatley (eds.), *Formulaic language*, Vol.I, *Typological studies in language*, 273–96. Amsterdam/Philadelphia: John Benjamins.

Wittgenstein, Ludwig. 1953. *Philosophical investigations*. New York: Macmillan.

Wray, Alison. 2000. Holistic utterances in protolanguage: the link from primates to humans. In C. Knight, M. Studdert-Kennedy, and J. Hurford, *The Evolutionary Emergence of Language: social function and the origins of linguistic form*, 285–302. New York: Cambridge University Press.

2002. *Formulaic language and the lexicon*. Cambridge: Cambridge University Press.

Wray, Allison, and George W. Grace. 2007. The consequences of talking to strangers: evolutionary corollaries of socio-cultural influences on linguistic form. *Lingua* **117**: 543–78.

Ziegeler, Debra. 2004. Grammaticalisation through constructions: the story of causative *have* in English. *Annual Review of Cognitive Linguistics* **2**: 159–95.

Zwicky, Arnold, and Geoffrey Pullum. 1983. Cliticization vs. inflection: English *n't*. *Language* **59**: 502–13.

Index